ARCHAEOLOGY

UNEARTHING THE MYSTERIES OF THE PAST

ARCHAEOLOGY

UNEARTHING THE MYSTERIES OF THE PAST

Kate Santon

p

This is a Parragon Publishing Book
First published in 2007

Parragon Publishing
Queen Street House
4 Queen Street
Bath, BA1 1HE, UK

For photograph copyrights see page 304
Text © Parragon Books Ltd 2007

Produced by Atlantic Publishing

ISBN: 978-1-4054-8787-0
Printed in China

Contents

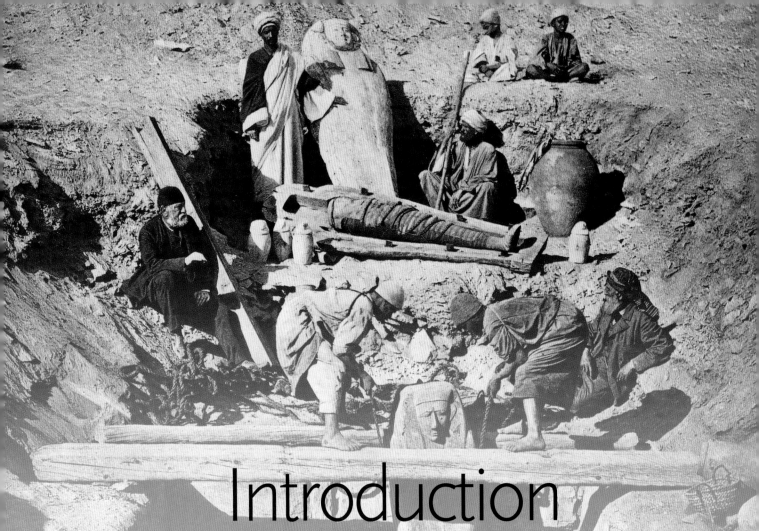

Introduction

Archaeology has often hit the headlines with tales of fantastic discoveries like the tomb of Tutankhamun. But it's not all golden treasures and Indiana Jones; much more importantly it's a window into the past, and often into the remote past where archaeology is the only way of understanding anything about what happened, about what our origins are, and how we developed the skills we have. Recent television programs have brought a more realistic understanding of what archaeology involves to a much wider audience, and it is more popular than ever.

People have always been fascinated by the past and by those who lived before them. In the past (and today) legends would be told; stories and poems recounted. Then, in the 17th and 18th centuries, some individuals began adopting a more considered attitude. Many of them were European and most of them were either professionals, like academics, clerics, or lawyers, or had a private income—or both. They began to survey obvious monuments such as megaliths and dug into others, like burial mounds, in search of whatever mysteries they contained. These men were the antiquaries, whose curiosity and enthusiasm for the past paved the way for archaeology as it is today. Over time their activities

EUROPE		12	HOCHDORF	21	MYCENAE
1	NEANDER VALLEY	13	MAIDEN CASTLE	22	ATHENS
2	LASCAUX	14	HADRIAN'S WALL	23	DELPHI
3	ALTAMIRA	15	VINDOLANDA	24	OLYMPIA
4	SKARA BRAE	16	SUTTON HOO	25	VERGINA
5	VARNA	17	JORVIK	26	CERVETERI
6	THE ICEMAN	18	OSEBERG	27	ROME
7	STONEHENGE			28	POMPEII
8	CARNAC		MEDITERRANEAN		HERCULANEUM
9	NEWGRANGE		WORLD	30	SABRATHA
10	TOLLUND	19	KNOSSOS	31	TIMGAD
11	LINDOW MOSS	20	TROY	32	LEPTIS MAGANA

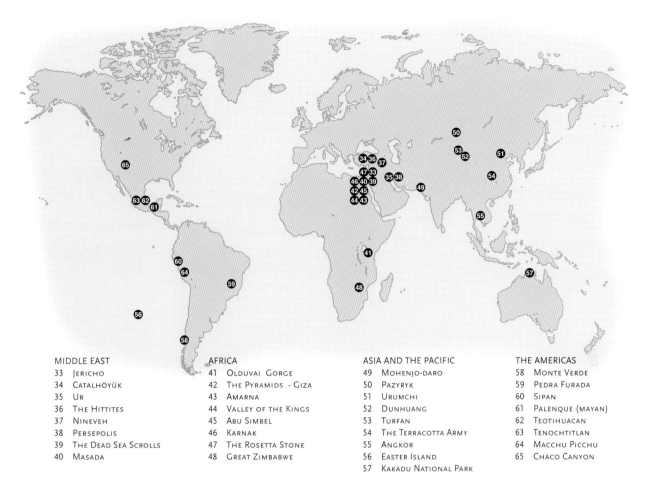

MIDDLE EAST
33 JERICHO
34 CATALHÖYÜK
35 UR
36 THE HITTITES
37 NINEVEH
38 PERSEPOLIS
39 THE DEAD SEA SCROLLS
40 MASADA

AFRICA
41 OLDUVAI GORGE
42 THE PYRAMIDS - GIZA
43 AMARNA
44 VALLEY OF THE KINGS
45 ABU SIMBEL
46 KARNAK
47 THE ROSETTA STONE
48 GREAT ZIMBABWE

ASIA AND THE PACIFIC
49 MOHENJO-DARO
50 PAZYRYK
51 URUMCHI
52 DUNHUANG
53 TURFAN
54 THE TERRACOTTA ARMY
55 ANGKOR
56 EASTER ISLAND
57 KAKADU NATIONAL PARK

THE AMERICAS
58 MONTE VERDE
59 PEDRA FURADA
60 SIPAN
61 PALENQUE (MAYAN)
62 TEOTIHUACAN
63 TENOCHTITLAN
64 MACCHU PICCHU
65 CHACO CANYON

became more systematic and careful. Simultaneously, interest in the physical remains of the classical civilizations of Greece and Rome flourished, and then extended to include Ancient Egypt, inspired by Napoleon's invasion of 1798.

In the 19th century, as more began to be known about geology and the immense age of the earth, scientific advances came into the picture. An understanding of stratigraphy—the fact that lower layers have to be older than layers that lie on top of them, and that these layers might take a very long time to accumulate—had a profound effect. The bones of extinct animals from very low levels, and the discovery of what appeared to be extinct forms of human beings, fitted with the theory that not only was the Earth older than anyone had previously thought, but that it had also been inhabited for a very long time. A major breakthrough came when Jaques Boucher de Perthes found the bones of extinct animals like mammoths in the same layer as stone tools at a site in France. Darwin's On the Origin of Species, published a little later, also had an impact, demonstrating the process of evolutionary change:

studying the past was beginning to become less of an intellectual amateur pastime and more of a discipline. Excavation gradually became a little more methodical and careful, sometimes with an emphasis on the stratigraphy of sites and on recording what was found.

By today's standards, however, much damage was done. Layard, exploring at Nineveh, burrowed huge tunnels and almost completely wrecked the site. The earthmoving in Schliemann's excavations at Troy was overseen by engineers who had worked on the Suez Canal and who had little concern for the way the site had been built up over thousands of years. Training was either nonexistent or done on the job, with younger archaeologists working under more experienced hands for a surprisingly short period of time before they went out on their own. There was a slightly wild air to it; romantic, yes, but also needlessly destructive. Between the two World Wars, many excavations—especially in the Near and Middle East—were gigantic, involving huge

Opposite: A photograph dated c. 1880 shows Egyptian laborers lifting out sarcophagi from a tomb at Saqqara.

teams of laborers and a few archaeologists directing the work. They could strip more soil from a site in a single digging season than a modern team would remove in many. At the same time, however, there were the beginnings of a more thorough approach. Starting in the late 19th century, this was typified by the work of German teams at Olympia and by General Pitt-Rivers in the UK. By the 1930s, Mortimer Wheeler was applying Pitt-Rivers' methods of organization and, as a side benefit, training many of the next generation of archaeologists in proper excavation methods.

Nowadays archaeologists are trained rather differently. They study a lot, obviously, but they are also trained in practical techniques such as surveying methods and computer analysis. They will work on many digs, under very close supervision, before directing their own, and they are taught to understand that the past is a finite resource. Archaeology is a destructive science and even the best excavation destroys evidence as it finds it. Meticulous analysis, recording, and publication

of the results are crucial parts of the picture. Environmental studies are critical, giving a much more rounded view of the past than that provided by artifacts and the remains of buildings. Excavation today is a meticulous, slow, thorough process and the conservation of finds, especially of organic material, has improved out of all recognition.

There are other things to consider, too, such as the role of local communities. An excellent example of working with local people came from the work done in Australia's Kakadu region by Rhys Jones and his team from the Australian National University, where the help and full involvement of the Aboriginal community was essential. Ethics are also given a more significant emphasis than they were in

Opposite: A photograph dated c. 1900 showing excavation work at Pompeii.

Below: Although the modern archaeologist can use advanced techniques such as radiocarbon dating, manual labor is still an essential part of the work.

the past, particularly—for example—when it comes to dealing with human remains. Another significant change is that where archaeologists once tended to be white, of American or European origin, and male, they are now often anything but that, as many more people from all cultures are joining the field.

It may seem that all the spectacular finds that can be made have been made, that the age of great discoveries is over, but that would be a mistake. The burial mound of China's First Emperor, whose armies of terracotta warriors are one of the greatest of recent finds, still remains to be opened; work on the KV5 tomb in Egypt's Valley of the Kings may produce surprising discoveries, as may continuing work at Pompeii and Herculaneum. Just as important, though, are the "smaller" things, the less apparently spectacular details which can reveal so much about how people lived their lives a very long time ago.

FINDING SITES

It cannot be denied that many things are found by accident. The extremely rich cemetery at Varna, Bulgaria, was found by workmen digging a trench; the Iceman was discovered by two hikers in the Alps. Some, like the burials at Sipan, have come to light as a result of grave robbing. Other discoveries have been made because of educated guesses and research, like that of the tomb of Philip of Macedon at Vergina. Meticulous surveying led Kent Weeks, director of the Theban Mapping Project, to the KV5 tomb in the Valley of the Kings which had been covered up for decades and never properly excavated.

Aerial photography was one of the earliest methods of scientific surveying, though it is generally used today to study sites that are already known. It is still important in surveying a wider area and providing a different perspective than is often possible on the ground. Features which cannot be distinguished at ground level are visible from above as low shadows, differences in crop heights or in soil color. Then there are surface surveys. These often take the form of walking a particular piece of ground in accordance with a formal grid (to ensure that fieldwalkers don't just concentrate on areas that look promising), but they can be of variable use, though they can be backed up—or back up—aerial reconnaisance.

A significant recent development is the use of GIS —Geographic Information Systems. These computer-based systems are designed for collecting, storing, retrieving, and analyzing data about sites and their location and can be linked to databases; they are invaluable for mapping and analysis but can have other applications. Some are based on predictive modeling and, in theory and sometimes in practice, can predict the possibility of finding sites in particular locations using their analysis of where sites have been found in the past.

There are various methods of surveying once a site or potential site has been found—echo sounding has been used at underwater sites, for example, and by Weeks and the Theban Mapping Project in Egypt. One of the most familiar methods to non-archaeologists is geophysical surveying. Geophysical surveys basically detect any changes in the soil below, like walls, burials,

Left: Excavations under the direction of Mortimer Wheeler on the site of the Roman city of Verulamium at St Albans, near London, in the late 1940s.

Opposite: An archaeologist works along the banks of the St Mary River at the site of St Mary's City, a settlement believed to be the first in Maryland, USA.

Opposite right: An archaeologist carefully examines a flake pile.

even ditches that have been filled in. They also measure the depth at which any changes occur, and three-dimensional maps can be built up before excavation commences. But nothing is certain ... it still comes down to digging.

PRESERVATION

Survival is a hit-and-miss matter. Sites and finds can be destroyed by environmental action, either from natural processes or man-made ones: floods, landslides, rising sea levels, and construction, among others. Some natural disasters can preserve sites, of course. Pompeii and Herculaneum are probably the most obvious examples but there are others, like the Neolithic village of Skara Brae on Orkney, which was buried in sand dunes. In general, preservation depends on so many variables that it can almost seem to be a matter of luck. But there are some conditions that can help.

Inorganic materials often survive well; for instance, stone tools have been found going back millions of years. Of course, it is possible that our early ancestors used wood and bone tools just as much as stone, but these would not have survived. Fired clay lasts, if the firing was efficient and thorough, and pots are one of the most important survivals in the archaeological record though acid soils can damage fired clay, and badly fired or porous ceramic material can be damaged by water or humid conditions. When it comes to metals, gold, silver, and lead generally survive very well in most circumstances. Copper and some bronze can be damaged by acid soils, becoming oxidized and leaving just a greenish trace behind. Oxidation also destroys iron, though colored marks can be found there too, rusty ones this time.

The survival of organic materials depends on the material they are in, usually earth, and the climate. Acid soils, once again, can destroy bone and wood while chalky soil will preserve bones. Salty conditions, such as those at the Iron Age mines of Hallstatt, are excellent for preservation; at Hallstatt, even the backpacks used by Iron Age miners have been found. Copper can also help the preservation of organic material. Excluding oxygen is also important, which is why the anaerobic conditions of a peat bog preserve skin and hair, though the acidity destroys a lot of the bone, as demonstrated by the Iron Age bog bodies found in northern Europe. That is also why the Vindolanda letters survived—they were in oxygen-free pockets in the right sort of deposit to chemically induce preservation.

On a wider scale, the interior of a cave is well protected from the vagaries of the climate outside and, in the case of limestone caves, can aid preservation: bones, plant fibers and footprints have all been found in Paleolithic caves, dating back thousands of years. So much survives from Ancient Egypt because of the arid conditions, and the same is true of the finds from Central Asia and the Pueblo settlements of the American south-west. Tropical climates, however, can be very destructive.

And, of course, once they have been found, the discoveries then have to be conserved to make sure they continue to survive. Conservation is a major issue for modern archaeology, not just of finds, but of sites too.

DATING

Telling how old things are has long exercised the ingenuity of people interested in the past, from the earliest days of archaeology. The Three-Age System was first proposed in 1836, by the Danish scholar Christian Jurgensen Thomsen; it is still in use today in a modified form. The original proposal was for a Stone Age, followed by a Bronze Age and then an Iron Age.

The Stone Age has now been divided into the Paleolithic and Neolithic, and the basic term "Stone Age" is seldom used. The Neolithic is differentiated from the Paleolithic by the development of domestication and—it used to be thought—pottery, and there is an interim stage between the two, the Mesolithic. The Neolithic and the Bronze Age are interrupted now by the Copper Age, to which both the Iceman and the finds at Varna belong, and the Bronze Age is followed by the Iron Age.

The terms can sometimes create an impression that development was constant over geographical areas, but this is not the case: it is quite possible for sites in one area to have an essentially Neolithic culture, while many miles away at the same time people were making a lot of bronze weapons and tools. Nor was change instant; in most cases it was a gradual process. There are other limitations: in Africa, for example, bronze was not used in large areas at all; in the Americas iron was not present (except briefly, in the Viking settlement) before the arrival of the European conquerors. The 19th-century academics also built up typologies—the arrangements of artifacts of similar types into sequences.

Tree-ring dating, dendrochronology, provided a major breakthrough. A tree adds a ring of growth every year, the thickness of which varies according to climatic conditions. It is possible to build up sequences stretching back thousands of years by matching and overlapping sequences of rings from different sources within a controlled area. It's reliable, but is limited to places where timber survives, and where complete sequences have been established.

Radiocarbon dating was first proposed in 1947 by Willard Libby, and has been used

extensively since; the early dates for Jericho were one of the method's earliest surprising revelations. The radioactive isotope Carbon 14 decays at a known rate after death and certain items can be dated by measuring how much remains. It is contained in organic material—plant remains and peat, bone, shell—and radiocarbon dating can give good results (with a certain degree of possibility, which is why dates are sometimes given as 'c.' or are shown with a plus or minus value, like 33,740 ± 430, for example) for dates going far back, to about 75,000 BP. But it does require appropriate material, of course.

For even older material there are other methods. When Louis and Mary Leakey made their early discoveries at Olduvai they used potassium-argon dating, now generally replaced by argon-argon dating which requires smaller samples. These are other means of measuring radioactive decay, this time following heating, and are very useful in dating volcanic rocks and lavas. If something lies on a volcanic deposit of one age, and is covered by another of a different age, you can tell how old the object in between must be.

THREATS

The world's archaeological resources are as under threat today as they have always been. War and vandalism have had a particular prominence in recent years, with the destruction of sites in Iraq and looting from museums there—but theft is probably the most significant danger.

Opposite: An archaeologist excavates using brushes, hammers, and fine dentistry tools at the Early Man dig in the Calico Hills, California.

Above: Taking accurate measurements in an important part of the role of the archaeologist.

When something is stolen, removed from its context—the source of priceless information about the culture than produced it—its archaeological value is largely gone. Yes, it may still be beautiful, rare or unusual, but it probably can't be dated, nothing is known of the circumstances in which it was found, deposited or created. It is effectively lost to humanity except as an object, and that's assuming it doesn't disappear into a private collection as most things do. Worldwide, the highly profitable antiquities trade has some very murky corners; sculptures are ripped from Cambodian temples, Etruscan tombs are still being robbed and frescos are stolen from the walls at Pompeii.

What attracts collectors is partly the same as what attracts everyone else: wanting to have some sort of connection to the past, to people who were here before us. But our past is a worldwide resource, not exclusive but valuable for all of humanity, and should be treated as such. And, of course, it should be enjoyed!

Europe

The Neanderthals

In 1856 quarrymen working in the Neander valley near Düsseldorf in Germany blasted out a small cave. While they were sorting through the debris they found bones: part of a skull, some long bones, and ribs. The workers thought they had found animal remains, but when they showed them to a local naturalist he realized the men were wrong. The skull had belonged to no ape, but it wasn't quite like that of a modern human either; for one thing, it had massive brow ridges. Gradually other similar specimens came to light and one had even been found earlier, at Gibraltar in 1848, though it had been ignored.

Neanderthals are now known from fossils from a wide area, ranging from Gibraltar in the south of Europe as far as Denisova Cave in southern Siberia; they have also been found in the Near East. They seem to have survived the longest in the west, until about 30,000 years ago, and the earliest fossils with clear Neanderthal characteristics probably go back to about 300,000 BP (before present).

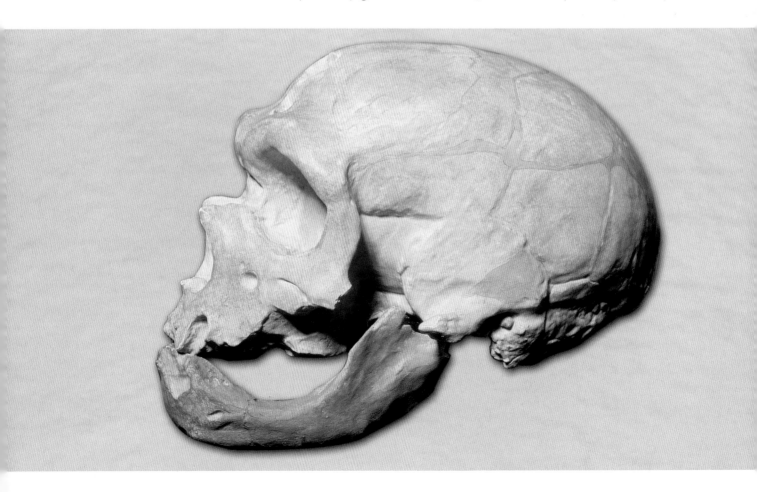

Recent DNA studies have shown that all existing humans are part of a genetically relatively uniform population, originating in Africa sometime in the last few hundred thousand years. Neanderthal DNA was investigated in 1997 and found to be significantly different, suggesting that though Neanderthals and modern humans may share an immediate common ancestor, probably Homo heidelbergensis, they are otherwise from different branches on the evolutionary family tree.

Neanderthals, shorter and stockier than modern humans, were well adapted to cold environments. They had powerful bodies: their bones show evidence of pronounced muscle attachments, so they would have been well suited to anything requiring physical strength. Nonetheless, a lot of the remains found show signs of having sustained physical damage—injuries, especially fractures, which were often healed. Many of the fractures relate to the upper body and modern parallels suggest that they may have been the result of hunting game animals at close range. Most of the bones that have been found also come from people under the age of 40.

Technologically, Neanderthals were reliant on stone tools, and the ones they used closely resemble those used by some of the contemporary groups of anatomically modern humans. Unlike those people, though, they only used stone, or occasionally wood for shafts or digging sticks, which would have restricted their activities. Without bone needles, for example, there would have been no sewn clothing. Many Neanderthal skulls have terribly worn teeth, worn more heavily than is likely from just eating even the toughest of food, so they probably used their teeth—and their powerful jaws—for grasping things, like pelts or plants, and stripping them. They lived in rock shelters, though open-air camps have also been found; like their technology, their occupation sites are not as adaptive as those of modern humans. There are only rare traces of artificial shelters, even in the coldest areas.

The question of how Neanderthals communicated with each other has also been raised, and the evolution of language is a controversial topic. Anatomical evidence seems to suggest that complicated speech—the ability to make the full range of necessary sounds—may not

Below: The name Neanderthal is derived from the place where some of the first Neanderthal bones were discovered, the Neander Valley.

Opposite: A Neanderthal skull, from Italy, clearly showing the characteristic brow ridge.

Right: A flint ax from Swanscombe in England. Handaxes of this type may have been introduced into Europe by Homo heidelbergensis, the probable ancestor of both H. neanderthalensis and our own species, H. sapiens.

have been entirely possible for Neanderthals, but this is debated. One thing that does seem clear from many Neanderthal sites is that some groups deliberately buried some of their dead. There are no convincing examples of Neanderthal art.

WHAT HAPPENED TO THE NEANDERTHALS?

During the time Neanderthals were alive, there were many climatic changes. They often seem to have been able to adapt enough, however, though they do appear to have left some of the coldest areas of central and eastern Europe around the end of the Last Interglacial period, about 70,000 years ago, as temperatures began to fall.

From about 40,000 years ago there was another factor—the arrival of anatomically modern humans, exploiting and occupying what was in effect the same ecological niche, and doing so more effectively. This may well have pushed the Neanderthals to the brink of extinction quite quickly, and they certainly seem to have retreated to remote locations like Gibraltar. There have been some suggestions of interbreeding—the two populations would certainly have been aware of each other—but this, especially in view of the DNA evidence, is probably unlikely.

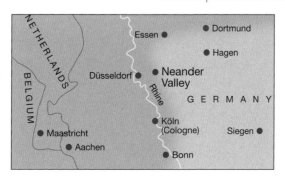

The Art of the Ice Age

Some of the earliest art in existence, dating back to the Ice Age, was discovered as early as 1833. These were two small, portable pieces: an engraving, possibly representing a bird, and a decorated harpoon. Another engraving, of deer on a reindeer bone, turned up a few years later. These pieces of art dated back to the Upper Paleolithic, to some time between 35,000 and 10,000 years ago. More were found, and some were displayed at the Universal Exhibition in Paris in 1878.

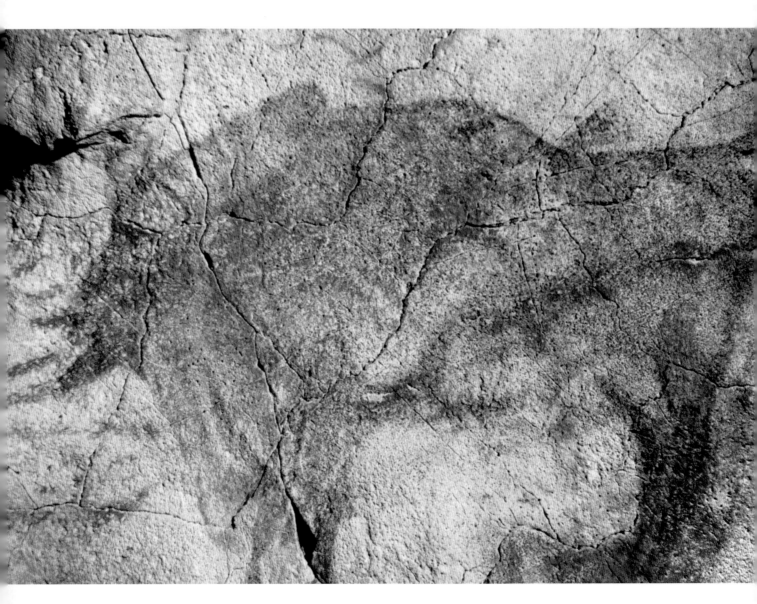

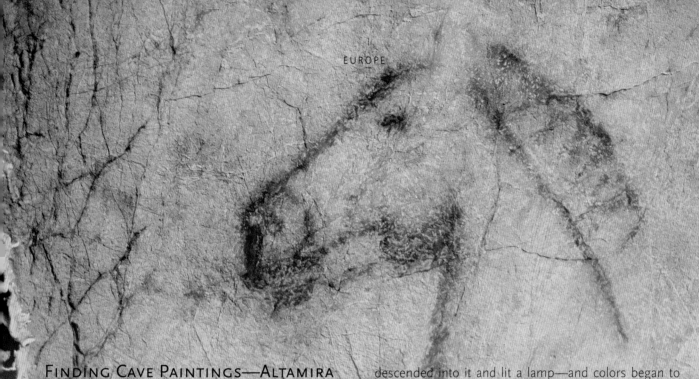

Finding Cave Paintings—Altamira and Lascaux

They were seen in Paris by Don Marcelino Sanz de Sautuola from northern Spain; as a keen antiquarian, he was fascinated. The following year he returned to a cave at Altamira where he had previously noticed dark marks on the wall, thinking he might find some small pieces similar to those he had seen. He had his daughter Maria with him, and she was playing in the cave when she looked up—and noticed a lot of bison painted on the ceiling. There was a strong resemblance between these bison and some of the portable art De Sautuola had seen in Paris, and he was sure these were of a similar age. Unfortunately his ideas were dismissed out of hand by the archaeological establishment of his day. Gradually, however, more and more discoveries were made and gradually the specialists came round. By 1902 De Sautuola's theories were accepted and the paintings in caves were recognized as belonging to the Paleolithic.

Discoveries then came quickly, not just of paintings in caves, but of reliefs, even works in clay. Many were found in France, in places like Pech Merle and Montespan, and more were discovered in Spain. One of the most beautiful and remarkable was Lascaux, to date still probably the most magnificent. It was found during the Second World War by four teenage boys exploring near Montignac in the Dordogne area of France. The boys were investigating a strange hole they had found in the woods, descended into it and lit a lamp—and colors began to appear on the walls wherever they shone their light. The preservation at Lascaux is astonishing; even the sockets for scaffolding still exist in one high and narrow painted passage. The cave itself has had to be closed to the public because the sheer number of visitors was causing serious deterioration, but an excellent replica has been constructed nearby. There are about 600 paintings at Lascaux and 1500 engravings, all startlingly clear. Lots of horses and deer are represented, and the four large bulls which dominate the Hall of the Bulls are up to 16 feet in length, the biggest representations of animals yet found.

Recent Discoveries

Finds are still being made—there's an average of one a year—and each new discovery is capable of radically altering our view of art and of the Upper Paleolithic. In recent years, for example, four have had far-reaching implications. In Portugal, rock engravings were found in

Opposite: This beautiful colored bison is one of those from the ceiling of the Spanish cave of Altamira.

Above: The outline of a horse from the cave of Tito Bustillo in Spain. Monochrome outline drawings like this are the commonest form of painting in caves.

Left: At present the most important finds of cave art are in southern France and Iberia.

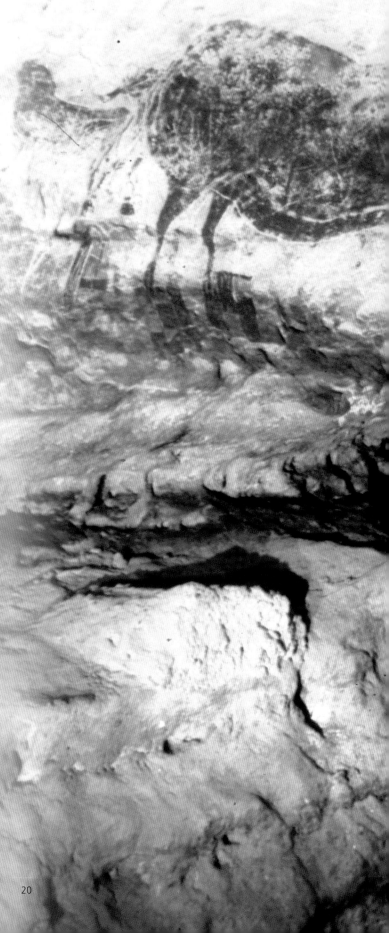

the open air along at least 10 miles of the Côa valley, and in nearby Spanish locations. They are an indication that much Ice Age art may have been outside; the art in caves may just have been better protected from the passage of time, not more common. Cosquer, on the Mediterranean coast of France, is a cave with an entrance which is now underwater, and parts of it are flooded. The entrance would have been on dry land when the art was created, about 18,000–127,000 years ago, and it's a useful reminder that much evidence may be lost through climatic change. Cosquer has some unique features and preserves depictions of sea animals such as seals. In 2003, Paleolithic engravings—notably the outline of an ibex – were found at Cresswell Crags in the UK, extending the known range of cave art northward by about 270 miles. Portable art was already known in Britain, but this was the first time any cave decoration had been found, and it's discovery was the result of a considered guess by experts in the field. At the present, it looks as though Cresswell could have been the northern limit of a landscape exploited by mobile hunter-gatherers.

CHAUVET

Probably the most important of recent discoveries is Chauvet cave in southern France. In December 1994, Jean-Marie Chauvet and two friends were hunting for suitable caves in the Ardèche region when they came across a small rock shelter on a hill, essentially an overhang with some rubble at the back. They thought they could feel air coming through the rubble, moved enough of it and found the opening of a narrow tunnel leading down into the hill. It was the start of a complex cave system and they were eventually able to make their way down into a vast underground chamber, where they spotted the red imprint of a hand on the wall. Similar examples exist in other Paleolithic caves, and they knew they were looking at a handprint made tens of thousands of years previously.

Right: A view of the paintings in the cave at Lascaux in France, which were discovered by children during the 1940s. The beautiful paintings at Chauvet cave in France were only discovered in the 1990s. Radiocarbon dating of the charcoal used for the black color and from hearths on the floor of the cave has given a very early date—about 32,000 BP (before present). This is, however, controversial, especially as the paintings are so stylistically sophisticated.

Above: Human figures are comparatively rare in cave art. This one, from Lascaux, has been variously interpreted as a shaman, a sorcerer, or a hunter, and the painting is probably most cautiously described as a possible hunting scene, though with highly symbolic elements. The bison certainly appears to have been wounded by a spear in the stomach.

Then they found glorious images of animals: bison, rhinoceros, lion, horses, and even woolly mammoths. Some were painted and some were engraved. They also found the bones of cave bears, which appear to have used the caves, but some of the bears' bones had been deliberately arranged. On the floors of the cave were signs of places where there had been fires, and there were soot marks caused by flaming torches being held against the walls. There were also footprints: the original painters had walked across a muddy surface, and their tracks were still visible.

The paintings are wonderful. There are groups of animals, drawn to show the effect of perspective, and carnivorous predators stalk across the surface of the walls. There are lions, a panther and even a possible hyena; the latter two are unique, not known from elsewhere. Nor is a long-eared owl, also depicted at Chauvet. There are many other animals: in total, for example, there are 47 rhinoceros and 36 large cats. The art of Chauvet is sophisticated; the surface of the cave wall was frequently prepared before painting by being scraped down, and additional scraping was used to give some painted outlines more prominence. The natural shape of the walls was deliberately used to create a more dynamic impression and the colors were skillfully applied to increase the impression of depth. Pigment was spread about, especially on the black animals, creating shading—this is called the "stump" technique.

Red ocher had been used, giving a deep terracotta-like red, and there was plenty of black. This proved to be charcoal and that, together with fragments of charcoal from the hearths on the floor of the cave, was used for radiocarbon dating. The results astonished everyone: the oldest images had a date of 32,410 ± 720 years. If this is correct, these become the oldest known representational images, the earliest evidence of painted art yet found—but the dates are controversial and have been questioned. If they are indeed right, then they are crucial to understanding how art emerged. This early date also brings them back much closer to the first appearance of modern humans in Europe.

THE TECHNIQUES OF CAVE DECORATING

Engraving is probably the most common way of decorating the surfaces within a cave, and was probably one of the most straightforward: the surface would be marked using a sharp stone, maybe a flint. Simple painted outlines of animals are also comparatively common; multicolor or bicolor paintings are rarer, as are clay modeling and relief sculptures.

Bumps, lumps, bulges, and cracks in cave walls were often incorporated into designs and, as at Chauvet, the wall might have been prepared first. Colors would be applied using fingers or implements—pads, soft sticks, other things which would have a brushlike effect. Paint was also sprayed onto the surface, most notably with hand stencils: a hand would be held against the cave wall and pigment sprayed around and over it. Once the hand was removed, the colored outline of its shape would be clear on the surface. Excavations in some caves have revealed the actual pigments used, and analysis of paint samples has shown that there were different ways of

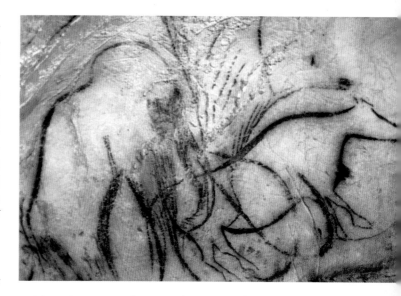

mixing pigments with minerals. Iron oxide was the base for red paint, for example, and most of the blacks are now recognized as charcoal, which can be used for dating. One thing this has shown—apart from the early date for the Chauvet cave—is that paintings in a single cave seem to have been worked on at several different times. They are not just a work completed at one point and then never altered again; images seem to have been retouched and areas reused.

Horses, wild cattle, and bison are commonly represented, as are ibex and deer. Large and dangerous animals appear to be more common in art from the earliest part of the Upper Paleolithic, and birds and fish are more commonly found in portable art than on cave walls. The animals depicted there are always adults, and are shown in profile. People are rarely illustrated, but there are a lot of abstract motifs, which are known as "signs." They can be simple, dots and lines, or much more complicated, and many interpretations have been suggested, from astronomical information to marks indicating the presence of a specific tribe. There have also been many ideas about the placing of art in caves, and in several caves links have been found between the most heavily decorated areas and those which have the best acoustics.

Left: A hand stencil and possible symbolic "signs"—the red spots—from Pech Merle in France. To achieve an effect like this, color would be sprayed around the hand, using either a tube or the mouth. This has been dated to around 25,000–24,000 BP.

Above: Animals from Pech Merle.

THE WORLD OF THE ICE AGE HUNTERS

Europe was a very different place in the Upper Paleolithic. Large areas of the north were covered by ice, and Britain was still joined to Europe, across both the Channel and the North Sea. The land which now lies beneath that is known as Doggerland, after the raised undersea area, the Dogger bank, from which much evidence has been dredged. It seems to have been particularly rich in potential prey animals, and there is also evidence of human occupation. Coastlines everywhere were different, and cold, dry climatic conditions seem to have prevailed.

Across the tundra or steppe-like landscapes of the north roamed massive herds of reindeer, wild horse, and bison. Mammoths were present and in some places, notably in more eastern areas, their bones were used to construct houses in the absence of wood. Many Upper Paleolithic sites seem to have specialized in exploiting a particular kind of prey, depending on local conditions. Southern areas of western Europe were much more wooded and have a focus on red deer, ibex, or chamois exploitation, whereas in the more northerly colder regions reindeer and wild horses were more important.

The people were highly mobile; evidence from flints, seashells and fossils which can be traced back to their places of origin confirms this. They seem to have moved great distances with the seasons, and would therefore have been familiar with animals from many different areas. There is evidence that camps were deliberately located in particular places which would have served as animal migration routes; their occupants certainly seem to have understood—and been able to predict—animal behavior. Exploiting large migrating herds would also have required a certain level of communication and social organization; coordination and cooperation would have been necessary. Some of the settlements found, notably ones like La Madeleine in France and Dolni Vestonice in the Czech Republic, were large. This suggests they may have been occupied by groups of several families living and working together, though there could—always—be alternative explanations.

Below: Wild goats and horses from the Lascaux cave.

Explaining Paleolithic Art

Ever since the first discoveries of Paleolithic art in the 19th century, there has been endless speculation about its purpose. Was it a simple record of what the artists saw? Was it symbolic and, if so, symbolic of what? Most of the possible explanations which have been suggested say more about the times in which they were put forward than they do about art in the Ice Age.

Some of the earliest explanations, from the earliest years of the 20th century, simply used ethnographic parallels and came up with hunting and fertility magic. In the 1960s André Leroi-Gourhan devised a complicated solution based on the philosophy of structuralism; he saw the cave paintings, particularly, as representing either "male" characteristics or "female" ones. Horses, for example, stood for masculinity; bison were feminine. He said that depictions of "female" species were concentrated in the central parts of the caves, while "male" ones were more widely distributed. According to this theory, the most dangerous animals were found in the most inaccessible places. For a while Leroi-Gourhan's theories were influential, but full analysis and discoveries since then have shown that animals are actually more randomly situated than he supposed.

A little later there came a focus on astronomical observations, and most recently—in what has been called the Information Age, after all—has come an emphasis on the paintings being a way of passing on essential information. Added to that, another strand of recent interpretations has laid a considerable weight on shamanism, the use of mind-altering drugs, and hallucinatory experiences.

In reality, not only will we never know, we must also not forget that this art was produced over an extraordinarily long period—probably about 20,000 years—and that it comes from a wide geographical area. What motivated an artist at one place and time may have been completely different from what prompted another to do something similar much later and far away. In fact, almost any of the explanations so far put forward might contain an element of truth. There is likely to have been more than one single reason for creating art, and whatever these were, they would have been sophisticated. One thing is certain: it is impossible to know for sure.

Below: This small ivory head, about the size of a thumb, comes from Brassempouy in France. It is one of the few finds from Western Europe on which the features are indicated. It was found early in the 20th century, and its exact provenance and context are unknown. As a result there has been some debate about its authenticity.

Portable Art

Painting and engraving on rock is not the only form of art that survives from the remote past of the Upper Paleolithic, over 30,000 years ago. There is also much portable art, as it is known—small sculptures or engraved and carved pieces. In fact portable pieces were the first to be recognized as belonging to this period.

Some of the carvings, such as that of a bison licking its side, on a reindeer antler from the French site of La Madeleine, are very realistic and bear witness to the observational skill of the artist. Things such as this bison, and the animals used to add decoration to functional objects like spear-throwers, did not seem to need an explanation—though magical motivation was suggested as early as 1887. Others are less clear, and among these are the many sculptures of women, known as "Venus figurines," and a strange part-animal, part-human figure.

Above right: Small figures of women, known as "Venus" figurines, are found all over Ice Age Europe, and one of the most well-known is this, the Venus of Willendorf. The statuette was found on the banks of the River Danube, and has been carved from limestone which may once have been colored red.

Right: Many of the Venus figurines show similar characteristics. This one, made of ivory, comes from the French site of Lespugue, a shallow cave overlooking a gorge. The figure was reportedly found in a hearth inside the cave.

A piece of mammoth ivory was used to create a small sculpture, 11 in tall, of a human figure with a feline head; this was found at Hohlenstein-Stadel, a cave in southern Germany.

Just as with the Chauvet cave, there are some surprising early dates for pieces of portable art, and the cat-headed figure has been dated to 32,000 years ago. A similarly early date has been ascribed to a statue of a woman known as the Dancing Venus of Galgenberg which was found in 1988 at the site of an Upper Paleolithic camp by the River Danube. Despite the name it has been given, it is rather different from the other Venus figurines, which are some of the most widely known examples of Ice Age art.

The creation of these seems to have been concentrated over about 4000 years, from 27,000 to 23,000 BP (before present), an artistic tradition lasting a very long time. One of the most famous is the Venus of Willendorf, also from the banks of the Danube. This figure is about 4.5 in tall and has been carved from limestone; it seems to have a headdress or braided hair. Figures were generally carved from soft stone like steatite or mammoth ivory, while the Black Venus of Dolni Vestonice is made from fired clay. Most of these figures place a strong emphasis on the breasts and buttocks.

Not surprisingly, there has been much speculation about their purpose—speculation which probably says more about the preoccupations of those putting forward the theories than it does about the figures themselves. Among other explanations, they have been seen as fertility or childbirth charms, general symbols of womanhood or representations of a goddess. There is no context for many of them, no records of what they were found with, or even precisely where they were found. Of the rest, some French ones seem to have been secreted in caves, some were placed in pits, and some, like the Black Venus, were found in Paleolithic refuse. Some of them show signs of having been colored with ocher, giving the impression of items of clothing. They do appear to vary geographically; there's much less emphasis on the breasts, for example, in Siberian figures, which give more attention to facial details. There is a tremendous amount of variation, and putting all these figurines together and generalizing about them as a group is probably a mistake. They may well have had different functions, maybe more than a single one, and a variety of different meanings, even though the theme—women—may have been held in common.

The End of the Ice Age

The overall temperature began to rise and ice sheets began to retreat. Sea levels rose as meltwater was returned to the oceans, and forests started to expand northward. This would have been, of course, a gradual process, but it caused irrevocable and radical change. Northern and central Europe had been tundra or steppe, and these were replaced by dense forests. The great herds of reindeer would have gone, replaced by other species—red deer, wild boar, wild oxen—more at home among the trees. Hunting practices would have had to be altered, and from the archaeological record it does seem that people were soon living in smaller groups, dispersed much more widely. Everything changes.

Below: An ivory carving of an animal from the Vogelherd cave in Germany. This has been interpreted as a bear, a cave lion, a hyena, or even a rhinoceros.

Skara Brae

During the winter of 1850 the islands of Orkney, off the north coast of Scotland, were swept by an exceptionally fierce storm. It stripped grass from a high dune by the Bay of Skaill and exposed an immense midden—a prehistoric dump consisting of peat ash, shells, fragments of broken bones, and similar refuse mixed with sand—and some surprising ruins.

HOUSES OF THE NEOLITHIC

The ruins revealed by the storm were the remains of ancient dwellings. This proved to be a settlement going back to the Neolithic and dating to between 3100–2500 BC, contemporary with many of Orkney's megalithic remains. Homes had been created within the huge midden and were remarkable not just for their age, but for the fact that so much survived. There were standing walls; backed by the midden these could be up to 10 feet thick. Even more unusually, the furniture and fittings also survived; they had been made from stone. This had been used because Orkney, bleak and exposed, is a place where few trees grow to any height and wood would have been at a premium, whereas good-quality stone was abundant. There are beds and cupboards made out of flagstone, giving an extraordinary impression of what a house would have looked like 5000 years ago.

Skara Brae consisted of several houses connected by covered passageways, and they all conformed to the same basic pattern. Each had a single doorway about 3 feet high and a central hearth, around which furniture was built into the walls and floor. Stone bed bases were on either side—these are likely to have been covered with bracken and furs to make them comfortable—and there were also stone "dressers." These shelved cupboards could have been used to hold personal items, food, or cult objects; there's no indication of what precisely was stored in or on them. Also uncertain is the purpose of stone-lined pits in the floors, though it has been suggested that they were used to hold water as they had been made watertight along the joins. They could have been used for storing shellfish, possibly limpets, which might have been used as fishing bait or even for food.

Below: Skara Brae is on the Orkney Islands which lie off the north coast of Scotland.

Opposite: An aerial view of the Neolithic settlement at Skara Brae, originally exposed by heavy storms in 1850. Further damage was done to the site by the weather in 1925 which led to the building of a sea wall to secure its foundations. The aerial view emphasizes the interconnectedness of the houses, mostly linked by still partly covered passageways.

Above: Inside one of the houses at Skara Brae, showing the bed bases and "dresser." Opposite this is the entrance, only about 3 feet high. The lower opening in the back wall goes into a narrow passage, running between this house and its neighbor, leading to a small cell. Here, in 1928, were found about 2400 beads, several pins and pendants, and a little whalebone dish filled with red pigment.

ORKNEY ISLANDS
ROUSAY
● Birsay
● Skara Brae
Finstown ●
Kirkwall ●
Stromness ● MAINLAND
HOY

EVERYDAY LIFE

The furniture and fittings from the houses were not the only signs of the life lived by the community at Skara Brae. There were other finds of items in stone, but bone had also been used and pottery was found. Cattle and sheep seem to have been kept and the people appear to have eaten a lot of seafood, game, and plants. Pots were used to store food (and could, of course, have been used to store other things as well), and tools for preparing skins were made from bone. Beads have been found—made from stone, animal teeth, bone, shell, and walrus ivory—and bone and ivory pins have also been discovered. Whalebone was utilized, and several dishes made of this have been found; two small ones—at least—had been used to hold red pigment. Perhaps the inhabitants used red ocher to decorate either themselves or the things they made. On a more prosaic level, the settlement had covered drains to remove sewage.

Above: The long slab lying on the floor of this hut had probably originally been a pillar; fragments of a pot were found beneath it which seems to have been broken when it fell. The skeletons of two elderly women were found beneath the foundation of the walls; they had clearly been deliberately interred there. It is possible that their spirits were intended to sustain the settlement.

Right: The interior of the burial chamber at Maes Howe on Orkney. The passageway is aligned with the setting sun at the winter solstice, almost in parallel with the alignment of the central house at the nearby Neolithic settlement of Barnhouse, which has some resemblances to Maes Howe in its construction and aligns to sunrise at the summer solstice.

RECENT DISCOVERIES— AND THE MEGALITHS

Skara Brae, remarkable though it is, is not unique on Orkney, though it is very well preserved. Other similar dwellings have been found, and some of them have revealed startling new evidence. There is a house near the Knap of Howar dating to about 3600–3100 BC which was full of cereal grains; this could suggest that farming had been going on even at this very early date in these northern latitudes, and traces of fields have been found on the nearby Shetland Islands.

A group of houses, similar to the group at Skara Brae, was found at Barnhouse. Here a group of huts was arranged around a large circular building whose entrance faced the point at which the sun rose on the morning of the summer solstice. This is unlikely to have been accidental or a coincidence. The Barnhouse settlement is very close to the Stones of Stenness, a major megalithic monument, and to Maes Howe. Maes Howe is an artificial hill covering a stone burial chamber and there are some similarities in the way both this and the large building at Barnhouse were constructed. At Maes Howe the burial chamber is aligned so that the last rays of the setting sun at the winter solstice shine down the entrance passage.

Very recently two more houses were found. One is close by the Ring of Brodgar, another stone circle, and more were found close to another passage grave. There has been some speculation that the people who lived at Barnhouse "controlled" the Stones of Stenness, and the same could easily be true of the house by the Ring of Brodgar and other monuments. While there may well be a connection, there is— as yet—no evidence for any unusual activity at the settlements which might indicate a special purpose.

Right: Recent archaeological work on Orkney has revealed the presence of a Neolithic house close to the Ring of Brodgar, here seen under the snow which emphasizes the conditions which can prevail on Orkney.

Varna

In 1972, workmen digging a trench for cables near the town of Varna in Bulgaria, in a place which was once the shoreline of a bay of the nearby Black Sea, exposed a grave. But it wasn't recent. It was the first one to come from a large Copper Age cemetery which proved to be astonishingly rich in grave goods—goods often made from gold.

Between 1972 and 1986 about three-quarters of the estimated extent of the cemetery was dug in excavations led by Ivan Ivanov. The Varna cemetery has been dated to between 4500 and 4000 BC, making it the earliest-dated major find of gold in the world. There was also copper in the burials, as well as flint and shell artifacts which could be traced to their places of origin—the people who buried and commemorated their dead at Varna evidently had extensive trading networks.

THE BURIALS

The finds were so extraordinary that describing them inevitably involves using percentages and figures. There were 281 burials excavated at Varna, sixty-one of which included gold. A few of the burials—twenty-three—had no grave goods but about 60 percent of the graves, included between one and ten items. Most of the rest had a lot more.

Of the 281 burials, 20 percent were symbolic burials, cenotaphs with no trace of human remains. Most of the gold was actually found in these symbolic burials, and three of them were particularly rich. One had 216 gold objects; the second contained 339 items; and the third had the most—857 objects.

Another rich burial was Grave 43. This contained the skeleton of a man who had been aged between 40 and 50 when he died, and who had been 5 ft 6 in tall. This burial contained almost 1000 gold objects as well as copper axheads and a "scepter," the wooden handle of which had been sheathed in bands of sheet gold. The man had been wearing large arm rings around his upper arms, beads around his neck, and a gold penis sheath.

Most of the gold objects found in the burials were ornaments—they would have been sewn onto fabric, worn in the hair or on the body itself—or of a symbolic nature, like mask decorations. Everything included in the graves seems to have been intended for display. This applies to the copper and stone items too; they could easily have been carried or played a ceremonial role. The flint tools were made from long pieces of high-quality stone, and axheads account for most of the copper, though there were also a lot of other things like pins and rings. Many of these copper objects were copies of items usually made from more everyday materials like antler or stone.

WORKING WITH METAL

During this time, people in Europe were becoming much more expert at firing pots at high temperatures. The skills needed to do this were easily transferred across to working with metals, and both copper and gold items begin to appear in the archaeological record. Gold was comparatively straightforward to work with; the basic technique of the Varna goldsmiths consisted of hammering gold into thick leaves and working with those. Copper was a different matter. Reducing ores to extract the metal requires temperatures of about 1800°F, heat-resistant containers and a reducing agent like carbon monoxide, though that can be obtained quite easily by burning wood. Like other "ages" the Copper Age did not happen simultaneously everywhere. The earliest attempts at working metals have—to date—been detected in Iran; in Europe the earliest evidence comes from the Balkans, with the ore coming from the Carpathian Mountains.

Opposite: Grave 43 from Varna. Its occupant was buried with almost 1000 gold objects, including the many small—and not so small—gold disks which would have been fastened onto fabric.

Below: The large holes on this gold bull from Varna were probably intended to enable it to be attached to clothing.

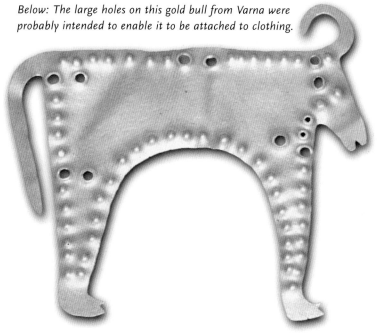

The Iceman

Two German mountaineers hiking near the Similaun glacier high in the Austrian Tyrol made one of the most remarkable recent discoveries in archaeology. On September 19, 1991, they spotted a body partly embedded in the ice. They thought they had found the corpse of someone dead perhaps twenty years, and reported their find immediately. A few days later the body, together with objects found nearby, was taken to a forensic laboratory at Innsbruck. There it became obvious that this was no recent casualty; the body was exceptionally old. Tests soon confirmed that the man had, in fact, died about 5000 years before.

Originally it had been thought that the Iceman, as he became known, had died of exposure. However, X-rays taken in 2001 revealed the real reason for his death—a flint arrowhead lodged beneath his right shoulder. Blood was found on his knife and garments, and on a broken arrow in his quiver; it came from four different individuals. He had a deep, debilitating cut on his hand, and had evidently been involved in a fight; it may have been two days before he succumbed to the arrow wound. The level of preservation was extraordinary and pollen remains indicated that his death had happened in early fall. A range of radiocarbon dates were undertaken for greater reliability, and these confirmed that he had died sometime between 3300 and 3200 BC.

Fragments of some garments remained. He appeared to have been dressed in fur leggings, a leather loincloth, a coat or cape made of tanned goat hide, and a woven grass cape. He also had a cap and leather shoes stuffed with grass; clothing perfect for the Alpine climate outside the worst winter months. Aged between 25 and 45, he had suffered from serious illnesses in the months before he died, and also had arthritis and an intestinal infestation. Tattoos on his left leg, right ankle and knee,

and lower back may have been done for therapeutic reasons, maybe to alleviate the pain from the arthritis.

Lying around his body were his possessions, including a copper ax hafted to a yew handle, an unfinished yew longbow, and a deerskin quiver containing a dozen unfinished arrow shafts as well as two flint-tipped arrows. He had also had a backpack made of hide and larch planks, a leather scabbard, and a dagger with a flint blade, a calfskin pouch hanging from his belt, and other items including a white marble bead threaded in an arrangement of long twisted leather tassels.

The Iceman seems to have been local. Scientific analysis of his teeth, bones, and stomach contents showed that he had probably grown up in a nearby valley, but had moved slightly higher when he was older, though he may have been involved in the seasonal movement of flocks instead. He could have been a shepherd; it is certainly one possibility. Some archaeologists have suggested that he might have been a shaman: also possible. What is certain is that this unique find brings us face-to-face with the distant past, and that more will be discovered about him as research continues.

Opposite: The Iceman had been preserved by a natural freeze-drying process. The body is fragile and can only be examined at intervals to ensure that it deteriorates no further but studies have established that he had been shot in the shoulder – the arrowhead was still lodged in his back – and had suffered a serious wound to his hand. He was found with a range of clothing and equipment, another unique survival. Grass capes, like the one he had been wearing, were still in use in northern Italy as recently as the 18th century.

Right: Reproduction tools made for a documentary about the Iceman.

Above: The Iceman was discovered by Helmut and Erica Simon near the Similaun glacier in 1991.

Megaliths

The great megalithic monuments of Europe—places like Stonehenge in the UK, Newgrange in Ireland and the stone rows of Carnac in France—have long excited attention, study and, often, wild theorizing.

These monuments, which alter the landscape in which they are installed, were constructed during the Neolithic, from broadly the fifth to the third millennium BC. By the early Bronze Age they were passing out of use, though they still remained visible, inspiring awe and starting legends. They are concentrated in the north and west of Europe and are especially significant in Ireland, northern and western Britain, and Brittany in western France.

Circles of standing stones are present specifically in Britain; enormous elaborate tombs are found in all areas, and there are also arrangements of standing stones, and single ones known as monoliths.

The word megalith comes from the Greek words megas, meaning great, and lithos, stone, so it simply means "large stone," and such stones are a defining feature of any megalithic structure. They are not, however, used as though they were just bigger versions of ordinary masonry (masonry using large stones which have been shaped is called Cyclopean masonry), but almost as though they were stone equivalents for great baulks or supports of wood instead. The enormous stone "lintels" at Stonehenge, for example, are even held in place by mortise and tenon joints, and there is some archaeological evidence that some sites, like Stonehenge, may have existed in a wooden form before stones were erected. What they meant to their builders and the people of their communities is uncertain, and there have been many theories.

Megalithic Europe
7000 BC–2000 BC
★ major site

Maes Howe ★
Callanish ★
N
Newgrange ★
Arbor Low ★
British Isles
North Sea
Avebury ★
West Kennet ★ Stonehenge
Atlantic
Ocean
France
Carnac ★
Alps
0   200 km
0   200 miles
Puy de Paulhiac ★

Opposite: Stonehenge from above. The area around the circle is exceptionally rich in contemporary archaeological remains.

Above: A lone stone situatated in Cornwall, England.

Left: A map showing major sites of megalithic monuments.

THREE PRINCIPAL TYPES OF MEGALITH

There are essentially three main types of megalithic monument: large tombs, stone circles and standing stones, either solitary ones or groups, and most were constructed relatively close to Europe's Atlantic coast. Some are found farther inland, in Spain, Portugal, and France, but many more are very close to the sea or open water, and often seem to have been located in particular coastal settings, like the Ring of Brodgar and the Stones of Stenness on Orkney. Not surprisingly, it has been suggested that the sea was an important means of communication, and islands which might seem isolated today, like the Orkneys or the Hebrides in Scotland, might have been thought of very differently in the Neolithic. There was certainly extensive trade. Beautiful jadeite axes, made with stone from the western Alps, have been found in burial mounds dating back to the fifth millennium BC near Carnac on the Breton coast and have also turned up in Scotland. They must have been valuable items: they do not seem to have had an everyday, practical purpose but to have been prized for their appearance; they have a highly polished finish. Other polished stone axes from other known sources were also traded between Britain and France.

Opposite: One of the massive upright stones at Stonehenge. Stonehenge is the largest of the English stone circles, measuring over 1300 feet across and containing more than 100 stones.

Below: The entrance to the great Irish tomb of Newgrange, showing the opening above the lintel which permitted sunlight to enter the passage at the solstice and shine down it into the burial chamber. Though Newgrange has been heavily restored, it still retains some of its atmosphere.

Why were Megalithic Monuments Built?

In stories and folk tales, from all over the places where they are present, megaliths have been ascribed to giants. In more recent times, however, there have been other ideas. In the 19th century, racial explanations were common: they were the work of a single group of people who had arrived in Europe from elsewhere. A modified version of this, in which migration was replaced by influence, became popular in the early half of the 20th century. It was thought that the "megalithic idea" had spread from Crete and the eastern Mediterranean by way of trading links through Spain and up the Atlantic seaboard. If this was true, then the monuments in the Mediterranean would be older—and, with the use of radiocarbon dating, this was found not to be the case. They are actually more recent.

It was then suggested that they had a specific function, and that this was why they had been built. Perhaps each communal tomb, for instance, would serve as a focus for a specific community. This idea was further developed by adding in a possibility that constructing one could serve as a territorial marker, that it would emphasize or even legitimize ownership or control of an area: in the case of a large tomb this could be expressed as "this is ours, it has the bones of our ancestors guarding it." Another strand of thought believed that the monuments were indeed connected to control, but to reinforce the right of one section of society—an elite—to control the rest.

More recently a lot of consideration has been given to the symbolic aspects of the monuments, and analyses have been very complex. There have been attempts to define spiritual "realms," areas of the landscape devoted to the dead—the ancestors—and the living, and these stress the importance of the overall area and the landscape in which the monuments sit.

There have always, of course, been other explanations put forward; the sophistication of the monuments has always seemed to require special, even exotic, theories. We are unlikely ever to know for sure, but megalithic monuments still have an undeniable effect. Today flowers and incense are sometimes left at places like West Kennet chambered tomb or Avebury stone circle; they can even be found at less well-known ones, such as in the double-chambered tomb in the small Welsh village of Dyffryn Ardudwy. There is no doubt that many people still feel a fascination and awe for them, feelings no doubt that were shared by the original builders.

TOMBS

Megalithic tombs are of different types and, inevitably, show differing levels of preservation. Some are almost intact, with huge mounds of earth still rising on top of them, while all that is left of others are the remains of their burial chambers. Most, however, were originally quite large, even enormous, and impressive. The earliest kind was the passage grave in which a stone-built passage led into a burial chamber. The passage was often narrow, low, and quite long, but it did allow repeated visits to the burial chamber.

The great Irish tomb of Newgrange is one of the best known; here, and in some other Irish tombs, access to the passageway entrance was gained via an open courtyard. Similar to passage graves are gallery graves, which have a corridor inside with side chambers leading off it. These were also covered by mounds of earth, and West Kennet long barrow in southern Britain is a very clear example. The mound at West Kennet is about 325 feet long, and it has five burial chambers leading off its central passage.

West Kennet contained the disarticulated remains of 46 people, but evidence of actual burial is not always present, and in some tombs animal bones are also found. The bones often seem, as at West Kennet, to have been used in some way, or maybe just moved. Sometimes they were sorted into types—long bones together in one place, skulls in another—but many tombs were investigated so long ago that there is no firm

Opposite: A carved stone from Newgrange has a clear design of lozenges among other, more swirling, designs. Initially the design would be scratched out with a small tool, possibly made of quartzite or some other very hard material. It would then be engraved more deeply and finally rubbed with a larger stone to give a smooth finish.

Above: The interior of the chambered tomb at West Kennet in England. This contained the remains of 46 individuals, but their bones were disarticulated and had evidently been moved. Even though the passages in these tombs may appear narrow and awkward, they would still have permitted repeated access, and the evidence shows that many were used repeatedly over long periods of time.

Left: The megaliths which form this stone circle at Callanish on the Hebridean island of Lewis are made from a relatively local rock that splits naturally into long thin sections.

Megalithic Art

A lot of megalithic monuments have been decorated. Some tombs in Portugal seem to have been painted and this may have been true of others, but most of the decoration visible today is in the form of incised carving. Simple motifs—crosses, ax shapes—have been found in passage graves in Brittany which are early in date (4800–4000 BC), but there are more elaborate examples from later, from the period of most passage grave building between 4000 and 3200 BC. These are especially abundant in Brittany and Ireland, where Newgrange is a particularly striking example.

This monument has been subject to heavy restoration but would still be impressive without it; the mound is 40 feet high and 325 feet in diameter, and the burial chamber inside is nearly 20 feet high. Both Newgrange and Knowth, not far to the west, are noted for the intricate designs carved on to the stones. There are concentric circles, spirals, wavy lines, lozenges, interlocking triangles, U shapes: all of it abstract and not representational. The designs cover stones around the mound, as well as the surface of those in the passage and in the chamber. In Brittany the tomb at Gavrinis is another fine example with stones entirely covered in carved designs, but there are some where the individual motifs are carved in isolation. It is striking that similar motifs, with only small variations, occur throughout the megalithic world. Tombs in Brittany have some decorations which do seem to be more representational, including a shield-like shape which appears rather human; this has been interpreted as being an idol, but that is really just speculation.

There have been many other guesses at the meaning of megalithic art. Some commentators, mindful of the astronomical alignments of many monuments, have suggested that the designs might be a way of symbolizing the movements of celestial bodies. Others have suggested that the designs of axes could stand for masculine authority, while yet more people have come up with the idea that the swirling abstract designs are the result of using hallucinogenic drugs. As with other "mysterious" aspects of archaeology, such as the possible reasons why Upper Paleolithic people decorated caves with paintings, the ideas put forward often say more about the individuals suggesting them, and the times in which they live, than they do about the subject under discussion. As far as the deeper meaning of megalithic art goes, yet again one thing is certain: we shall never know.

evidence of what lay inside. It may be that the disarticulation of the skeletons in some bears witness to two-stage burial, which is known to have happened in some societies in the recent past; initially the body may have been exposed and then the bones put inside the chamber. At the very least these chambers were used successively, with burials made at different times. They do seem to have been places for collective burial, and were visited for many years.

Many are deliberately designed to correspond with a particular time, notably sunset or sunrise at the solstice, the winter solstice for both Newgrange and Maes Howe on Orkney, for instance. The excavator of Newgrange, Michael O'Kelly, found a small opening rather like a window above the lintel of the passage entrance. This aligned with sunrise on the winter solstice, December 21, so that the sun would shine directly down the passage and light up the floor of the burial chamber deep within the tomb. It must have taken a lot of effort and planning to get the effect exactly right; a small change in the position of the roofing slabs would have ruined it, and the level of the floor of the passage even rises gradually to match the beam of light.

STONE CIRCLES

The most famous of all megalithic monuments is a stone circle, the undeniably impressive Stonehenge in southern England. In its final phase this was also deliberately oriented to align with the solstices: with sunrise at midsummer and with sunset in winter. At dawn on the summer solstice the sun rises above—actually slightly to

the left of—the Heelstone, a monolith standing just outside the circle, and shines directly along the main axis of the monument. This was noticed as long ago as the 1720s, when it was remarked upon by the antiquarian William Stukeley, and draws crowds to the place today. It is repeated in reverse at the winter solstice when the setting sun in the southwest shines through the circle from the opposite side, and some recent work has suggested this may actually have been more important.

This astronomical alignment may only have become significant in the latter stages of Stonehenge's development, however. Originally Stonehenge was a timber monument, with 56 wooden posts arranged at roughly regular intervals within a circular ditch and bank.

Left: Avebury, which is not far from Stonehenge, is the biggest stone circle in Britain.

Above: One of the massive Stonehenge trilithons. The engineering problems these—particularly the lintels—present have provided the inspiration for many attempted reconstructions.

Opposite: The Ring of Brodgar on the Scottish Orkney Islands is one of the more remote, but powerful, circles. Orkney was a focus for much activity in the Neolithic and has been extensively studied; the remains include houses as well as megalithic monuments.

Though there was a gap in this earthwork toward the northeast, it could not have framed the sun at any time of the year. Moonrise might have been significant, but more work remains to be done on that possibility.

At some time around 2500 BC work began to transform Stonehenge into a stone circle with a definite solar orientation at both summer and winter solstices. Some of the stones used, the 82 "bluestones," were transported to the site from quarries in Pembrokeshire in South Wales. Precisely how the people moved the stones the 240 miles between the two places has been the subject of much debate and some (inconclusive) experiments, but the most practical solution would have been to use a mixture of river, sea, and overland transport. The larger blocks, the 84 sarsen stones, were generally believed to have come from about 18 miles away on the Marlborough Downs, but it is now thought likely that there was more than one source. The sarsens appear to have received their final shaping on site and a lot of hammer stones and mauls of various types have been found at Stonehenge; they were used to hold the uprights firm in their foundation holes. Sarsen stone is very hard and does not break off in large pieces, so the hammer stones were usually also of the same hard material. There is evidence that gangs of workers had shaped the stones; some of them show parallel lines which seem to have been made by groups of people. The whole monument was realigned at this time and a large double earthwork, now called the avenue, was created on one side and the Heelstone, an unworked sarsen block, was erected at the end of it. Stonehenge is very much part of a complicated Neolithic landscape, and appears to have been its focus.

There are many other stone circles in Britain, and though Stonehenge is impressive, some of those on the Scottish islands—notably the Ring of Brodgar on Orkney and Callanish on the Hebridean island of Lewis—are among the most striking. This is partly because the local rock splits beautifully into tall thin stones, giving the circles made from them an air of otherworldliness. Avebury, not far from Stonehenge, is the largest of the English stone circles at over 1300 feet across, and contains more than 100 stones. Avebury also has two parallel avenues of standing stones; one was recognized only recently when two isolated stones were identified as belonging to it.

How to Lift a Large Stone

A lot of thought has gone into trying to determine how the megalith builders moved and erected such large and heavy stones. In many cases stones were transported long distances, sometimes over difficult terrain, but moving them was not the only problem. They also had to be set in place, something which appears to us to have been very difficult—especially in the case of the large stones topping the uprights at Stonehenge.

When it comes to moving them, many people have suggested that they would be transported on sleds running on rollers, which seems likely. Quarrying a stone and moving it onto rollers would have been relatively easy but moving that stone onto a sled would have been more awkward, and it has been suggested that this could have been accomplished by cutting away the earth beneath the stone and using levers. At Vestra Fiold in Orkney, a Neolithic quarrying site, excavators found a monolith which had been pulled over a rock-cut pit and onto two masonry supports. Unfortunately these had collapsed and the stone had been abandoned; maybe the quarrymen had been trying to maneuver it onto a sled. Like some other quarries, the stone at Vestra lies in bedding planes which could have been separated fairly easily, given enough labor to wedge the stones and lift them up. Erecting large stones on site seems to have been generally done by a gradual process of tilting them up and into prepared holes, though this would have had to be carefully controlled to avoid accidents.

There have been many different suggestions for the methods by which large stones were lifted on top of others; the big Stonehenge trilithons—with two uprights and a horizontal "lintel"—are the focus for many of these. Some ideas seem to be impractical: for instance, it has been suggested that the lintel and uprights were lashed together and hauled upright as a single unit, but this would be extraordinarily difficult if not almost impossible. Ramps, either of earth or timber, have also been suggested, but they would have left traces in the archaeological record, and so far no definite ones have been found.

Various experiments and reconstructions have been attempted, and one likely solution came from a Czech engineer, Pavel Pavel. He began working with a small scale model of Stonehenge and then, when his idea appeared to work, built a full-size replica of the parts of a trilithon in concrete. He and his team leaned two large oak beams against the top of the uprights, which had already been set in position. Two other beams, slightly smaller, were placed on the other side of the uprights to act as levers. The lintel was resting across the bottom of the first, substantial, pair of beams which were smooth and well lubricated with animal fat. Another, separate, beam crossed the big beams behind the lintel to stop it sliding backward, and it was attached by ropes to the levers. These were operated by two teams of people. As they hauled down on them, the lintel stone was dragged up the main pair of beams. The stop beam which lay behind it was also moved upwards, keeping pace. The lintel was easily raised and placed on top of the uprights—and the whole operation took ten people just three days.

In 1955 Alexander Thom published his theory that a single unit of measure, which came to be known as the "megalithic yard," had been used when constructing many stone circles. He had carefully measured 46 of them and subjected the results to statistical analysis, leading to the idea that a common basic unit had been employed when the circles were planned; this, he said, was about 33.7 in. Thom's figures have since been criticized, but it is possible that a measuring unit of some kind was used. If it had been a set one, used in common, then the circles would actually have been more regular. As it is, it could simply be something like a human pace, which would, of course, vary with the height of the individuals involved.

STANDING STONES

There are many individual standing stones, and a lot of them are solitary, apparently unrelated to any others. One is the immense Rudston monument, still standing nearly 26 feet tall in a churchyard in Yorkshire. The Grand Menhir Brisé (or the "great broken menhir") in France would have stood almost twice as high, if it had ever been erected. At present it lies on the ground in four huge pieces, but it would have been 65 feet tall.

Sometimes standing stones have been arranged to form rows or alignments. These can be single lines, and may appear to link up with other megalithic monuments, or they can appear in multiple rows. The most well-known example of this is Carnac in Brittany, where ten or more parallel rows extend for over half a mile. Another Breton site, Ménec, has 11 rows of a similar length, and is made up of 1099 individual granite stones.

Whatever the type of megalithic monument, it always seems to have had some sort of relationship with the landscape. Sometimes they are part of a dense concentration of other megaliths and contemporary buildings, even houses, as on Orkney, or in the area of Newgrange and Knowth in Ireland. Sometimes they are linked to only a few other monuments or maybe a single one; sometimes they have a relationship to a specific landmark and some, it is thought, may have been designed to be seen from the sea. Whatever their deeper significance to the society that produced them, they cannot be divorced from their environment.

Opposite: The main circle at Stonehenge, probably the world's best-known megalithic monument.

Above: The stone rows at Carnac in Brittany still have considerable impact, stretching as they do for over half a mile. There are ten or more rows, and they are almost parallel.

Bodies from the Bogs

Water, and wet places, played a significant part in European religion during the Iron Age, and this tradition may well have had its roots in earlier times. Items of high value dating back to the Bronze Age have been recovered from bogs, but the most surprising finds from wet places have been people.

Peat bogs are excellent preservers, and this applies to corpses just as much as it does to other things. Soft tissue survives very well, though bones do not, the opposite of what happens in most soils. When sphagnum moss forms peat, bacteria are unable to flourish, so anything deposited in it is free from microbial attack. Anaerobic peat bogs like this also contain what is effectively a natural tanning agent, preserving skin but changing its color to—usually—a deep dark brown. Peat also builds up quite quickly, covering anything buried in it more and more deeply as time passes.

Bog bodies are not a recent phenomenon; they have been turning up for centuries, revealed when people cut peat for fuel. There are accounts going back to the 17th century, but recorded finds became more numerous in the 19th century. The most famous discoveries were made in the 20th century, often in the commercial excavation of peat, and have been subjected to a battery of scientific tests and even attempts at facial reconstruction. Detailed forensic analysis, combined with the excellent level of preservation, has produced a lot of information. Most of the bodies so far studied go back to the Iron Age, about 2000 years ago, and particularly to the period between the first century BC and the first century AD.

TOLLUND MAN

In May 1950, two Danish farmers were digging peat for winter fuel in Central Jutland when they uncovered a face. As frequently happens, they thought they had found a recent murder victim and reported their discovery to the police. The local police were aware that ancient bodies were sometimes found in the peat and asked people from the local museum to accompany them, and when they in their turn saw what had been uncovered they consulted an expert, Dr Peter Glob. He went to the peat bog immediately and came face to face with the body that would become known as Tollund Man, possibly one of the best-preserved bog bodies ever found.

The dead man, who was lying on his side, looked very much as though he was sleeping. He was naked except for a belt around his waist and a pointed cap made from skin; this had been fastened around his neck and his hair was short, almost completely concealed by the cap. There was short stubble on his cheeks, upper lip, and chin. When more peat was removed it revealed something else: a noose made by plaiting two long

Opposite: Tollund Man. The most extraordinary thing about Tollund Man is the level of preservation, but his peaceful expression is also remarkable. It has been suggested that his stubble is actually post-mortem growth.

Above: Offerings were not just made in Danish bogs; there are many examples from elsewhere and particularly from Wales. This iron firedog is from Capel Garmon in north Wales.

leather thongs together, which encircled his neck and lay behind him. The body was removed from the bog the following day and transported—along with a lot of the surrounding peat—to the laboratory of the National Museum in Copenhagen, where it could be studied properly.

Tollund Man's head was especially well preserved and, though there was slight decomposition of parts of his body and some damage had been done to his back by peat cutting, the overall level of preservation was excellent. This included his internal organs, and it was possible to tell what the man had eaten for his last meal. It seemed to have been a vegetarian soup or gruel, made with barley and linseed among other things, and had been eaten between 12 and 24 hours before his death.

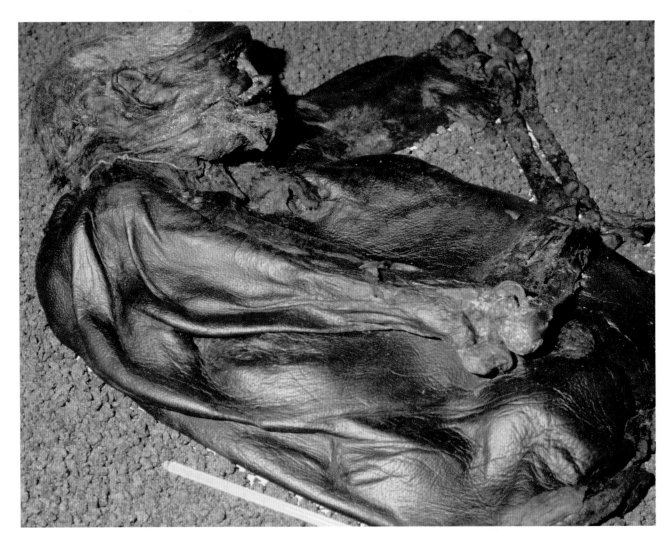

LINDOW MAN

Although those from Denmark are very well known, bog bodies are not a uniquely Danish phenomenon. They, or traces of them, have been found in other places and in 1984 one particularly good example was found near Manchester in the UK. Again the discovery came as a result of cutting peat, but this time on a commercial scale, which meant damage was done to the body due to the automated processes involved.

In 1983 part of a skull had been found on a conveyor at the commercial peat diggings on Lindow Moss to the south of Manchester; the site manager took it to the police. It was initially thought to belong to a local missing woman and supposed murder victim, but it was dated to the early part of the first millennium AD. The following year part of a foot was noticed on the conveyor, and again the police were involved, as was the county archaeologist. He visited the place from where the peat containing the foot had been extracted, and noticed that

skin was still visible in the cutting. A block of peat was removed which would contain any remains; this was taken to the British Museum once it had been established that the skin was not of recent date, and archaeological investigations began.

The peat block contained the upper half of a male body (facial hair made his sex obvious), naked except for an armband made out of fox fur. At the time this was thought to be all that had been left by the peat cutting operations, apart from the foot found on the conveyor, but more body parts have been found since and seem likely to belong to this individual. Even so, it was possible to tell quite a lot about the dead man, including what he had eaten—and how he had died. Inevitably, he became known as Lindow Man.

He had been between 5 ft 6 in and 5 ft 8 in tall— this was calculated from the length of his humerus, the upper arm bone—and had probably weighed about 141 lb. He seemed to have been fit and healthy though he had mild arthritis in his lower spine, and had been in his mid-20s when he died. His hair was straight and had been roughly trimmed just before death, as had his beard and mustache, probably using shears. His fingernails were undamaged, suggesting he had not been involved in heavy or rough work, and he may therefore have had a privileged position in his community. Shortly before he died he had eaten what seemed to have been a griddle cake. Then, or maybe just beforehand, he had been taken to Lindow Moss. There he had been hit twice on the head with a blunt

instrument, causing fractures each time. He had then been garotted, using a twisted garotte and a stick to tighten it, which broke his neck. Following this his throat was cut just above the garotte, though it is possible that the final twist of the garotte was only administered after his throat was slit. He also had a broken rib, which might have been caused by one of the people involved, probably someone using the garotte. This killing appeared to have happened during cooler weather, one winter perhaps, some time between the first century BC and the first century AD.

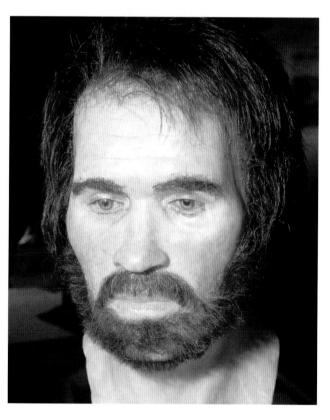

Opposite: The upper body of Lindow Man. The compression and staining of bog bodies can sometimes make them difficult to visualize, and even though Lindow Man was well preserved, it was decided to attempt a facial reconstruction.

Above: The facial reconstruction of Lindow Man produced by the highly experienced team at Manchester. Some aspects are conjectural but likely, such as the color of the hair and eyes, whereas others—the shape of the skull and shape and position of the features—are reached through painstaking research and work. The same team also did a facial reconstruction of the Yde Girl.

Right: The Battersea Shield was found in the River Thames, London, and appears to have been a votive offering.

OTHER BODIES, OTHER DEATHS

Like Tollund Man and Lindow Man, most bog bodies seem to have suffered violent deaths, sometimes with multiple possible causes. While Tollund Man had been hanged—the position of the noose was not thought to be consistent with strangulation—Lindow Man could have died in any of three ways. Grauballe Man, another Danish bog body from the first century AD, had sustained a non-accidental forehead wound and broken leg as well as having his throat cut. The Yde Girl, from the Netherlands, also dating to the first centuries BC/AD, had been strangled with a woolen band which had been twisted around her neck three times. It had a slipknot which had been tightened below her left ear. However, below the mark of this ligature was a stab wound, a cut about 1.8 in long and 0.8 in deep, running from the middle to the left of her throat; she too had multiple potential causes of death.

WHY DID THEY DIE?

The Roman historian Tacitus described executions among the inhabitants of Germany. He said that some criminals—those guilty of "unnatural vice," which may mean promiscuity as well as homosexuality—were "pressed down under a wicker hurdle into the bog" and this has led to the idea that the bodies in the bogs might be those of criminals. It is also quite possible that they were sacrifices, however. There is a long tradition of making offerings in wet and boggy places in the areas where they were found, and the deaths certainly seem to correspond to some sort of ritual. Many of the victims appear to have belonged to a high social group; their hands are generally smooth, uncallused and well kept, indicating that their lives did not involve much manual labor. They were also usually stripped before being placed in the bog, though whether before or after death is not known, and show signs of having received special care, such as having their hair trimmed. It has been suggested that the societies from which they came would have been experiencing stress at the time, with the aggressive expansion of the Roman Empire, and that this could have led to a perceived need for special sacrificial offerings. In the end, whether they were criminals or sacrificial victims is not known, but they certainly died in a ritualistic manner.

Bog "Deposits"

Making offerings by means of water and wet places had been done for many years and, as well as the bodies, many artifacts have been retrieved from such locations. In the UK, objects such as the Battersea Shield, which came from the Thames have been found in rivers or in peat bogs and lakes. There are many from Wales, for example, including the iron Capel Garmon firedog, found in a bog in Flintshire.

Some of the most elaborate come from Denmark, where the beautiful Trundholm sun chariot—dating to much earlier, to about 1650 BC – was discovered in a bog in 1902. Other precious objects have been retrieved, including bronze lurs or ceremonial trumpets. An extraordinary silver cauldron was found at Gundestrup; this is roughly contemporary with most of the bog bodies and, in fact, was found close to a place where some bodies have also been discovered. The cauldron was not made locally, but most probably came from southern Europe. It was certainly of high value, and equally certainly was placed deliberately in the bog; it may well have been a votive offering to the gods.

Opposite: The Trundholm sun chariot was retrieved from a Danish bog, but dates back to the Bronze Age; making offerings in bogs has a long history. This is made of bronze, with one side of the sun disc covered in gold; the bronze is engraved. It was certainly an object of high value and significance.

Right: The Gundestrup cauldron was also retrieved from a bog in Denmark, and was deposited there at around the same time as many of the bog bodies—between the first century BC and the first century AD. It was made in southern Europe but may have been designed for a Celtic patron; certainly the motifs seem to correspond with what is known of "Celtic" armor, and trumpeters are shown blowing distinctive instruments. How it reached a Danish bog is not known.

The Iron Age

Iron began to be used increasingly in Europe during the first millennium BC, especially after about 700 BC, but bronze continued to be used as well, and many bronze objects have been recovered from Iron Age sites. Skills in working with other materials, notably gold, also developed and extensive trading networks were built up, some of which ran down to the Mediterranean world. While most of the people would still have been involved in farming, the trading generated considerable wealth and contributed to the establishment and growth of local elites. There is a great deal of archaeological evidence from this time, ranging from chariot burials to hillforts and larger settlements, from industrial and mining sites to hoards of treasure. Some of the most unusual evidence relates to offerings made in bogs.

Biskupin in Poland is a fortified town that was constructed in the eighth century BC. Its preservation is unusually good; Biskupin was built on a low marshy island and the inevitable waterlogging has permitted the survival of a lot of wood. It was surrounded by a solid timber stockade, originally about 22 feet high with a walkway for defenders, and had been protected from the lake surrounding it by a breakwater. Inside were tightly packed houses, terraced along parallel streets. The streets were also made of wood, split oaks and pine logs, and had been surfaced with soil and sand. Dendrochronology—tree-ring dating—has shown that the 80,000 trees involved in its construction were cut in a single winter, that of 738–737 BC, and the sheer scale of the task implies some local central authority. The existence of some sort of hierarchy becomes more and more obvious throughout the millennium, and as time progresses evidence also comes from classical authors.

Opposite: Hillforts appeared in the Bronze Age though their real flowering came later, in the fifth and sixth centuries BC. Many fell out of use but some continued in occupation or were reoccupied later. That is true of this one, South Cadbury in Somerset, whose occupation after the Romans left Britain, together with its location in the west of Britain, led to its being described as the "original Camelot."

Above: The Iron Age hillfort of Maiden Castle in Dorset, UK. The hilltop was fortified in depth, protecting the top with elaborate earthworks. It was probably captured in AD 43 by Vespasian's Second Legion.

Right: Bronze continued to be used; it was not completely replaced by iron, as these British examples illustrate. This bull with two "busts of goddesses" on its back comes from Maiden Castle.

Industrial centers developed in the middle of the millennium, such as Sticna in Slovenia, which has a lot of evidence for iron smelting and founding, and Hallstatt in Austria, where salt was mined. At Hallstatt the damp, salty conditions preserved many artifacts made from leather, wood, and fur, including leather backpacks which were used to take tools into the mine and bring salt out. Hallstatt wasn't just important for the mines, however: many extremely rich burials have also been excavated there, and the mines appear to have acted as a focus for wealth gained through trade. Sticna was also more than a center for smelting high-grade iron ore; it was a large fortified site with a big cemetery.

HOCHDORF

Elite burials are a feature of central and northern Europe in the Iron Age, and have been found in many places; the tomb found at Hochdorf in western Germany in the 1970s was particularly remarkable. The excavation of a burial mound, which had originally been as much as 22 feet high but which had eroded away to almost nothing, revealed a wealthy and intact burial dating to 550–500 BC. The excavations were difficult, largely because of the sheer density and richness of the items in the tomb, and in some cases blocks of soil were removed and excavated in a laboratory.

In the middle of the tomb was a wood-lined burial chamber of a double skin construction, the two layers being separated by stones. It contained the body of a man lying on an extraordinary bronze bed which has been described as a "recliner." This is shaped rather like a bathtub with one long side cut away and stands on eight legs, in the form of the figures of women who appear to hold the bed up with their hands. The back and sides are decorated with embossed designs of dancers and wagons, together with their horses, and it had been lined with fabrics and furs.

The man whose body had been laid on it was about 5 feet 11 in tall and had been buried wearing a gold hoop about his neck; his clothing was also decorated with gold objects. Among the other finds in the chamber was a bronze kettle which scientific tests showed had contained mead; this was of foreign origin, possibly coming from one of the Greek colonies in southern Italy. Opposite the bronze couch was a four-wheeled wagon, nearly 15 feet long, made of wood and covered in iron with harnesses for two horses. Other European burials from the Iron Age have also included wheeled vehicles—in some cases the dead person was placed in the box of a chariot—but the iron sheathing on this one is, so far, unique.

HILLFORTS AND TOWNS

In Britain hillforts are among the most noticeable Iron Age survivals. A naturally prominent site would be further strengthened by enormous earthworks requiring a massive investment in both manpower and time. Many were occupied, often by quite substantial communities. Not all of the hillforts were in use at the same time, and many were abandoned by the third century BC, while a few rose to dominant positions. They first began to develop in the Bronze Age, as they also did in southern Germany, but the sixth and fifth centuries saw them flourish. They were clearly the result of communal effort, and are most likely to have been organized by some form of controlling power such as a tribal ruler. One of the best known is Maiden Castle, excavated by Sir Mortimer Wheeler; another two which have been dug are Danebury and South Cadbury, investigated by Barry Cunliffe and Leslie Alcock respectively.

Urbanized communities began to develop in Europe, and the dominant British hillforts may have shared some of their characteristics. These European settlements, known as oppida, were described by Caesar in his account of his campaigns in Gaul (now Belgium and France). They were large—between 0.1 and 1.16 square miles—and were surrounded by walls. Houses were crammed inside, and there were workshops as well.

THE CELTS

Ancient Greek writers used the term Keltoi to describe the peoples of Europe living north and west of the Alps; it essentially conveys the same meaning as barbarian: people not like us. The Romans distinguished between some of these groups, though with a broad brush, and called the inhabitants of France Galli, or Gauls, differentiating them from the Germans on the other side of the Rhine. These terms were used as generalizations, and the people concerned seem to have used other names to describe themselves, such as Boii, Parisii or Brigantes—names reflecting tribal affiliations, though the tribes were often very large and are possibly better described as peoples. There's no evidence that they ever described themselves collectively as "Celts." In fact, there may never have been a single homogenous Celtic people corresponding to that described by classical writers. Nevertheless it is a term used as convenient shorthand by archaeologists, historians, and art historians, and over the last 200 years or so has also acquired political overtones. The whole issue is one which continues to be hotly debated, and there is no doubt that some things that are considered to be distinctively Celtic—like heavy neck rings, torcs—occur across a wide area of northern Europe.

Left: A gold torc which comes from Snettisham in Norfolk. The first finds from a field in eastern England were made in 1948 and 1950: five gold torcs. Since then, a find made by an amateur enthusiast using a metal detector has resulted in the whole field being stripped of topsoil and carefully excavated. Five major hoards were found including many torcs—there were 9 in gold, 15 in electrum (a mixture of gold and silver), 14 in silver and 25 in bronze—and many other items.

Opposite: Mortimer Wheeler excavates at Verulamium.

Sir Mortimer Wheeler

Mortimer Wheeler, who was born in 1890, became one of the 20th century's greatest archaeologists. He studied at the University of London and fought in the First World War. As director of the National Museum of Wales he began applying some of the systematic excavation methods of the Victorian archaeologist General Pitt-Rivers, one of the first to do so. He improved on Pitt-Rivers' methods with techniques of careful stratigraphic open-area excavations, making it possible to expose entire systems of things such as street layouts or fortifications. During the years before and after the Second World War he developed his approach to excavation at sites in the UK such as Maiden Castle in Dorset, an Iron Age hillfort, and Verulamium, the Roman town of St Albans. He also did a lot of work elsewhere, notably on the Indian subcontinent. He died in 1976, and his impact on the following generation of archaeologists was marked. Not only did many work with him on his sites as young volunteers or students, but he also began popularizing archaeology in the media.

Hadrian's Wall

The Roman Empire covered a vast area and continued to expand for many years. The Emperor Augustus had tried to limit further expansion in AD 9 but the emperors who followed him, desiring the military glory which could consolidate their position at home, continued the pattern of conquest and control. The Emperor Hadrian, who ruled from AD 117 to 138, was the first to recognize that the empire could not go on expanding indefinitely and worked to consolidate the frontiers. Two areas were particularly problematic—northern Britain and Germany—and Hadrian decided to create fixed frontiers in both. In the latter, military campaigns had extended the frontier between the Rhine and the Danube, and Hadrian made this line permanent, constructing a pallisade wall from near Bonn on the Rhine to Regensburg on the Danube. In Britain he decided to build a high stone wall. The result today is one of the most impressive archaeological sites in western Europe.

Like many of the other manifestations of the power of imperial Rome, Hadrian's Wall never entirely disappeared. Early chroniclers, writing only about 500–600 years after it was built, decided it had been constructed for protection during the last days of Roman Britain. As with many other sites, serious excavations and study only really began in the second half of the 19th century; before then it had proved an excellent source of building material or a good foundation for the road leading from one side of Britain to the other.

The Emperor Claudius's troops had conquered Britain in AD 43 (Julius Caesar, nearly a century earlier, had only raided the island), and in the next 40 to 45 years the army managed to establish some sort of control over the the south and east. Other areas were more difficult to subdue, and at the start of Hadrian's reign northern Britain was still troublesome. Serving there must have been demoralizing; the pattern of tentative forays northward and retreats south would have sapped army morale. Hadrian's pragmatic solution—a definite frontier from coast to coast—would probably have served to restore that, involving his skilled troops in a major undertaking, as well as providing a defensible line. The Romans certainly extended their influence to the north of the Wall, and Hadrian's successor Antoninus Pius tried to push a frontier line much further north, but this did not last.

It is likely that the main purpose of Hadrian's Wall was to supervise and control movement across the border, providing a policing presence rather than a base for warfare. It has even been compared to a customs zone, but it may have fulfilled many functions during its approximately 250 years of operational existence. Construction followed a regular plan, with a small fort called a Milecastle extending on the south side roughly every mile and with two turrets evenly placed between each Milecastle. Forts were built along its length a little

later about 6 or 7 miles apart, and in some places this meant demolishing and rebuilding parts of the newly built wall. At about the same time a huge, flat-bottomed ditch with earthworks on either side was constructed to the south; this is known today as the Vallum and is still visible, winding across the landscape. Usually it was

Opposite: Hadrian's Wall at Housesteads. It is a mistake to think of troops from Italy being miserable in northern British weather; many, probably most, of those serving on the Wall came from parts of the Roman empire where the weather would have been similar. There are records of auxiliary soldiers coming from Belgium, Gaul, Germany, and Romania—among other places—being stationed on or near the Wall.

Above: A view of the Wall at Walltown Crags enables the visitor is able to understand how impressive the edifice would have been, even without the wooden parapet.

Below: A map showing the extent of Hadrian's Wall.

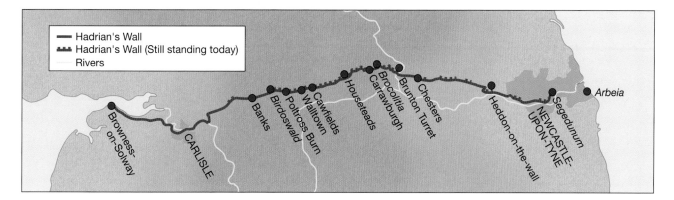

The Roman Army

Without the army, there would have been no Roman Empire, no conquest and no continuing occupation of places like Britain for hundreds of years. It was an efficient and professional fighting machine, but fighting was not its only purpose. Roman soldiers were also engineers, administrators, surveyors, and builders.

There were two main parts of the Roman army, the legions and the auxiliaries. The men in the legions were Roman citizens and highly trained; most of them were infantry, but there was a small contingent of cavalry. The auxiliaries, on the other hand, were not citizens, though they qualified for this status after 25 years' service. They were locally raised troops from various parts of the empire and did not generally serve in their country of origin. In the records from Vindolanda, for example, references are made to Tungrian and Batavian troops who came from northern Europe, from around the River Meuse and by the mouth of the Rhine respectively. Auxiliary units could be either infantry or cavalry, and did less specialist and technically demanding work. Hadrian's Wall, for example, was constructed by the legions while the auxiliaries manned it, operating the system which the legions had determined.

Legions were around 5000 men strong, and there were about thirty of them in the Roman army. A legion was divided into ten cohorts; the first cohort was different, but the other nine were divided into six centuries each. A century had 80 men and was commanded by a centurion—men who were vital to the running of the army. Auxiliary troops were organized in smaller groups. There was also, sometimes, a third group involved with the army: the irregular soldiers, probably hired as extra manpower along with their leaders in times of special need.

about 110 feet behind the Wall, but this can vary. The Vallum's exact purpose is unclear, but it has been suggested that it defined the southern limit of the zone of direct military control.

The stone used to build the Wall itself came from local sources, and though the finished width can be assessed today (it varies from east to west), determining the final height is less easy: it was probably at least 11 or 12 feet tall. Nor do we know for sure whether it was topped by a walkway protected by a parapet. There is evidence, however, that a white lime mortar or whitewash may have been used to cover the surface, which would have made the frontier visible from a distance. This would also have afforded some protection from the weather and made it easy to spot any deterioration. Behind the Wall and Vallum were a variety of forts and supply centers which could have provided administrative back-up, barracks and storage facilities—the granaries at one, Corbridge, are particularly clear, but the best known of these is Vindolanda. The military command of all of northern Britain, including the Wall and its forts, was based at York. This was the headquarters of the sixth legion.

The most spectacular part of the wall visible today is the central part, where it was built on top of the Whin Sill, an outcrop which runs for some distance and gives wonderful views to both north and south. The fort at Housesteads controlled this sector. All forts were generally constructed on the same basic plan and Housesteads was no exception: within the walls everything conformed to a grid pattern. In the middle was a headquarters building and the commanding officer's house. Around this center were granaries, barracks and service facilities such as kitchens, a hospital, and a latrine. Main bathhouses—the commanding officer's house usually had its own—would generally be outside a fort. Also outside was the

Above: The latrine block at Housesteads is one of those archaeological remains that gives a real impression of a living community. Seats would originally have run around the sides, with drains beneath, and the sewage would have been swept down and out under the wall with the dirty water from the channel in the floor. It is highly likely that it would have been used as fertilizer.

Below: The remains of the hypocaust of the bathhouse at Housesteads.

Opposite: Castle Nick Milecastle, otherwise known as Milecastle 39, on Hadrian's Wall not far from Housesteads. Milecastles were miniature forts and had a little accommodation for a few soldiers, generally about 12 though with a maximum of thirty men, but they were really little more than fortified double gateways through the wall. Recent work just to the west of here has shown that white lime mortar had been applied to the Wall, though whether this was to make it more visible or protect the masonry is unknown.

civilian settlement (a vicus), some areas of cultivation and a few other specific buildings like a temple to Mithras, a god particularly popular with the military. Burials would also have taken place outside.

One of the areas of Housesteads which has been excavated most clearly is the latrine block lying in the south-east corner. It was a communal facility, though it is not large enough to have been adequate for the whole garrison; barrack blocks may have had their own arrangements. It had wooden seats running around three of the walls and a paved floor. Next to the building was a large cistern, and this would have provided the water which was necessary for washing; it ran around the room, fed by gravity, in a channel at foot level. Dirty water ran off into a deeper passage beneath the seating, and this would have flushed the contents out through a channel in the wall of the fort. The commander had his own latrine as well as bathhouse; during excavations a gold ring was found in it, trapped in a crack in the sewer.

The vicus or civilian settlement at Housesteads originally lay further to the south, beyond the Vallum, but it was evidently allowed to move next to the fort in the third and fourth centuries. It is only partly exposed, though more has been excavated than is currently visible, and bumps and ridges in the grass show where more buildings lie. Soldiers' families would have settled in the vicus, as would people whose livelihoods depended on the fort such as merchants and tradesmen. One building, which can still be seen, was rather surprising to excavate. It appears to have been built about AD 300 and abandoned about seventy years later. One end gave onto the main southward street of the vicus and housed a shop; behind this was a large room. In 1932, the excavators found two bodies there. They were a man and a woman, and the point of a sword had been broken off between the man's ribs; a new clay floor had been laid above them. Roman law expressly forbade burial within a settlement, and the name the building was given by the diggers—the Murder House—seems entirely appropriate.

Left: Conservation work is on-going along the length of Hadrian's Wall. In common with many other important archaeological sites, those responsible for the preservation of the Wall must consider how to deal with the effects of tourism and environmental factors such as the weather. At the same time, archaeologists continue their work at Vindolanda during the summer months each year in order to make further discoveries.

Vindolanda

Vindolanda was one of the "support" forts in the immediate hinterland of Hadrian's Wall. The organization of the fort itself was typical, conforming to pattern, but here a lot of the civilian settlement has been excavated. Other finds make Vindolanda, a relatively unimportant part of the Roman Empire, absolutely unique.

Since 1969 Vindolanda has been excavated by Robin Birley, and an extraordinary variety of evidence has been recovered from the site. A lot of this, remarkably, has been organic material. There are worn-out shoes and sandals, tent fragments, bags, leather straps and offcuts; there are wooden items such as bowls, tent pegs, the top of a trestle table, and combs; and remnants of bigger things like flooring planks, oak beams, and walls made of wattle and daub. The shoes include ones which would have been worn by women and children; there's a child's sock and insole and even a woman's wig, so there would have been plenty of civilians around. Even metal objects—spearheads, nails, needles, rings, and coins—were found in excellent condition, generally not corroded.

To some degree this level of preservation was possible because the fort had been rebuilt several times and each time the floors were packed and levelled. A combination of factors allied to this—the materials used such as the bracken and straw which were part of floor coverings, the incorporation of material from the process of tanning, the presence of natural springs—

kept the lowest layers permanently damp. When these levels were exposed, some of the bracken was still green. The packing included general refuse, human excrement and urine (which were probably connected to tanning and leather waste rather than squalid living conditions), and fly pupae and internal parasites were discovered. Organic remains like these are remarkable in themselves, but far more unusual are the numerous documents which were also retrieved. Running the Roman army must have involved a lot of bureaucracy, but not much evidence of it has been found. Most of what information there is comes from Egyptian and Syrian papyri, and nothing at all had been discovered in Britain. This changed in 1973 when Robin Birley first noticed ink lettering on a scrap of wood.

By now over 1500 written documents have been found. Many were embedded in the compact layers of

Above: A reproduction of a Roman fort at Vindolanda, giving an impression of Roman masonry. The crenelated parapet is conjectural but probable: a contemporary souvenir from the Wall known as the Rudge cup shows towers with crenelated tops like these—though precisely which part of the wall is shown in this way is unclear.

Left: Much of the site of Vindolanda is as yet unexcavated but the walls and gates are visible as well as the Headquarters building and the Commanding Officer's Residence.

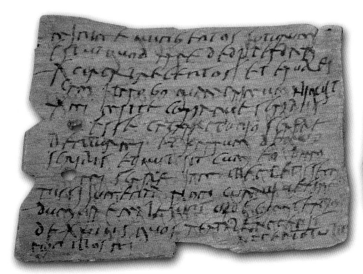
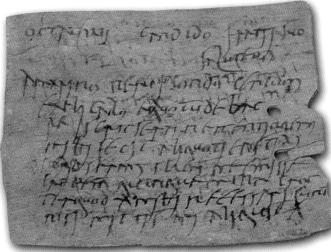

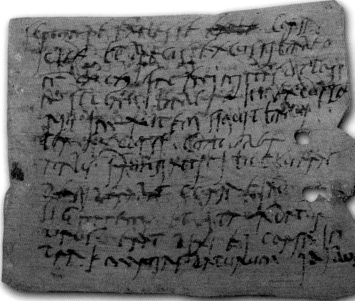

flooring; some have burned edges so they may have come from bonfires. One large group of 300 certainly did. In 1993 they were excavated from what had been the base of one; they had evidently been unwanted archives destroyed—incompletely—by troops leaving the area. Written material comes from all over the site; documents have been retrieved from drains, refuse pits, and old water tanks as well as the floor packing.

Some are wax tablets in wooden frames; they would have been written on using a metal stylus. These have proved impossible to read since they have several superimposed texts, although some addresses are legible. Most, however, are on fine slivers of wood, usually birch or alder. They have been folded (which would have been

perfectly possible when they were new) and the address was written on the back. Some of the longer records of accounts are made of several pieces, fastened end to end with matching tie holes, and privacy would have been preserved on the smaller ones by binding them shut. The writing surface is fine and smooth, and the ink was made from carbon, gum arabic; a pen was used for writing. Writing implements for both these and the wax tablets have also been found at Vindolanda.

There are roster lists, revealing the operational reality of the Roman army. The first cohort of Tungrians, for instance, had a nominal strength of 752. Of these, 456 were absent. Some were serving as guards at Corbridge or with the provincial governor; other detachments had gone to York to collect pay or even to Gaul. Thirty-one were unfit for service; fifteen were sick, six were wounded and ten were suffering from eye inflammation.

There are ration lists, requests for leave, petitions for promotion or clemency, a demand for more beer for the soldiers ("the lads have no beer, please send some"), receipts, accounts, and lists of household equipment. Some of these seem to have been written by slaves who may have acted as record keepers or secretaries. There are drafts of official letters, correspondence about clothing ("I have sent you two pairs of socks from Sattua two pairs of sandals and two pairs of underpants"), letters from one soldier to another ("I am surprised that you have written nothing back to me for such a long time"), and even a medical prescription. Many concern the movement of goods; one very long one concerns problems connected to paying for and collecting some hides: "I would already have been to collect them except that I did not care to injure the animals when the roads are bad." There's also a note about fighting the Britons, who are described as "Brittunculi," a perjorative way of describing them: "There are very many cavalry. The cavalry do not use swords, nor do the wretched Britons mount in order to throw their javelins."

One of the most remarkable is a party invitation sent to Sulpicia Lepidina, the wife of Flavius Cerialis—commander of the cohort of Batavians stationed at Vindolanda—by Claudia Severa, wife of another local commander. "On the 3rd day before the Ides of September [September 11], sister, for the day of the celebration of my birthday, I give you a warm invitation to make sure that you come to us, to make the day more enjoyable for me ..." This letter, most of which was evidently dictated, ends in a different hand. This is likely to be Claudia Severa herself, writing "farewell, sister, my dearest soul ..." Another letter from her to Lepidina has an equally flowery ending. This is the earliest known example of Latin writing by a woman, and both the correspondents were evidently literate.

Opposite: A letter from Octavius to Candidus, in which he explains why he has been unable to collect some hides. Octavius starts by promising "The hundred pounds of sinew from Marinus—I will settle up" and asks for cash to cover a deposit for some grain. It is a long and rather gossipy letter which covers quite a lot of business dealings: "I told him I would give him the hides by the Kalends of March. He decided that he would come on the Ides of January. He did not turn up nor did he take any trouble to obtain them..." and "I hear that Frontinius Julius has for sale at a high price for leather-making the [things] which he bought here for five denarii apiece."

Below: The birthday invitation from Claudia Severa to Sulpicia Lepidina. The address was on the back, and the change in the style of the writing can be seen quite clearly at the bottom of the right-hand leaf; this is the note that Claudia Severa added in her own hand. She also sends greetings to Lepidina's husband, the commander at Vindolanda, and greetings from her own husband, Aelius, and their "little son."

Sutton Hoo

A landowner from Suffolk in eastern England, Edith Pretty, had an interest in archaeology. She also had several large burial mounds on her estate. In 1938 she commissioned Basil Brown, an archaeologist who knew the area, to investigate these. Four were opened, and the objects found were obviously Anglo-Saxon in date, coming from the latter half of the first millennium AD. But it was the largest mound, Mound 1, that was to provide a range of marvelous discoveries.

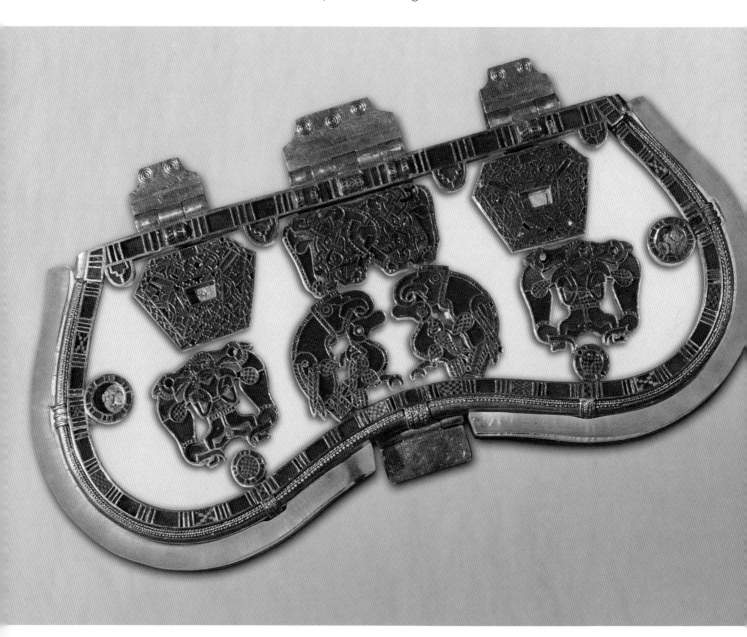

EXCAVATING THE SITE

Digging on Mound 1 began in May 1939, after Mrs Pretty had indicated which of the mounds she would like excavated next. A wide trench was cut across the mound and five iron ship nails were recovered. Brown, who had a lot of knowledge about East Anglian archaeology, suspected he had uncovered evidence of a ship burial and, sure enough, traces of the outline of the bow were soon revealed. The wood of the ship itself had not been preserved in the acid conditions of the sandy site so the archaeologists were faced with a not uncommon task, excavating a "shadow" marked by changes in soil color and, in this case, rows of nails. The size of the ship which had been beneath Mound 1 was already apparent and Brown called in additional experts. Over only ten days, a highly experienced team of archaeologists worked on the site and found more than 260 objects, many of which were unique.

The ship had been large—about 90 feet long—and had been clinker-built. There was no trace of it having had a mast, but traces of some sort of unusual timber structure were found by Brown just before he called in the specialist help. This proved to be the wall of a burial chamber, roughly 18 feet long, constructed in the middle of the ship. It had originally had a sloping roof, with the eaves resting on the ship's sides; the two ends of the chamber appeared to have been gabled and, at its peak, it had stood almost 13 feet above the keel plank. The mound had been piled around and above the funerary boat, but the chamber itself was left free of sand. Eventually it could no longer withstand the weight of sand that had been piled above it and gave way, collapsing probably within a century of the burial. The sand which then poured in preserved many of the objects that had been placed inside.

Opposite:
One of the
most beautiful finds
from Sutton Hoo was this
lid of a purse. It is decorated
with glass enamel, garnets, and gold.

Above: One of a pair of shoulder clasps from Sutton Hoo, decorated in a similar style to many of the other items from the burial. The two halves, shown in their linked position here, are joined by inserting a pin down the middle.

Below: One of several buckles from Sutton Hoo, decorated in enamel and gold.

Excavating and removing these during the dig was a delicate task, and excavation continued with "paint-brush and packing-needle." The sand was damp, and some items—like those in leather and fabric—had to be prevented from drying out. These were often removed in a block and were sorted and cleaned in a laboratory, a much more suitable environment.

THE BURIAL

The finds from Sutton Hoo included many beautiful and precious objects. Gold items were in extremely good condition—gold withstands most corrosion—but some of the other metal objects needed careful conservation, as did the leather and fabric. This was due partly to

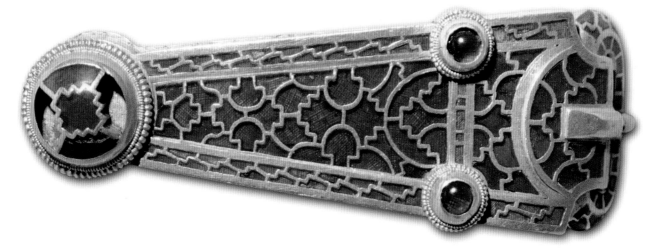

damage sustained when the chamber collapsed, and partly to the effects of the damp sand. Among the many items found were coins, and these made it possible to date the burial with a degree of certainty to some point between AD 620 and 650. England, at that time, was ruled by several regional Anglo-Saxon kings and this burial may have been connected to one of them.

There is, however, no trace of the body itself. The acid conditions of the site could easily have destroyed all trace of it, and tests have been carried out to try and determine whether or not there ever was one. These, unfortunately, proved inconclusive. It may be that the ship was a memorial, a cenotaph or symbolic burial, and that no body was ever included. In support of this theory is the fact that no intimate personal items—rings, pins holding clothing in place—have been found: had a corpse been interred, then these might well have been present. Against the cenotaph idea are the traces of iron coffin fittings which marked out an empty rectangle in amongst the grave goods.

Above: A solid gold buckle from Sutton Hoo. The beautiful interlinked patterns of animals cover almost the entire surface, and the whole object weighs nearly one pound.

Opposite: The helmet from Sutton Hoo was only partly intact, and some parts were never recovered.

Below: A map showing the location of Sutton Hoo.

THE GRAVE GOODS

The dead king had been buried—or commemorated—with a wide variety of items, many of which were in precious materials. There were also plenty of textiles: the remains of wall-hangings, linen cushion covers and cloaks, some of which had been carefully folded; some items in the chamber had also been wrapped in textile, strips of woven tape, before being buried. There was a cap made from otter skin, the remains of four shoes and other items of leather clothing. A silver dish lay near a yew bucket which contained a smaller bucket; and beneath the silver dish were two more silver bowls. There were also bone combs, a set of bone-handled iron knives and a wooden box with iron fittings. Some objects could be used in feasting: two bronze hanging bowls, drinking horns with silver fittings, and bottles made of maple wood decorated with silver-gilt mounts. There was even a lyre, in a bag

made from beaver skin. There was also a large decorated whetstone which could have been part of a scepter; it was topped with a bronze figure of a stag standing on a rotating iron ring.

The king had been provided with weapons: spears, an ax-hammer head and a fine sword in the remains of a scabbard. This would originally have hung from the sword belt equipped with buckles decorated in semi-precious stones and gold, and there were also the remains of a shield with gilt-bronze decoration. There were clasps in gold and garnet that would have held together the two halves of a leather cuirass (a breastplate and backplate fastened together); it had long since vanished, but the clasps remained. Next to these lay the remains of a helmet. The original excavators believed it might have hung on the walls of the chamber as it was found not in one piece but in parts scattered over a wider area, so it might have been damaged when the chamber collapsed. This unusual find, with its decorated face mask and band running over the top, is similar to the helmets described in the great Anglo-Saxon poem Beowulf.

Many of the items recovered from the burial chamber came from some distance. At the west end of the chamber a heavy bronze bowl was found, for example: it had originally come from Coptic Egypt. Most of the silver was Mediterranean in origin. There was a total of 16 pieces, and it has been suggested that some of them may have formed part of a diplomatic gift, possibly from Gaul. One of these silver items—a large bowl more than 27 inches in diameter—has a mark on the foot which is the stamp of the Byzantine emperor Anastasius, and there were other bowls, and ladles and spoons bearing Greek names.

There has been speculation about the identity of the person who had been buried or commemorated beneath Mound 1 at Sutton Hoo. He appears to have had a certain importance or contacts outside England, so is likely to have been a ruler, and there are contemporary chronicles which list kings. However, in the absence of any truly personal artifacts it is impossible to say for sure. The most significant fact about the finds at Sutton Hoo is that they demonstrate the sophistication of Anglo-Saxon society. Prior to the discoveries at Sutton Hoo the Anglo-Saxons had essentially been thought of as crude warriors, but this somewhat simplistic view could no longer be sustained. Some of the other burials at Sutton Hoo do, however, bear testimony to the harshness of this society.

NOT JUST SHIP BURIALS...

Recent work at Sutton Hoo, from the 1960s and 1980s, has shown that the Anglo-Saxon cemetery of which Mound 1 was part lay on top of a prehistoric settlement. The cemetery itself was pagan, and contained a series of different kinds of burial, including other ship burials but also flat graves and cremations. Traces of the occupants, no more than shadows in the soil, were found in some. One of these had contained the bodies of a horse and a young man who had been buried in a coffin; a

harness of leather, gilt-bronze and iron was included in this burial. Other burials contained rich items too, such as a silver chain, small buckles, and a chatelaine (something like the bunch of short chains holding useful items and attached to a belt which was worn by women in later times) recovered from what is likely to have been a female grave. This was found in the eastern part of the site, as were 23 graves of people who seem to have been executed; they could have been sacrificial victims. Some had their necks broken or their limbs tied together, and they were contemporary with the rich burials.

The Vikings

The popular idea of the Vikings as bloodthirsty raiders is only partly true. They may have had a reputation for violence but they were also farmers and settlers, traders and merchants. Exploration was one element, but they also began attempts at colonization in places as far apart as Russia and Newfoundland.

VIKING SHIPS

Central to Viking expansion—and to Viking culture—were their magnificent ships. A particularly beautiful one, known as the Gokstad Ship, was excavated from a mound near Oseberg on the Oslo fjord in 1880. It dates to about AD 900, and was shallow with a deep keel so it would have been easy to sail in coastal or shallower waters. It would also have been able to land on a sloping beach; there would have been no need for a specific harbor. This supported records left by those who survived Viking raids; they often report their shock at being attacked when far from a harbor or by a river that was supposedly unnavigable.

In 1903, another ship—even more beautiful—was also found near Oseberg. It lay beneath a mound like the earlier find, and it too had been very well preserved. It was also of a similar size to the Gokstad Ship, about 20 feet wide and 78 feet in length. Both of them had burial chambers constructed within them, but while the Gokstad Ship had contained the body of a man, the Oseberg Ship—as it became known—contained two women, one young and one older. Both the ships had been robbed, but some things remained. The man from the Gokstad Ship had been buried with a peacock, six dogs and twelve horses; a sledge, some small boats, and a large cauldron. The Oseberg Ship had also contained at least ten horses as well as two oxen, three sledges, beds with associated textiles, and a carved cart; the ship itself was wonderfully carved. The grave-robbing both had suffered was probably a common hazard; there are references to it in Norse sagas. These poetic stories and legends also contain, of course, references to the glorious and frequently menacing ships, as do the surviving accounts of those who were on the receiving end of their attentions.

INTERNATIONAL TRADERS AND SETTLERS

Most Vikings sailed in search of profit. This could well come from raiding, but trade was an equally important factor, probably more important in the long term. Following rivers eastward led Norse explorers into Russia and gave them access to the Muslim world: many goods—furs, honey, walrus ivory, and slaves—were exchanged for Arab silver.

Opposite: The Gokstad Ship, used as part of a male burial. The ship, though not as elaborately decorated as the Oseberg ship, still reveals its beautiful construction.

Right: The prow of the magnificently carved Oseberg Ship. It was found beneath a burial mound, and had contained a burial chamber. In this were found the remains of two women, but most of the artifacts that would also have been included were stolen, probably close to the time at which they were buried.

Below: Heavy arm rings from Denmark.

Westward, the coasts of Northern Britain were an immediate target, but Viking sailors also reached Iceland in the 860s and 870s. Greenland was visited about 900 and a settlement there was established in the latter part of the tenth century. This was a useful staging post for more journeys even farther west, and the sagas record the existence of somewhere in the far west called "Vinland the good." The Greenland settlement established by Erik the Red could not support many settlers, even though the climate there was less severe than it is today, and Erik's son Leif moved on westward. He certainly reached Baffin Island and Labrador, and a settlement has been discovered in Newfoundland. The precise location of Vinland, however, remains a mystery; its description certainly doesn't match the Newfoundland settlement.

VIKINGS IN NEWFOUNDLAND

In 1960 a Norse village was found at L'Anse aux Meadows in Newfoundland, only about 325 feet from the shore of a shallow coastal bay. It has been dated to about

AD 1000, which fits with the slightly earlier date of Erik the Red's establishment of the parent settlement in Greenland. No other traces of Viking settlement have been found anywhere near this, and it seems to have been used as a base for additional exploration southward: for example, two butternuts—a form of wild walnut—were found there but do not (and did not) grow locally. There were eight buildings at L'Anse aux Meadows, some small and some quite spacious with several rooms. All were built of sods with a timber frame. There could have been as many as 70–90 people at the site, and there were workshops, including a carpenter's, a boat repairer's, and an iron smithy; in fact, the earliest evidence for iron smelting in North America was found here. There is no evidence of farming or farm

Opposite right: A stele—an engraved, upright stone slab—showing Vikings in a ship and warriors on foot at the top.

Opposite left: Viking metalworking was sophisticated and often elegant, like this silver brooch in an interlaced design from Trollakogur in Iceland.

Left: A runestone from Sweden. Dating to the sixth century AD, this stele with runes and a carved warrior is one of the earliest Scandinavian engravings of the runic script used at the time.

Above: This brooch, part of the Hornelund hoard from Denmark, demonstrates the Vikings' mastery of engraving.

buildings. Ships were pulled up on the shore for maintenance, and iron nails and scrap still remained. Little else, however, did.

The settlement at L'Anse aux Meadows had a somewhat short life, being deliberately abandoned not long after it was established. Almost everything had been systematically removed by its occupants, and the excavators found very little, all items that might have been lost or accidentally dropped: there were 99 broken nails, a single intact one, a knitting needle, a bronze pin, a whetstone, a spindle, and a solitary glass bead. Quite why this abandonment happened is impossible to say, but the village was too small to be sustainable in the long term. The harshness of the environment may have been a factor, too, as might hostility from local inhabitants and the Greenland settlement itself was too small to continue to support L'Anse aux Meadows as well. That lasted somewhat longer, ending in the late 14th century; ultimately Norse culture was not flexible enough to adapt successfully to life in the increasingly demanding conditions of Greenland. The form of farming that was practiced could not be sustained in a worsening climate and the settlers' later relations with various local inhabitants, whom they called skraelings—wretches—went from poor to appalling.

Jorvik

The Roman city of York—Eboracum—had never been completely abandoned, and when the Vikings took the place in AD 866 they found a town rather than a crowded city, and one dominated by the old walls of the Roman fortress. Excavations in the modern city, especially in Coppergate, have revealed much of the city the Vikings created between then and 1067, when the Normans arrived. The Viking city was known as Jorvik.

The inhabitants of the Viking town made extensive use of the Roman ruins. A wealthy cemetery was established within the walls of what had once been the headquarters building, the Principia, and parts of the ruined barracks were used for workshops, like one in which jet had evidently been worked. Churches in Jorvik were stone-built, but houses and workshops were thatched and made of timber—masses of wood has survived due to the excellent preservation conditions at the Coppergate site. These also permitted the survival of a lot of other environmental evidence. Old cesspits, for example, revealed the unsurprising existence of flies and beetles as well as providing evidence of intestinal parasites, and the presence of lice was used to determine which buildings had been houses and which workshops. Sheep lice indicated the presence of wool preparation, and waste from dye baths was found in thick layers in some places. There were loom weights which were also suggestive of cloth production, though this could have taken place in homes as well as workshops, and silverworking had been an important industry. A lot of fabrics were found and some of these had clearly been imported, like silk, some of which could have come from Byzantium. There has been speculation that the silk found might have been brought to Jorvik by Viking traders from Russia who had contact with the Central Asian Silk Road.

Opposite: A carving of a smith and his client from Hylastad church in Norway; the scene actually appears to represent a story from a pagan myth.

Right: An animal head post from the Oseberg Ship.

The
Mediterranean
World

Knossos
and the Minoans

The island of Crete occupies a vital position in the eastern Mediterranean, perfectly situated for trade, and it was highly likely that it might have had considerable importance in the past. Greek myths seemed to reflect that possibility, too, with their stories of Theseus and the Minotaur. But until just over 100 years ago, nobody had any real idea that it had actually been the center of a lively and sophisticated civilization in the Bronze Age.

ARTHUR EVANS' EXCAVATIONS

Some basic archaeological discoveries had been made on the island by Minos Kalokairinos in 1878, and Heinrich Schliemann—the excavator of Troy and Mycenae—had also been tempted by Crete's possibilities, but had been unable to agree a deal. Arthur Evans, however, was eventually successful in his negotiations, and began work on the barren hilltop of Knossos on March 23, 1900. Evans had originally been attracted to the place by stone walls which looked as though they might be ancient, though he was chasing the sealstones that interested him so much rather than myths and legends, like Schliemann. Within only a week an inscribed tablet appeared. Shortly afterwards a lot more came to light; Evans had hoped for "entire deposits of clay archives," and here they were. Though the tablets couldn't be completely deciphered, they did prove that the excavators were dealing with a literate culture, one apparently keeping administrative records and accounts. Digging continued. Then the discoveries became more and more astonishing.

Opposite: When Arthur Evans began digging at Knossos, he had no idea whatsoever of the ultimate extent of the site. Its complexity is evident in this aerial view, which clearly shows the large central courtyard common to Minoan palaces.

Bottom: The exterior of the palace at Knossos, while impressive even today, generally gives little impression of the richness within.

Right: A libation jug from the Katsabas tomb. Minoan pottery was often exuberant, and this rather bizarrely decorated pot is a perfect example, with its combination of raised surface decoration and swirling paintwork. It shows a considerable level of skill.

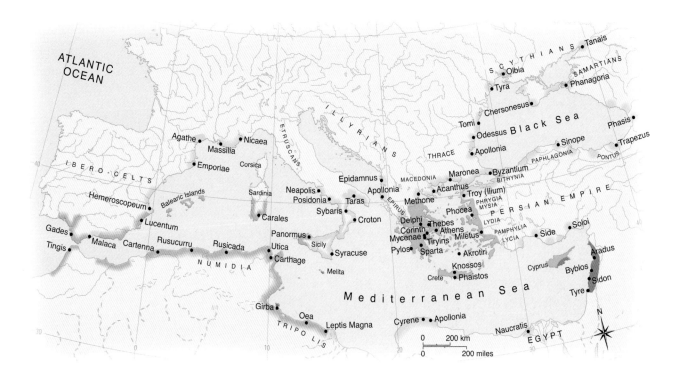

THE PALACE COMPLEX

The area of the hilltop actually hid a massive citadel, a vast "palace complex" on many levels with elaborately decorated rooms and huge stores for grain and oil. This was like nothing seen before; it revealed a completely unexpected civilization with amazingly high levels of artistic skill and craftsmanship. Following Schliemann's linking of archaeological sites to Greek myths and legends, similar associations were inevitably made on Crete. King Minos had been Crete's legendary ruler, and Evans dubbed the civilization 'Minoan' after him, and called the palace complex the "palace of Minos." It is a substantial site, and 'palace' is a useful word to describe it, but we don't actually know if Minoan Crete was ruled by a king as such; there's no direct evidence one way or the other. Ritual seems to have been very important to the Minoans; there could have been a religious ruler, for example, or some other way of organizing society. The sophistication of Minoan culture is not in doubt, however. The palace at Knossos was arranged around a central

The Mediterranean

Phoenicia, c. 750 BC

Greece, c. 750 BC

Phoenician settlement, from the 9th century BC

Greek settlement, 8th–6th century BC

courtyard, and at first appeared rather chaotic; in fact "labyrinthine" (echoing the myths) was a frequent description. There is actually an underlying order. Grander rooms were on the upper floors, reached by masonry staircases, and other important rooms opened off the central court. Double doors folded back into recesses, so that rooms could be partitioned or opened up as required. In a cutting into the hill on the south-eastern side, a magnificent series of rooms rose three stories high, connected by an imposing "grand staircase." Deep light wells, shafts running straight down, provided both light and ventilation for the lower floors. When Evans discovered the staircase, the elegant tapering columns and wooden beams had rotted away but he was able to restore it, after much study, using skilled engineers. Many rooms in the palace were decorated with elaborate wall paintings, and there was a complicated system of water supply and drainage.

Opposite and above: Evans' reconstruction of the palace of Knossos is controversial—he used concrete, metal girders and bricks—but it does convey a vivid impression of what was once there. Getting light and air to the lowest levels of the palace necessitated leaving space in the buildings for four clear shafts—light wells, which allowed both sunlight and fresh air to reach down. Nonetheless, the lower levels must have been comparatively dark, even on the brightest day.

In addition it became obvious that the palace was multi-functional: there were the elaborate formal rooms, the "state apartments," but craftspeople were also based there, as were the bureaucrats who kept all the records. There is also a lot of evidence for an elaborate religious cult, though positively identifying "religious" items can be difficult without any written records, and the scripts found were—and two of them still are—undeciphered. The palace itself was surrounded by other buildings on a much smaller scale.

Legends of Crete

Minos was the ruler of Crete, about three generations before the Trojan War, according to the tales. He struck a deal with the god Poseidon, asking him to send a mighty bull from the sea as a sign of his right to rule, and promising to sacrifice it to the god. When the bull appeared, Minos won the kingdom—but refused to kill the bull in return. A catastrophic sequence of events then resulted in the birth of the half-man, half-bull known as the Minotaur, the child of Minos' wife Pasiphae and Poseidon's bull.

King Minos commissioned the building of a vast maze of a palace, the Labyrinth, to contain the monster, and regularly sent seven young men and seven young women to it as food and, effectively, as a sacrifice. These victims were Athenians, sent to Minos by the king of Athens as tribute because he had killed Minos' son. On one occasion, Theseus, the Athenian prince, was selected or volunteered to be among them. When the 14 potential victims arrived in Crete they were confined in the Labyrinth, but Theseus had been seen by the Cretan princess Ariadne. She fell in love with him and found a way to give him a ball of thread so that he could trace his way in the confusion of the Labyrinth; using this he was able to discover and kill the Minotaur, and find his way out again. He fled the island at night, together with Ariadne and his original companions.

THE FIRST PALACE AT KNOSSOS

The first palace at Knossos was probably built around 2000 BC, but was modified, expanded, and rebuilt before it was destroyed by fire sometime about 1425 BC. It was constructed using a lot of local stone, and timber beams and posts were incorporated to give additional flexibility, a necessity in this earthquake-ridden region. It was large—population estimates have ranged between 15,000 and 50,000—and the "new period" palace alone covered some 140,000 square feet. Simply building something on this scale would have required a substantial labor force, both general 'muscle' and more skilled specialists. The countryside around the citadel would have supplied food and other necessities, and there is plenty of evidence for trade on an international scale. The storerooms Evans found were enormous, with ranks of clay storage jars—pithoi—nearly six feet high, used for olive oil, wine, and grain. Comparable evidence, though not on the same scale, began to appear from other places on Crete and, as time has gone on, Minoan sites have also been found on other Greek islands. Evans had uncovered what appeared to have been a maritime 'empire', with a reach across the Aegean and international links.

Without any clues from texts—Linear A was the script used during most of the time Knossos was occupied and has not been deciphered—much of our understanding of Minoan society depends on other evidence, like the wall paintings. People feature in many of them: youths carrying large jars, women with elaborate hairstyles and clothing, athletes leaping over a charging bull. Dolphins, birds, plants, and flowers appear frequently, and there are scenes of everyday life. Frescoes have been found in buildings outside the palace at Knossos, and at other Minoan sites. A cat stalks birds at Agia Triada, and a pair of boys have a boxing match at Akrotiri on the island of Thera, where another young man carries strings of fish.

Opposite: The grand staircase at Knossos: the restored wall paintings are especially evocative, and many of them use decorative motifs, like these shields, rather than representing particular scenes. Shields of this shape are shown on many finds from both Crete and the mainland, throughout most of the Bronze Age.

Right above: Marine creatures and waves appear frequently in Minoan art, craft and decoration, and often occur with great flair and exuberance as in this fresco, stressing the importance of the sea in this maritime culture.

Right: A bull's head in painted terracotta. Stylized bull's horns, often called 'horns of consecration', appear in a wide variety of contexts, from being an important part of buildings to appearing on pottery or seals. They may have originally been used to indicate the presence of a shrine.

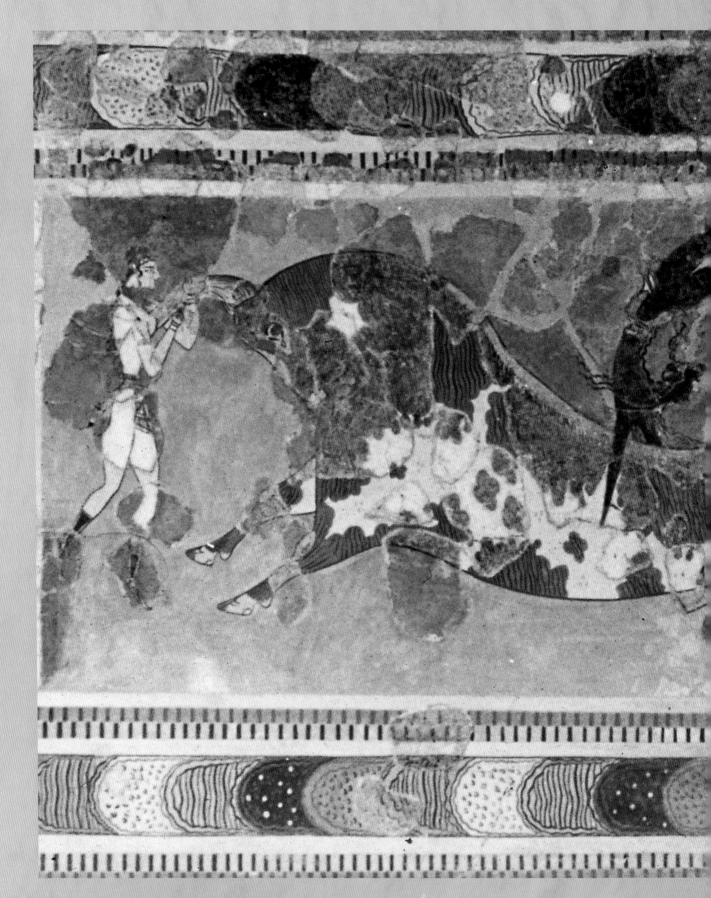

The Bull Dance

Bulls were obviously significant to the Minoans. Stylized bull's horns are a frequent motif in art and decoration; bulls appear in ceramics, metalwork and on seals; there is a particularly impressive ritual vessel (a rhyton) in the form of a bull's head—and the importance of bulls in Crete is even marked in Greek legends about the island. The 'bull dance' is the most unusual manifestation of this. Young athletes jump over the bull—it is often called "bull-leaping"—using the horns for leverage and somersaulting over the animal's back before landing safely.

There has been some debate about whether it is actually possible for anyone, however fit, to leap over the back of a charging bull using the horns, but there's no doubt that it's a popular scene. And it's not just the frescoes, either: for example, a small ivory figure of a bull-leaper was found at Knossos. The young man's muscles and veins are realistic, though his body is somewhat stretched, presumably to emphasize his athletic grace.

Left: A restored wall painting from Knossos, showing young athletes and a charging bull. Traditionally, women are shown with paler skins in Minoan art, and there can be little doubt that some of the bull-leapers were female.

THE TEMPLE AT ANEMOSPILIA

Many things have been described as "having a cult significance," though whether they were actually used in ritual is presently impossible to determine. Women feature in some of these, but it is unclear whether they represent priestesses or worshipers, or even goddesses. One very unusual site provides startling and controversial evidence, though. It dates from about 1700–1650 BC, and involves deaths during an earthquake—probably the upheavals that saw the end of the earliest palace phase at Knossos. A small Minoan temple was found at Anemospilia near Archanes in central Crete, unusual in itself as most "temples" were either in palaces or on mountains. It had been destroyed by an earthquake and then swept by fire, which may have been caused by the oil lamps in the temple being knocked over in the tremors. In the entrance hall, the excavators found 150 vases, suggesting that the area was used for the collection of offerings. Just in front of the entrance to the central part of the temple was a skeleton, crushed by falling masonry—the first definite earthquake victim found on Crete. The only trace of any god or goddess was a pair of feet which appeared to have fallen from a platform at one end of the central part of the temple; there were more vases in front of this platform, too.

HUMAN SACRIFICE

The eastern part of the temple contained the biggest surprise. It was empty—except for three skeletons. In one corner was a young woman just over 5 feet tall, lying face down. A man, about 5 feet 10 inches tall and probably between 30 and 40 years old, lay on his back near by; his legs had been broken by falling debris. On the little finger of his left hand

he had a silver and iron ring, which would have been a rare and valuable item in the Bronze Age, and he was also wearing a beautiful engraved amber seal on one wrist. What seemed to be a sacrificial victim lay on another platform (described as being "altar-like") near the man. As they began work, the excavators, Yannis and Efi Sakellerakis, thought this would be some kind of animal, as animal sacrifices are often represented on sealstones. However, it gradually became clear that it was the skeleton of a young man. He was about 18, and was in a position indicating that his arms had been tied up behind his back. His legs were doubled up and resting on his body was a superb bronze blade, about 15 inches long and engraved on each side with an animal head.

The discovery caused consternation; even though human sacrifice was described in history, and referred to very clearly in the legends connected to Crete, the reality

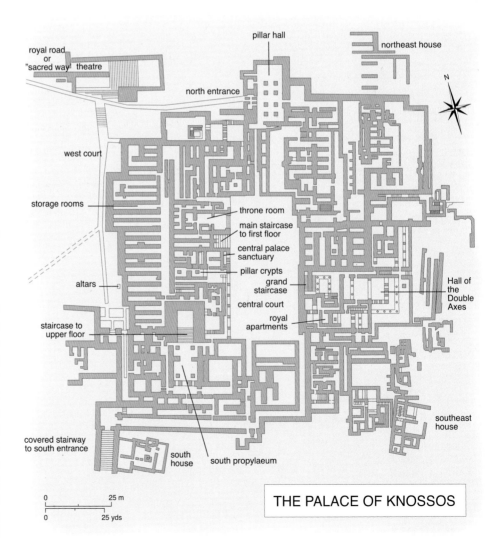

THE PALACE OF KNOSSOS

still came as a shock. The excavators suggested that it had been an extreme measure, something done to appease the deity who had been causing the earth to shake—and that it had been unsuccessful, the participants being caught in another, fatal earthquake. The person whose skeleton had been found in front of the entrance, they suggested, had been trying to escape from the collapsing building following the sacrifice. They also suggested that the man with the ring

Below: The "snake goddess" figurines have been the focus for much debate about the status and role of women, but there can be no definite conclusions at present. There are many similar representations— on wall paintings, seals or in metalwork—but whether they depict a specific goddess, a priestess or a worshiper remains uncertain.

Right: Two boys engage in a boxing match in a wall painting from Akrotiri.

Above: Buildings in the once-thriving town of Akrotiri, buried in pumice and ash about 3500 years ago by the eruption of the Thera volcano. The arrangement of door and nearby or adjoining window is very common; the entrance often opens on to a small lobby from which a stone staircase leads upwards in two flights.

had been carrying out the sacrifice and had fallen back, raising his hands to protect his face when the earthquake hit, and that the woman had run to the corner seeking protection. Since this discovery, made in the 1970s, there have been other digs that have produced evidence supposedly indicating human sacrifice or similar rites, but these have been questioned. As yet, there is no other formal explanation for what the Sakellarakises found.

THE END OF THE MINOANS

The Mediterranean has always been subject to earthquakes and volcanic activity, and about 3500 years ago—the precise dating is still being debated—the volcano on the island of Thera (Santorini), about 60 miles from Crete, sprang back into life. At first there were earthquakes, forcing many inhabitants of Thera to flee,

and then things settled down again. Repairs were begun, but the volcano erupted, sending fine ash and pumice over everything. Buildings were now completely abandoned and filled with ash and volcanic debris.

Then the island blew itself apart. It has been claimed that the explosion was far greater in size than Krakatoa; certainly not much remains of Thera today, and there is still some volcanic activity. Ash deposits from the explosion have been found in Crete, lying over Minoan fields, and in deep-sea cores; the distribution suggests the ash was carried on the region's summer north-westerly winds. It is highly likely that tsunamis would have been generated by an explosion of this size, and there is some possible evidence of their force—at Amnisos on the north coast of Crete, huge blocks of stone have been torn out of position, for example.

It is never completely clear why civilizations collapse, in archaeology or history, and this is true of Minoan Crete. There is seldom one cause. There is certainly evidence of some catastrophe on Crete; towns, palaces and villas in the countryside were destroyed, generally by fire—but the ash levels from the explosion are lower than the destruction layer, and so must have been deposited well beforehand.

Writing

The strange script found on sealstones first drew Arthur Evans to Crete, and clay tablets covered in writing began turning up almost immediately excavations began at Knossos. The tablets meant that the culture which was being uncovered had been literate, but nobody could read the language they were written in. Or languages: there appeared to be three.

The one from the lowest, earliest levels has been called "Minoan hieroglyphic" as it uses some Egyptian symbols, but the language itself is completely different. It's still undeciphered. So is the next script, called Linear A, which is found throughout Crete and on some other Greek islands. The numbers on Linear A tablets can be understood as they are adapted from the Egyptian system, but not the words.

The last script comes from the final occupation levels at Knossos, and is called Linear B; Evans discovered over 4000 tablets in this language. It's found on the Greek mainland too, at Mycenae and other sites. Again, Evans was able to read the numerals, and identify ideograms, signs that indicated what was being listed on the tablet—symbols like people, horses, or ears of corn—but he couldn't break the code of the script itself. The tablets did, however, seem to be administrative records.

In 1936 Evans gave a public lecture and described the baffling Minoan scripts. A 14-year-old boy called Michael Ventris was in the audience, and he became determined to solve the mystery. He published his first attempt only four years later, but progress was interrupted by the Second World War. Ventris still worried away at the problem, following what he thought were links to the Etruscan language, but in 1951 he came to realize that he was actually dealing with a very early form of Greek. Everything began to make sense. By this time Ventris was working as an architect, and he enlisted the help of a specialist, John Chadwick; they announced the decipherment together in 1952. Many scholars and academics expressed doubts, but confirmation came from Carl Blegen, the excavator of the Mycenaean city of Pylos. He had dug up lots of inscribed tablets, and now found he could understand them; a double-check came from the ideograms, the signs—images of animals, foodstuffs, or people—showing what the tablet listed. They tallied with the information from the script.

Ventris' decipherment changed archaeology in the eastern Mediterranean, demonstrating continuity between the Bronze Age world of the palaces, the world described in the great poems of Homer, and the much more familiar classical Greek civilization. Tragically, Ventris died in a car accident in 1956, before he could extend his detective work to Linear A.

Left: The Phaistos Disk, approximately 6 inches in diameter, was stamped with 45 different symbols on both sides, making a spiral text; it was then fired in a kiln. These pictograms are in an archaic form, related to the "Minoan hieroglyphics" of the earliest period. There are 241 signs, divided into 61 "words" by incised lines, and many attempts have been made to translate them. None have succeeded; there isn't even any general agreement on whether translation should start on the outside and work in.

THE EXPLOSION AT THERA

The archaeologist Spyridion Marinatos argued that the Thera explosion was the cause of Minoan collapse, and set about proving this. He thought that excavations on what remained of Thera itself might support his theory and, despite the problems caused by thick layers of volcanic ash, was able to locate a potential site. Akrotiri, in the south of the island, had fields where the farmers said they were unable to plow because of the quantity of stones just below the soil. This was a useful sign, and Marinatos began digging in 1967.

The archaeological site at Akrotiri is an extraordinary place. Pumice and ash filled the streets and abandoned buildings, which stand up to two or three stories high—it is a Minoan version of Pompeii. Unlike Pompeii, however, there is no trace of the inhabitants; hopefully they were able to escape from the island in the earlier stages of volcanic activity. There are few valuable artifacts, suggesting that the people carried those with them when they fled, but bronze tools and lead weights have been found. The ground floors of the houses were used for work and storage, and smarter rooms seem to have been on the upper floors. Pouring plaster into cavities showed where furniture had once been, and there were jars which had held food and wine. Paintings are preserved on many walls, vividly illustrating scenes of everyday life and echoing the style of frescoes on Crete.

But this was an independent culture; the pottery is quite distinct, of local manufacture, though there are Minoan imports. And these show quite clearly, from their distinctive style, that Akrotiri—undoubtedly abandoned at exactly the time of the Thera explosion—was buried at least twenty or thirty years before the final destruction of sites on Crete.

So we still do not know what finally happened to Minoan civilization for certain. The effects of the Thera explosion—ash smothering fields before harvest and possibly causing famine; tsunamis hitting the coasts, smashing boats and affecting trade—must have been severe, but they do not seem to have been the immediate cause. Knossos survived longer than other Cretan palaces, and there are signs of a new administration there—using Linear B, the early Greek script also found on mainland sites like Pylos and Mycenae.

Opposite: The level of preservation at Akrotiri was very high, and many wall paintings remain. The fresco of the fisherman from Akrotiri highlights the importance that the sea had for the people of the town.

Below: Steps and streets on two levels in the town of Akrotiri, giving an impression of the sheer size of the site; it covers about 32 acres.

Arthur Evans
Excavator of Knossos

Sir Arthur Evans (1851–1941) was fortunate to have an archaeological background; his father was a distinguished antiquary who encouraged his son's interest in classical history from the start. However, Evans actually began his career as a journalist, working in Bosnia where he became a political activist, supporting the Balkan quest for independence from the Turks. He then became a special correspondent for the *Manchester Guardian*, and criticized the Austrian occupation of Bosnia—as a result he was imprisoned and then banned from the country.

He had maintained his fascination with classical history, and an encounter with Schliemann seems to have rekindled his specific interest in coins and sealstones, particularly inscribed ones. Many of the ones which he found in the Athens flea market came from Crete, and Evans soon made his way there. He first saw the site of Knossos in 1894, but his attempts to purchase it ran into problems, partly connected to Crete's attempts to win its independence from the fading Ottoman Empire. In 1900, Crete finally became independent and Evans, who had supported the independence movement (predictably, given his

earlier experience in the Balkans), was able to begin serious work on the site. He recognized that he wasn't an experienced digger, and enlisted the professional help of Duncan Mackenzie. Surprising discoveries came almost immediately.

Arthur Evans' reconstructions of some parts of the palace of Knossos, and the restoration of many wall paintings, were controversial from the beginning. His engineers used modern materials like metal girders and bricks, and it was felt that some of the artists had been somewhat overenthusiastic with the frescoes. In addition, the reconstructions have destroyed or obscured many important features and, in some specific cases like the throne room, can be misleading.

However, Evans did face conservation problems from the beginning—the throne room, with its fragile frescoes, began to deteriorate the first winter—and some work was necessary early on. A certain amount of care was taken. The Grand Staircase is especially successful, and it certainly stood there (the remains of it were found, burned and collapsed, below ground level). But Evans gradually came to want to restore Knossos to what it "might have been" instead. Some of the later layers of occupation were sacrificed. This meant, for example, that the remains of a Mycenaean megaron, a throne room like the ones from the mainland, were demolished. It was incorrectly determined to be "classical" and the foundations became part of one of Evans' less accurate reconstructions.

Despite this, Knossos today conveys a powerful impression of Minoan decorative detailing, and of how it may have appeared at the height of its power. This is largely down to the reconstruction work, although much of it is the result of one man's imagination.

Right: A detail of the lily fresco from the House of the Ladies at Thera.

Troy

The city of Troy has long been known in legend. In classical times it was believed to have been a real place, situated close to the Dardanelles at the Aegean end of the straits. The city of New Ilium, which existed from about 700 BC to AD 500, was widely thought to have been built on or near Troy. Various locations in Turkey were suggested in the 19th century, most notably Bunarbashi and Hissarlik.

Frank Calvert was able to buy part of the settlement mound at Hissarlik and conducted promising trial excavations, but could not raise enough money to continue. Investigations commenced at Bunarbashi under a German team, and produced nothing. Then Calvert met Heinrich Schliemann.

SCHLIEMANN'S EXCAVATIONS AT HISSARLIK

Schliemann had the resources Calvert lacked and, equally convinced, began extensive excavations at Hissarlik. The site is on the edge of a plateau, stands well above the surrounding land to the north and west, and is not large. Today, most of the place is destroyed, both because of the activity of classical builders who flattened the top—and because of archaeologists. Archaeology can be very destructive, and this is especially clear at Troy, where the digs were on a grand scale, and the site very complex with many layers of occupation.

Excavations, by both Schliemann and his successors, established that there were several successive cities on the site, each built on top of the remains of the previous ones. These were numbered Troy I–IX. They cover a long period of time, from 3000 BC for Troy I to AD 500 for Troy IX. Though the city started out as a small place, it quickly developed into a significant one—and probably a regional power—by about 2500 BC. This is the city known as Troy II.

THE TREASURES OF PRIAM

Schliemann believed this to be the city known to Greek legend; he was wrong, it's too early by over a thousand years. He found gold artifacts, however, and called them the "Treasures of Priam." There was a lot of gold jewelry, some pieces of plate, silver flasks, several gold and silver cups, and other objects in precious metals. Many archaeologists believe that Schliemann might have gathered this Early Bronze Age treasure from several places, and possibly from several levels; his accounts are baffling and contradictory. It does, however, seem most likely to have come from Troy II. Stylistically it fits with that period, and later re-excavators in the 1930s reported finding gold scattered in almost every room of Troy II, as if the people who lived there had fled suddenly. Whatever its precise origin, some items seem to have been destined for recycling: many pieces were unfinished, damaged, or broken and there were some notched "ingots," perhaps for the manufacture of beads. It may well be that some of them were simply the remains of a gold worker's store. One thing is certain: they are certainly not a treasure hidden for safekeeping during the Siege of Troy. Like Troy II, they were over a thousand years older than that.

Opposite: The walls of Troy VI, probably the city recalled in the Greek oral tradition and immortalized by Homer.

Right: The Treasures of Priam.

Troy VI

Of the other levels of the city, the one that has received a lot of attention is Troy VI. During the Middle and Late Bronze Age this was a fortified citadel, enclosing some major buildings, which had an extensive settlement outside the walls. Though the highest point of Troy VI had been flattened to permit overbuilding by later occupants, many traces remained and the defenses were of a very high standard, over 13 feet thick and about 30 feet tall in places. Roads within the citadel all led to the summit, where the palace must have stood, but very little remains of that. Immediately below were about twenty-five large houses, which may have belonged to members of a royal family, other important families or senior officials. One of these is called the "Pillar House" and is over 75 feet in length and nearly 36 feet wide. It had a main hall and a cooking area, and stone pillars supported the roof. The upper story would most likely have been timber-framed.

Dorpfeld, who worked at Troy with Schliemann and continued to work there after Schliemann's death in 1890, was certain that this city was the original of Homer's Troy—it even appeared to have been destroyed by force. Others asserted that the destruction was due to a major earthquake, which had certainly happened at other levels. However, if it was an earthquake, why were the great houses not rebuilt? Some archaeologists have spoken of it looking as though a large population had to be sheltered in a hurry, and have even evoked a siege. The defenses were repaired to some extent, but in many places wreckage lay where it fell. There are other differences; in fact, the whole character of the settlement seems to change. In addition, there is evidence of a fire, of arrowheads and human remains. Carl Blegen, who worked at Troy after Dorpfeld, but before he found the Mycenaean site of Pylos, came down in favour of Troy VIIa being the "right" one, Homer's city; it also seems to have been violently destroyed. The debate continues, but at present Troy VI is probably the more likely contender, in view of current dating and with doubt being cast over the earthquake hypothesis. The exact relationship between Troys VI and VIIa is somewhat confusing. While Blegen was definitely not a supporter of the "Troy VI as candidate for Homer's city" argument, he did believe that the Pillar House had been converted into a barracks or armory during the final phases of occupation.

More Recent Excavations

There have been more recent excavations at Troy, beginning in 1988. The Late Bronze Age shoreline has now been identified, and close to this over 50 cremation burials were found—cremations with Mycenaean grave goods and pottery dateable to the early 13th century BC (late Troy VI). The remains included women and children, so this may have belonged to some trading colony rather than a camp of a besieging army, however.

On the other hand, much of the recent work seems to confirm some of the more puzzling details in the *Iliad*, references to water sources, the location of the Greek harbor, and suchlike. More independent evidence in support of some conflict at around the correct time comes from the diplomatic records of the Hittite Empire, which are beginning to be fully analyzed. Though much debate continues about place-name equivalents, these also talk of military campaigns in about the right place at about the right time. There is also material from Mycenaean written records.

While much more is becoming known about Troy and its setting, there is still no proof linking the archaeological Troy to Homer's city that is beyond doubt. Work continues ...

Below: A golden cup with twin handles, sometimes called the "sauceboat," which comes from Troy II. It dates to at least a thousand years before the Trojan War might have happened.

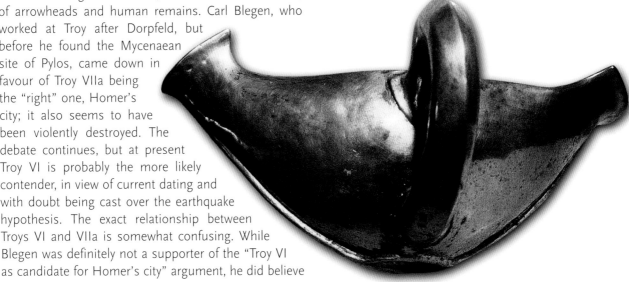

Heinrich Schliemann
Excavator of Troy and Mycenae

Heinrich Schliemann (1822–90) was born a pastor's son in Germany. He made a large fortune from trading in indigo dye and was able to retire early. His interest in Homer's *Iliad* and *Odyssey* caused him to travel in Greece and Turkey, seeking places associated with these great poems. Schliemann was convinced that the war Homer evoked had actually taken place, and that he had been describing real places and people.

His researches and contacts, notably Frank Calvert, led him to the settlement mound at Hissarlik in the northwest of Turkey, which he also decided was the probable site of Troy. He dug there for four seasons, and for the last two (1882–3 and 1889–90) he had professional help from Wilhelm Dorpfeld, who had been trained in excavation and recording techniques. The dig was on a suitably epic scale: between 1871 and 1873 Schliemann employed 150 workers who drove massive trenches into the Hissarlik mound. The site was extremely complex, but he identified seven cities and thought that the second had been the Homeric Troy. Dorpfeld, later, decided this was the sixth; this is still debated. It is

certain, however, that Schliemann was wrong; the second level is far too old.

Schliemann was a great writer and self-publicist, but he did change many details of his life, lied about the discovery and composition of 'Priam's Treasure' and "forgot" to credit the contribution that other people, notably Frank Calvert, had made to identifying Hissarlik as the site of Troy. He claimed the credit for himself alone—and that is how he is frequently remembered, as the sole discoverer of Troy.

Schliemann smuggled most of the treasures out of Turkey, much to the fury of the Turkish authorities, who declared him persona non grata as a result. He was fined—and he paid up—but was unable to return to Hissarlik immediately. In 1881, Schliemann gave the treasures to the city of Berlin (he received formal citizenship in return), where they got caught up in a more recent war: individual items were packed away for safekeeping in 1939, but disappeared in the last days of Nazi Germany. In 1993 they surfaced in Moscow, and are now on display in the Pushkin Museum there, having been fully authenticated.

The Mycenaean World

When Homer wrote down the tales of the Trojan War, he was preserving stories that had been passed down by word of mouth. The Illiad and the Odyssey were probably composed about 700 BC, maybe by a single poet or maybe by several, and the oral tradition they came from must go back well before that. This origin was generally recognized, but there was no actual evidence that the world Homer evoked, one in which iron was a precious metal, not something used every day, and where mighty warriors fought each other with bronze weapons, had ever existed.

THE CITY OF MYCENAE

Mycenae, the city Homer connected with Agamemnon, the Greek—or "Achaian" – leader, was known, however. Homer had called it a "well-built city" and said it was wealthy, but by his time it can have been neither, as it had been destroyed in the Late Bronze Age and had never fully recovered. Interestingly Homer also gives a list, in Book 2 of the Illiad, of 164 towns that were said to have sent troops to Troy. Some were still well known when he was writing, but several are listed which had been completely abandoned by then, and whose exact location was unknown. Archaeological and historical research has since shown that they were real places, and had been accurately described by the poet; one is the Mycenaean palace of Pylos. Mycenae itself seems to have been the center of a series of similar, if often smaller, sites; other palaces have been found in various places in the Peloponnese in southern Greece, and there was a network of well-built roads.

The site of Mycenae had been described by the Greek travel writer Pausanias in the second century AD; many more recent, 18th and 19th century, travellers had visited it as well. The massive fortifications, called "Cyclopean" after the mythological race of giants, and the impressive tholos or beehive tombs could still be seen. None of these travelers ever imagined a real link with the supposedly fictional world of Homer, however, until the end of the 19th century.

Opposite: Inside the citadel walls at Mycenae. Grave Circle A, where Schliemann found the gold masks and other burial goods, is surrounded by the curving wall in the center.

Above: Completed in the mid-13th century BC, the Lion Gate formed a new main entrance to the citadel, and is one of the most imposing archaeological remains ever discovered. The lintel and the threshold stones weigh over twenty tons each; the door jambs are smaller.

SCHLIEMANN'S FIRST EXCAVATIONS

Heinrich Schliemann, who had been prevented from continuing to excavate at Troy, turned his attention to the site and began digging, opening a large trench in September 1876. He was inspired by Pausanias' declaration that Agamemnon and his companions had been buried inside the citadel and, sure enough, he soon found several shaft graves—large, deep rectangular pits with burials at the bottom—in a circular enclosure just south of the main gateway to the citadel, the Lion Gate. They contained 19 bodies, probably nine women, eight men and two children. These people had been richly supplied with extremely spectacular grave goods—golden masks, gold, silver, and bronze jewelry, plate and weaponry. One of the masks allegedly inspired Schliemann to declare that he had "gazed upon the face of Agamemnon" but it is now known that these burials actually date from the earlier years of Mycenaean civilization. If there ever was such an individual as Agamemnon, he would have lived at Mycenae sometime around 1250 BC (opinions on dating differ), about 300 years later than the people whose bodies lay in the shaft graves.

Schliemann's circle of graves is known as Circle A; Circle B was found outside the walls of the citadel in the 1950s, and dates from even earlier times. There are some artifacts buried with the bodies there, but they are not so rich and there is only one mask. By contrast, in the three wealthiest graves from Circle A alone there was at least 28 lb of gold. The male bodies were buried with weapons, sometimes with elaborate daggers intended for show rather than actual use. The women had jewelry—necklaces incorporating beads made of Baltic amber were found, bearing witness to trading networks—and there were many other items such as pots or copper vessels. The source of all this wealth cannot be known, but it is impressive that so much of it could be removed from circulation and buried with the dead. There must have been a continuous supply.

Opposite: One of the gold masks from the shaft graves in Grave Circle A. This is the mask that supposedly led Schliemann to announce that he had "gazed on the face of Agamemnon." These are not necessarily accurate portraits, however, and date from much earlier than the possible time of the Trojan War.

Left: The almost heraldic sculpture of lions guarding a column fills the "relieving triangle" above the Lion Gate itself. The missing heads were originally held in position by dowels, and there has been much speculation about their appearance. They may have faced outwards, looking directly at anyone who approached.

Left below: A gold-plated box from one of the shaft graves in Grave Circle A, showing a lion chasing a horse and deer.

Mycenae of the Heroes

There are many versions of the stories surrounding Mycenae; poets and playwrights have added and ignored parts, emphasized others and changed the slant of the tales. They all agree that Agamemnon was the organizer of the campaign against Troy and supreme commander of the Greek forces there. His brother was Menelaus, whose wife Helen had been abducted by the Trojan prince Paris; he ruled in Sparta, and Agamemnon himself ruled Mycenae, "rich in gold."

When Agamemnon left for Troy, the fleet was prevented from getting there by adverse winds and it became obvious that the powers causing them would have to be appeased; Agamemnon sacrificed his daughter Iphigenia and the wind changed. The troops were away for ten years, with no word or news coming back to Mycenae, which had been left in the hands of Agamemnon's wife Clytemnestra. During this period she eventually took a lover, Aigisthos, and they ruled together.

However, the result of the war was announced by the lighting of beacons; Agamemnon was on his way back to Mycenae. He returned in triumph, bringing with him the Trojan princess Cassandra as booty. They were greeted by Clytemnestra and Aigisthos—and murdered. However, Clytemnestra's existing children by Agamemnon, Electra and Orestes, were determined to avenge their father's death and Orestes eventually did so, killing his mother.

THE TOMBS OF MYCENAE

Mycenae has been subject to much excavation over the past 130 or so years, and can appear confusing, with previous trenches posing problems for the next generation of archaeologists. Some parts of it, however, have remained obvious over centuries like the next series of tombs, next in terms of date of construction. These are the spectacular tholos tombs like the Treasury of Atreus, and the greatest of these were built in the 14th century BC. Almost nothing of their contents has survived; they were too obvious to survive unplundered, so we don't know whether they contained anything as dramatic as the items from the shaft graves. The tombs themselves are such an impressive statement of power and wealth that it is possible the grave goods were equally so—but there's no definite evidence. It has been suggested that the tholos tombs might have been used by several members of a family or ruling group, rather than just one individual. Certainly this is true of some of the shaft graves, which contain more than one body, buried at different times and with older ones pushed aside so that another person could be included.

Mycenae isn't just about tombs, though. It sits on a hill, protected by deep gorges on the north and south sides, and has a reliable water supply from a nearby spring. The views from the citadel itself are not as comprehensive as might be expected, but those from the watch point on the summit of Aghios Elias above Mycenae are excellent, and this is easy to reach. From the earliest times the massive walls have impressed travelers, and excavations inside the citadel have revealed much more. The defenses themselves focus on the main gate, the monumental Lion Gate, through which visitors pass into the citadel proper past Grave Circle A. This was incorporated into the citadel by

extending the walls around it; it had originally been outside, as Grave Circle B still is. Some powerful ruler may have wanted to be identified with the people who were buried in the shaft graves, and emphasized this by bringing them within the circuit of the walls. Several stages of construction have been identified, and the height of Mycenae's power seems to have been in the 13th century BC, when the wall layout changed and the Lion Gate itself was built. The sculpture of the lions fills the space above the lintel of the massive gate formed by the "relieving triangle" which directed some of the weight of the superstructure away from the lintel itself. It's been suggested that lions are both symbols and guardians of the royal house of Mycenae; lion hunts are depicted on daggers, they appear on seals and elsewhere, and lion bones have even been found at several Mycenaean sites.

Right: A container in the form of a duck made out of rock crystal, which comes from the earlier circle of shaft graves at Mycenae, Grave Circle B.

Above: Many small ivories have been found at Mycenae; this one, of two women and a child, comes from the palace area. Though it is only about 3 inches tall, it reveals many details of female costume: the heavy flounced skirts, bodices, and jewelry are all clearly shown. It has been suggested that ivories like this were probably given as highly prestigious gifts.

Opposite: Another of the gold masks from the shaft graves in Grave Circle A.

Inside the Walls

Inside the walls Mycenae was packed with buildings, storerooms, workshops—and, of course, with the palace itself. The summit of the citadel is badly eroded, however, and the palace complex is not well preserved. The area around the throne room, or "megaron hall," has partly slipped into one of the ravines, for example. The other buildings, which are not quite so exposed, have survived better. A set has been described by one of Mycenae's recent excavators, George Mylonas, as a "cult center." These occupy a cramped site, south of Grave Circle A, and include a 'temple' and a room with a well-preserved fresco. The temple has a central platform and benches along the north wall (there are signs that the east wall, at least, had a textile hanging down it, suspended from a wooden slat). A clay figure still stood on a side platform, next to something described as a portable altar. Associated with this space was a sealed store, filled with large numbers of male and female figures and other "cult paraphernalia" like a sculpture of a coiled snake. In the room with the fresco, a beautiful ivory head was found which had evidently once fitted on to a wooden body. There was also another lion, with a socket in its underside, which may have been part of a scepter or a piece of furniture. The fresco showed two large figures face to face and a smaller one at

Opposite: There was an extensive oil store directly behind the megaron at Pylos, with large containers—pithoi—set into benches. The main entrance into the megaron can be seen in the wall opposite, behind the circular hearth. There was another store nearby, and a separate building held many jars, this time for wine storage.

Left: George Mylonas excavates a grave at Mycenae in 1952. The two distinctive pots seen in this grave—the jug with a "beaked" spout and the two-handled vessel—are relatively common at Mycenaean sites.

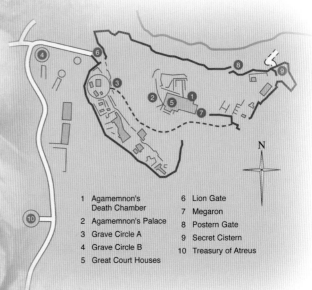

1 Agamemnon's Death Chamber
2 Agamemnon's Palace
3 Grave Circle A
4 Grave Circle B
5 Great Court Houses
6 Lion Gate
7 Megaron
8 Postern Gate
9 Secret Cistern
10 Treasury of Atreus

Pylos

Homer referred to Pylos as the palace of Nestor, one of the leaders of the Greeks in the Trojan War, but there had always been some confusion about where exactly Pylos lay. Schliemann attempted to discover it but was unsuccessful. Two tholos tombs like those at Mycenae were found in Messenia, in the southwest of the Peloponnese, early in the 20th century, and an expedition was formed to investigate further. Carl Blegen was one of the leaders, and he began trial excavations at a site he thought looked promising, finding Mycenaean pottery, fragments of painted plaster and clay tablets inscribed with Linear B on the first morning. Unfortunately this was in April 1939, and digging was interrupted by both the Second World War and the civil war which followed in Greece. It was not possible for him to return until 1952.

The palace complex Blegen went on to find was very similar to Mycenae, and to Tiryns, another Mycenaean site. In the center was a throne room with a large circular ceremonial hearth and four columns holding up the roof. A room like this is a common feature of Mycenaean palaces and is often referred to as a megaron. Storerooms were located nearby, and residential quarters opened off a courtyard which lay in front of the megaron. The stores contained thousands of cups and plates, and containers for wine, oil, and grain. Two rooms near the entrance to the palace contained very many clay tablets, and they had survived beautifully; they would normally have been recycled or weathered away, but these had been baked in the fierce fire that destroyed the palace in the late 13th century BC. These were instrumental in Michael Ventris' decipherment of Linear B, and could then be read; they proved to be administrative records which document the daily running of the palace—the rations given to weavers, the bronze used by the smiths, offerings made to the gods. A king is mentioned, but he is not named. Like other Mycenaean palaces, Pylos was surrounded by a settlement, but none of these "towns" has been thoroughly excavated.

modern archaeological techniques have made it possible for many aspects of life to be examined. It is now much more possible to determine, for example, what pots contained and thus what the Mycenaeans ate. There is also written evidence from clay tablets. The basic diet might have been rather bland, though in some respects a little like a "Mediterranean" diet today without those ingredients, tomatoes for instance, which were introduced comparatively recently. Excavations have found wheat, barley, vetch, lentils, broad beans, and peas, and it has been suggested that the grains were made into a sort of porridge. The records on clay tablets show that rations allocated to workers included olives and wine as well as grains, and some texts also specify figs and flavorings; the tablets from the "House of the Sphinxes" list ones like cardamom, celery, fennel, mint, and sesame. Wild herbs and other locally grown flavorings, like wild onions, are likely to have been used as well. There are shells from seafood—the local conditions are not appropriate for the survival of fish bones—and evidence of sheep, goats, pigs and some cattle. It is highly likely that dairy products also played a part in the diet; DNA testing gives the same result both for these "secondary products" and for the animal itself. Wild meat, game, is represented by deer, boar and hare. Rubbish heaps which date to the earliest phases of the citadel included a lot of animal bone—sheep and pig—and large amounts of oyster and mussel shells. Analysis of the organic residue in three pots showed that two had contained a stew made with olive oil, meat, and lentils and the other one a mixture of olive oil, wine, and fish. There is evidence from some Mycenaean sites for a fermented drink made with barley and honey; here many vessels had contained wine, including a resinated type.

floor level, and cannot be easily interpreted; in front of it was a platform (maybe an altar) with a group of nine pots next to it; these could have contained offerings. There was also a larnax, a large container. These have several interpretations—they could be used as coffins, chests, baths—but it has been suggested that this one was for ritual cleansing, given its setting. While some of this is informed guesswork and deduction, there is also, unlike in Minoan Crete, written evidence for religion in the Mycenaean world. Linear B tablets from Pylos, for example, refer to gods by name—and they are some of the classical Greek divinities like Zeus, Athena and Poseidon—and one set lists the contents of a temple storeroom like that found in the Cult Center.

On a more down-to-earth level,

Above: A gold rhyton—a vessel probably used in ceremonial or ritual—in the form of a lion's head from the Grave Circle A shaft graves.

Right: A stylized crown from the shaft graves in Grave Circle A at Mycenae. This has also been interpreted, the other way up, as being a belt decoration with hanging pendants.

The Treasury of Atreus

Pausanias mentioned this great tholos or beehive tomb, and it is remarkable; it takes its name from Agamemnon's father. It is undoubtedly the product of a culture that could call on a large labor force, and one which marked the prominence of particular individuals or groups of individuals. This tomb was probably built sometime in the second half of the 14th century BC. It was certainly constructed by skilled engineers and builders, and similarities between it and another, roughly contemporary, tomb at Orchomenos have led to speculation that the same highly skilled specialist team may have been responsible for that one too. The stone is the local limestone, which had to be dressed into shape with hammers, and finished by grinding. There is an impressive entrance, which must have been even more spectacular when it had its decorated green marble half-columns, two flanking the door and two the triangle above the lintel. That triangular space had bands of colored infill, as well. The doorway itself is about 17 feet high and there are signs that it had equally massive doors. The passageway leading

to it is lined with large blocks of stone, heavy and difficult to maneuver. It is highly likely that the stonemasons and builders used a combination of earth ramps and pulleys.

The main chamber is around 48 feet in diameter, and 43 feet high at the highest point of the beautiful corbeled vault, and there is a side chamber which was probably used for the burial itself. Corbeling, a technique of roof building which involves successive layers of stones, each layer projecting inwards slightly further than the last and finally meeting at the top under a capstone, requires skill and careful judgment, and it is stabilized by the large mound of earth over the top. The inside of the vault was originally decorated with bronze rosettes, and some were still in place in the 19th century, despite the looting of the tomb. The engineers' talent is further demonstrated by the use of a relieving triangle—the triangular space above the entire length of the lintel which enabled the weight of the whole vault to be transferred away from the lintel itself.

Warriors of the Bronze Age

Bronze is an alloy of copper and tin. It was circulated in the form of ingots, and these could then be used to make items ranging from decorative wire to shields and swords. Molds have been found, showing how the weapons were cast from molten bronze; once the metal cooled, it could be hammered into shape and given a sharp edge. "Classic" bronze has 10 percent tin, and "mild" bronze has only 6 percent. Classic bronze can be brittle once hardened, and was used to make large swords, socketed spear- and ax-heads, and even wheels. The "mild" form could be hammered into sheets, was relatively flexible and resilient, and was used to make armor.

Typically, a Mycenaean warrior had a couple of swords—which might be elaborately decorated—a dagger, and a spear. Both daggers and swords had an inherent design weakness where the blade joined the hilt, and there were adaptations over time. These could easily have led to a change in the way warriors fought: slashing instead of thrusting at their opponents. Armor is very rare in the archaeological record, though there is one set which was found in a contemporary tomb at Dendra, also on the Peloponnese; it covers the torso and has added shoulder pieces, arm guards, and skirt sections. A replica of this was made; though it was possible for the wearer to move and fight, the armor was cumbersome and heavy (about 55 lb), and there has been some speculation that most warriors would probably have used layered leather, perhaps with bronze plaques. The helmet certainly was made using leather—and the unusual kind described by Homer, and assumed to be imaginary, has shown up in the archaeological record. It was covered by plates made from boars' tusks, arranged in a decorative pattern, and there are small ivory heads of men from Mycenae wearing just this sort of helmet.

The only evidence of shields comes from wall paintings, images on pots and seals, and small ivory models. They are also shown on the "lion hunt" dagger, where two different types can be seen: the large "figure of eight" ones, and an equally large rectangular type. These were probably made from leather stretched over a wicker frame; patterning is often shown which looks like the markings on cowhide. Smaller shields appeared later, in the 12th century BC.

Left: A bronze dagger from Grave Circle A dating from the middle of the 16th century BC, showing hunters armed with spears, and a bow and arrow, pursuing lions. It is inlaid with gold and silver. Recent tests have shown the black background to be an alloy of bronze, gold, and silver.

THE END OF MYCENAE

Trying to work out what finally happened to the site of Mycenae, as well as to other Mycenaean sites, is complicated. The archaeology has not been helped by previous occupants of the citadel (who dug foundations for a few buildings in Hellenistic times) or by Schliemann's excavations; he cleared the palaces he excavated without keeping adequate records, especially of the pottery he found, which could have helped with dating. In addition, Mycenae particularly shows signs of having been damaged by earthquakes and fire on several occasions; the fires, of course, could have been a consequence of the earthquakes.

There is definite evidence from some Mycenaean citadels, including Mycenae itself, that the fortifications were renewed or improved at some point during the 13th century BC. The water supply was always a weak point during a siege, and late in that century the situation was improved at Mycenae by extending the fortification walls to include a natural terrace at the east end of the citadel, and building an entrance passage to the pre-existing cistern through the walls. Similar work was undertaken at roughly the same time at Tiryns, another Mycenaean palace, and at Athens. However, most Mycenaean palaces were either abandoned by their inhabitants or

Above: The large hearth in the middle of the megaron at Pylos, the main room of the palace, had four large pillars around it, a standard arrangement. The site of one of them is shown clearly here. Megaron hearths like this were repeatedly plastered and decorated with designs of flames and spirals; the walls would also have been covered in wall paintings. The floors were patterned, and it is highly likely that the ceilings would also have been painted.

completely destroyed toward the end of the century. Exactly why this happened is the subject of much debate. It is possible that there were attacks from foreigners—a popular explanation in the past—but it is probably more likely that local conflict played a critical part. Rivalry between different Mycenaean kingdoms, internal unrest, population pressure, failure of the harvest following drought: all of these, either together or singly, have been proposed as causes for the collapse.

Even after the destruction people still lived at some sites, notably Mycenae and Tiryns, but in a much more modest way. International trade did not stop completely, but all the characteristics of Mycenaean civilization at its height—massive buildings, elaborate decoration, sophisticated craft production and writing—disappeared. Mycenae, and the other sites, began to drift from history into legend.

Athens

No citizen of Greece in the classical era would ever have really defined themselves as 'Greek': they would have thought of themselves as Athenians or Spartans or Thebans. Though they shared a language, Greece was a land of independent city states. The Persians attempted to conquer Greece three times between 490 and 479 BC, but were defeated by an alliance led by Athens and Sparta, and within 30 years many occupied areas of Greece had been reclaimed. Wealth began to flow in, especially to Athens.

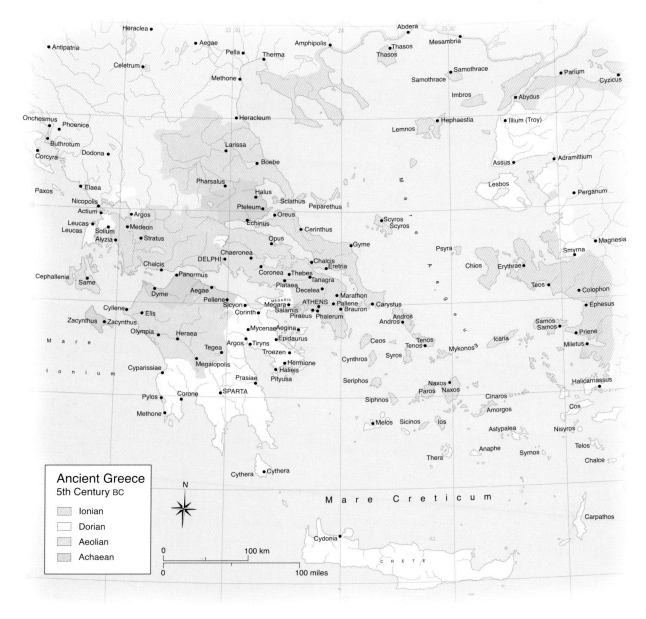

Ancient Greece
5th Century BC

Ionian
Dorian
Aeolian
Achaean

N

0   100 km
0   100 miles

Athens was the largest city state, and the city itself had been inhabited for centuries before the classical period. Wells have been found on the northern slopes of the Acropolis that date back to the Neolithic, but few other such early traces have survived. A series of Mycenaean chamber tombs have been found in the area and there may well have been a Mycenaean palace on the summit. There are signs of both Neolithic and Mycenaean activity in the area of the Agora, just below the Acropolis: this is one of the best excavated and researched areas, so it is not surprising that evidence for the earliest history of the city has turned up here.

In the fifth century BC, at the height of its power and influence, Athens had a large number of inhabitants. Some estimates have been very high, but trying to

Opposite: Most Doric temples had 13 columns along the sides but the Parthenon has 17 because it was longer than normal—there were two inner chambers, one for the gigantic statue of the goddess Athena.

establish exact figures is almost impossible. However, it was certainly a big city. It was sacked by the Persians in 480 BC, which fueled a spate of lavish rebuilding. Defensive walls were constructed; called the Long Walls, these ran down to the port of Piraeus so that Athens would not be cut off from its supplies in time of siege—by then the city was at war with Sparta. New temples were built on the Acropolis, including the present Parthenon which was started in 447 BC.

The Parthenon itself was the temple to Athena Parthenos, the patron goddess of Athens. It has been visible, and much visited, ever since it was built, though its appearance has changed over time; its sculptures would originally have been brightly painted, for instance. Despite this, much remains debatable, like the fact that one of the best friezes—an unusual feature on a building in the Doric style anyway—can only be viewed with extreme difficulty. There must be some reason for this, but we can only speculate; the precise nature of the subject matter is also uncertain. There was an enormous gold and ivory statue of Athena made by the sculptor Pheidias, who also created the colossal statue of Zeus at Olympia, and the Parthenon was used rather like a treasury, sheltering many gold and silver offerings to the goddess.

There had been another building on the site, and the plan of the Parthenon we see today is based upon it: the huge limestone platform which forms the base, for example, had been built for the earlier temple and just needed a slight extension. Many of the marble column "drums"—the individual sections—were also reused. There are more temples to Athena in her other personas (Athena Parthenos was the virgin Athena), such as Athena Nike (Athena the promise of victory) and Athena Promachos, the warrior.

Above: A silver Athenian coin, a tetradrachm, with the goddess Athena's head on one side and her symbol, an owl, on the other. The coins were, as a result, known as "owls."

Below: The Agora, with the vast Stoa of Attalos which was reconstructed by the American School of Classical Studies, who have excavated a lot of the site. This stoa seems to have operated as an area of shops; today it houses the museum. The reconstruction gives a good impression of what parts of the Agora would have looked like in classical times.

THE AGORA

Below the Acropolis was the Agora, essentially the city's marketplace and center. Many different activities took place here, from philosophical discussion "schools" to legal affairs and, of course, buying and selling. The Athenian Agora has been excavated since the 1930s, with some interruptions, by the American School of Classical Studies at Athens.

The administration of the city was concentrated in buildings along the western side of the Agora. Here was the Bouleuterion, the council chamber, and the Tholos, where meals were provided for the 50 members of the city council who were on round-the-clock duty at any time. Civic dinners were cooked in a kitchen annex and the digs in the area have found pottery shards from dining ware labeled "public property." There were law courts—bounded enclosures—and several stoas, buildings with open colonnades at the front. This feature made them cool in the heat of the day, while providing protection from sudden storms. Stoas are common

The Venus de Milo

Many beautiful sculptures from the classical age of Greece were destroyed or damaged in the following centuries, accidentally or deliberately; some pieces, like a statue of Herakles that came to light in the 14th century, were reburied. Some were salvaged and reused on the palaces and estates of Renaissance nobles, and some were only discovered much later. In the 18th century the collectors and cultivated gentlemen of northern Europe began acquiring statues to add to their private collections, or to donate to the fledgling national museums. Owning authentic statues brought a certain status. They could be found in some surprising places—E. D. Clark managed to persuade a local priest to help him extract a massive sculpture, originally from the sanctuary of Demeter at Eleusis, from a dung heap; it was presented to Cambridge University.

The statue known as the Venus de Milo—which actually shows the semi-naked Greek goddess Aphrodite—was found by a peasant on the island of Melos in 1820. It dates from the second century BC and is made from two blocks of marble. It was discovered with an inscribed plinth, which may not actually belong to it; if it does, it records that the statue had been made by a sculptor from Antioch. It was obtained by an officer in the French navy together with the French vice-consul, on behalf of the French Ambassador to the Ottoman Empire at Constantinople. He presented it to the then King of France, Louis XVIII, at what proved to be just the right time to insure its lasting popularity. Napoleon's defeat in 1815 had meant that much of the loot brought to France during his rule had to be returned. This included a marble statue called the Venus de Medici, which was sent back to Florence. The Venus de Milo turned up at the perfect moment to be publicized as an infinitely better replacement.

features of many classical Greek sites and were used for many things. Rooms in some of them, like the South Stoa, had doors set to one side so that dining couches could be fitted in, and city officials had their offices there. Tradesmen might rent storerooms and there would also have been shops in some; rooms on the Stoa of Attalos on the eastern side of the Agora were certainly used for this purpose—it has been suggested that they formed a kind of up-market shopping arcade. One of the stoas in Corinth had even been used as a fish market. Stoas also acted as meeting places, as indeed did the whole Agora, and the Stoic school of philosophy takes its name from the Painted Stoa where the philosopher Zeno had his base.

Entry to the Agora was a privilege; anyone in "bad standing" could be banned, down to the fourth century BC. There were boundary stones; one is still in place. Despite this possible restriction, buying and selling would have gone on in many places; there was a degree of civic control, as attested by official sets of weights and measures. There is even evidence of bronze-working. The casting bit for a bronze statue was discovered and inside were remains of a mold, apparently for a statue of a naked youth, a kouros, possibly destined for the nearby Temple of Apollo.

There were gods and goddesses everywhere in the Agora; this was by no means a secular space. The Hephaisteion, a fifth-century temple to Hephaistos and Athena, stood above the site and traces have been found of plants, apparently from formal rows of flower pots ranged around it. There would have been statues everywhere, of both gods and heroes. The major route across the Agora was the Panathenaic Way, along which the procession of the Panathenaia took place every four years. This was a festival in honor of Athena and it has been suggested that the almost-invisible frieze on the Parthenon illustrates the procession.

Opposite above: The woman shown on this jug from 490 BC has a full set of spinning tools.

Opposite below: Archaeologists excavate a site in Athens. During the construction work for the 2004 Olympic Games many new discoveries were made.

Right: Many houses depended on water carried from public fountains. These were sociable places, and, like the one depicted on this black-figure vase, were usually roofed with a colonnaded entrance. Water was generally fetched by women.

KERAMEIKOS

One of the most interesting areas of Athens is the Kerameikos district, the name coming from the pottery workshops that were nearby. It was divided in two by the city walls. The cemeteries lay outside the walls and this part of Kerameikos was distinguished by the marble tombs that lined the roads leading out of the city. Burials here date back to early times. At some periods most of the burials were cremations, at others they were inhumations; sometimes they were marked by massive kraters or amphorae, sometimes they were covered by grave mounds surmounted by statues or gravestones. In the Archaic period (about 700–480 BC) wealthy people might well put up a kouros, a statue of a naked standing youth, or a kore, a clothed young woman. These could represent deities or the people buried in the tombs; sometimes an inscription on the base makes the distinction clear. Some of the graves are lavish, and this level of expenditure was eventually curbed by restrictive laws, limiting excesses.

But the Kerameikos wasn't entirely the domain of the dead; it also had a much less quiet and respectable side. It was the red-light district. Some of the prostitutes whose presence is attested to by contemporary

playwrights such as Aristophanes may have used nearby brothels; some may have used the cemetery itself. Piraeus, the port of Athens, was also renowned for its streetwalkers, but Kerameikos appears to provide archaeological evidence as well, most clearly from the site known as Building Z.

OUTSIDE THE CITY OF ATHENS

Greek cities like Athens were reliant on supplies coming in from outside, either from the countryside under the control of the city state, or as imports from other regions, or from abroad. Considering how important the countryside was, remarkably little archaeological work has been done there, though this is now being rectified. Initial results have shown that rural Greece was actually humming with activity. There is a network of small sites, possibly individual farms, and villages, but many workers lived in the cities and went out into the countryside to work. A large part of people's everyday diet came from grains, vegetables, and olives produced there, and goat and sheep rearing would have provided both meat and dairy products. Grapevines were grown; wine was a vital element of Greek life. When it came to the water rather than the land, fish was often added to the diet whenever possible and this was also traded, as were sponges and salt.

Building Z

Just inside the city, drains from the Kerameikos led to a strange building excavated by Ursula Knigge. It was originally constructed sometime after the middle of the fifth century BC and went through many changes over a period of about 150 years. The basic plan, however, stayed roughly the same.

A door in the shadow of the city wall opened on to a large entrance hall. From this a narrow corridor went past small rooms and turned into a courtyard. More doors led off this, and directly opposite was the antechamber to a much larger and more impressive room with a mosaic floor. Through this room visitors could reach the west side of the house—a row of larger chambers with red walls, and another little courtyard behind them. There were more than 15 rooms, connected by corridors and open spaces, and the house must have been confusing to wander through. A large number of artefacts which were distinctively feminine were found; there was also an array of pottery, enough to entertain guests.

The building seems to have been severely damaged in an earthquake and when it was rebuilt the main courtyard was enlarged and the number of rooms increased. However, then the building was destroyed in a fire.

This time it lay derelict for a while but enough must have remained for the next building on the site to follow the same basic ground plan about 50 years later. Statuettes of foreign goddesses were found, suggesting that some of the inhabitants came from different places: Thrace, Syria, and Anatolia, the usual sources of Athenian slaves. If, as seems likely, Building Z functioned as a combination of brothel and inn, then some of the prostitutes may well have been slaves.

There is also a lot of evidence for weaving at Building Z, which actually adds weight to the brothel theory. Much weaving was done in the home, but it was also a trade. Women who worked had a bad reputation, whatever the nature of their work, and it may be that they had no other sources of income. But there was some link between the cloth trade and prostitution. There are paintings on vases which show women working on textiles in what are evidently brothels. One perfume bottle shows a woman spinning yarn while being propositioned by a man who is offering her money; on another vase a woman is shown putting her work away as a man approaches while a companion greets a male visitor. These are just two examples; there are others. It is quite possible that weaving was another way in which a brothel made money; much of a brothel's business would be done after dark—would slaves have been allowed to idle away the daylight hours? It is unlikely. This version of Building Z was also destroyed, in all probability by another earthquake, around the end of the fourth century BC. The finds seem to indicate that it struck during the day, while the women were working on their looms. Much is still uncertain, but weaving, women, and wine were all vital elements of whatever was going on in Building Z.

There were workshops at Laurion, too; once at the surface the ore was sorted, crushed, and processed. It may have also been smelted at the site, but furnaces have not yet been found. Laurion silver went into the famous silver coins of Athens, the "owls" with Athena's head on one side and her symbol, the owl, on the reverse. These were first issued in the sixth century BC; by the second century AD Pausanias was able to describe Laurion as "the place where Athens once had silver mines."

Opposite: This red-figure vase depicts a spinning woman who is attracting a lot of interest from a young man. The link between spinning and weaving and prostitution is sometimes depicted quite clearly in vase painting.

Left: The gravestone on the corner of the cemetery in Kerameikos commemorates the cavalryman Dexileos who died at Corinth in 394 BC.

Below: A tetradrachm with the goddess Athena's head on one side.

SILVER MINES

The state of Athens was particularly fortunate in having the silver mines of Laurion within its territory. Silver from these financed many of the state building projects, but it was mined in conditions of great hardship and misery, largely by slaves. Erosion would have originally exposed the ore deposits at the surface, where they could be easily worked. Veins would then be traced back underground, with the miners following the deposit and tunneling along it. But there were also other levels reached by vertical shafts, some of which were 300 feet—or more—deep. Once veins of ore had been located via these shafts they would be opened up, but these galleries were never more than a few feet high. Workers lay on their backs or sides, using simple tools like hammers or picks, and relied on torches or lamps for a bit of light. These would have smelled strongly and smoked a lot and this, together with the excessively dusty and cramped conditions, must have made working in the mines appalling. Sometimes secondary shafts were sunk in an attempt to improve ventilation, but some miners still suffocated. There are a few records of trouble with the slaves. They fled, for example, when the Spartans attacked Attica and the decline in activity during the third and second centuries BC was made worse by a slave revolt.

Delphi and Olympia

Certain sanctuaries were popular throughout the classical Greek world. There were four main ones on the mainland of Greece itself: Delphi, Olympia, Nemea, and Isthmia near Corinth. The first two are by far the best known ones today, and were probably the most significant in the past.

Sanctuaries were an essential part of Greek life and played an important political role. They could be centers for a cult tied firmly to a particular state, like the Acropolis at Athens, or places for major festivals and sporting contests where people from all over the Hellenic world could gather, like Delphi or Olympia.

Delphi

THE HISTORY OF DELPHI

The history of Delphi goes back beyond the classical period; there was a Mycenaean settlement and a group of figurines were found, apparently deliberately deposited, in what later became Athena's sanctuary. However, it does seem that the site was abandoned after the end of the Mycenaean period, probably until about the tenth century BC.

Its location, well away from many centers of population, might seem surprising, but in actual fact this relative remoteness gave Delphi a valuable neutrality. Even today the place has an undoubted power and impact. The Greeks believed Delphi to be the center of their world, and though it was peripheral to major centers of power it certainly was not isolated: it could be reached by one of the main land routes northward and was also accessible by sea. The first three temples to Apollo were made from laurel, beeswax and feathers, and bronze—according to legend. Certainly there was a substantial building in existence by the seventh century BC, which was replaced in the following century after it had burned down. This, in its turn, had to be reconstructed following earthquake damage. Though the site is best known as being sacred to Apollo, there was also an important sanctuary of the goddess Athena, and Delphi attracted pilgrims from all over the Greek world and beyond. Many of these came to consult the Oracle.

Opposite: The Temple to Apollo at Delphi is quite modest, considering its importance. The Oracle would have sat in the innermost sanctuary, presumably at the back of the main chamber.

Right above: The round Tholos in the sanctuary of Athena at Delphi is one of the most famous monuments at the site, but its purpose and use is uncertain. However, the name of the architect is known: Theodorus. There were originally 20 columns; three have been restored.

Right below: The Kastalian Spring was on the road down to the sanctuary of Athena. The water was used in purification rituals, and it was where the Pythia bathed before consultations. After she had done this, she burned laurel leaves and barley grains and then went to the Temple of Apollo where she would give her predictions sitting on a tripod.

THE ORACLE

Possibly the most significant occupant of the Temple of Apollo was the Oracle, known as the Pythia. By the eighth century BC the Oracle was certainly functioning and was being consulted on major political questions; by around 600 BC the Pythia had an international reputation. Originally the Oracle operated on only one day a year, but this was later extended to nine days. Those who wished to consult the Oracle had to purify themselves and pay a fee—make a substantial offering—after which an animal would be sacrificed. If the omens proved favorable, a questioner would then be able to enter the temple and make another sacrifice. Finally he would be able to make his inquiry of the Pythia herself. She was a woman of about 50, and was expected to devote herself to the god on being appointed. There are stories that "vapors" seeping from cracks in the ground inspired her replies but, though she may have gone into a trance, these do not seem to have had any basis in fact. Sometimes her replies to questions could be straightforward, even direct, but often they were ambiguous. Croesus of Lydia, for example, asked the Pythia what would happen if he marched against Persia and is supposed to have been told that he would destroy a great empire. He acted on the prophecy, attacked Persia—and lost. The empire he destroyed was his own.

The fortunes of Delphi have fluctuated. Since the height of its power it has been plundered—by Sulla in 86 BC, for example—and repaired. It has never faded from memory and one of the most persistent traditions since ancient times has been tourism.

Opposite: The Temple of Apollo at Delphi.

Below: The theatre at Delphi lies within the sanctuary of Apollo. It was used for general gatherings and for the musical contests at the games. There are 35 rows of seats which could hold about 5000 spectators.

The Wealth of the Sanctuary

The "fee" any potential questioner of the Oracle had to pay could be significant. The historian Herodotus lists some of the things Croesus is supposed to have sent; even allowing for wild exaggeration it is evident that large amounts of precious metals were involved. A number of Greek city states built treasuries at Delphi (Croesus' gifts were lodged in the Corinthian treasury) and, built in a competitive spirit, these could be spectacular and occasionally provocative, with sculptures illustrating the success of one state in battle over another. The use of marble and statuary was impressive.

It was also customary to make a donation to the sanctuary in gratitude for something like winning a contest or having a marked stroke of luck. The Corcyraeans dedicated a bronze bull after they had successfully landed an immense shoal of tuna, for instance. As a result bronze statues featured strongly, and one of the most famous is known as the Charioteer. It was found in the course of French excavations at Delphi in 1896 and had survived because it was buried in an ancient earthquake. This figure of a robed young man, still holding the reins of his horses in one hand (the other arm is missing), stood on a base showing that it had been part of a dedication from Polyzalos of Gela, the Sicilian tyrant, who had won a chariot race at Delphi's Pythian games in 478 or 474 BC.

Olympia

THE GAMES

Olympia is widely known because of the games that were held there. Like those at other sanctuaries, they took place on a four-year cycle, and the communities of the Greek world would send their best athletes and performers. There were training facilities for them as well as places for the various contests to take place. The tradition of the games was revived in the 19th century, with the creation of the modern Olympic Games.

At ancient Olympia the sports would have consisted of things like chariot racing, boxing and wrestling (and a "no-holds-barred" fight, the pankration), and athletic contests like running. During the games a temporary truce was in operation, enabling safe attendance and competition. Winners had the right to display their images in the sanctuary itself and also gained enormous status in their hometowns: they might be awarded free dinners for life, for example.

The present stadium at Olympia is an enlarged version of an earlier one on the same site. Up to 40,000 spectators could watch the contests, sitting directly on earth embankments—these were never upgraded to the stone seating which became increasingly common in other places. There is an umpires' stand quite a long way from the start (or finish) line—there is a line at either end of the nearly 192-meter-long course—and there were places for 20 runners. Contestants and umpires came into the stadium through a vaulted tunnel which they entered by a gate set into an arch. Married women were not allowed to attend the games, though the priestess of Demeter Chamyne was: she sat on a stone altar which has been reconstructed on the north embankment. In the second century AD four-yearly games for women were instituted, honoring Hera, the wife of Zeus.

Above: Competitors and umpires came into the stadium through this entrance, the arch of which has been restored. There were usually ten umpires to monitor the contests, and at the south end of the stadium there is a paved umpires' stand.

Left: Column drums from the temple of Zeus at Olympia show quite clearly how pillars were constructed in a series of sections.

POLITICAL AND RELIGIOUS SIGNIFICANCE

The prominence of the games that were staged there gave Olympia a level of political importance. Treaties between states were displayed and, as at Delphi, there was a degree of inter-state rivalry in building treasuries. Monuments were also put up marking success in war and there is evidence that precious objects were also donated to the sanctuary for the same reason. A gold cup has been found, for example, whose inscription records that it was dedicated by a Corinthian family after the sack of a Greek city of unknown location, named as "Herakleia."

Along with Delphi, the sanctuary at Olympia was one of the most significant ones in all of Greece. It was sacred to Zeus, the ruler of the gods, and his great statue in the temple became one of the seven wonders of the ancient world. His temple is impressive today; at its height it must have been astonishing. The colossal gold and ivory statue of the god sat inside on a rich throne, supported by a base decorated with gold figures. It dominated the main room, towering over worshipers. The sculptor was Pheidias, who had also created the great statue of Athena in Athens, and his workshop at Olympia was discovered by a German team of archaeologists during their longterm digs at the site. The building called the Workshop of Pheidias is certainly big enough to have housed a statue over 40 feet tall, and clay molds were found which could have been used for making the gold drapery of the great figure of Zeus.

There were other sculptures in the Temple of Zeus, notably the metopes—square panels from the frieze level of the building, up above the columns—which illustrate the 12 tasks of Herakles. Herakles was the mythical founder of the games and universally popular in Greece; he was also a local hero to the inhabitants of the Peloponnese.

Northeast of the temple lay the altar of Zeus. This was supposed to have been made from the remains of ash and bones generated by hundreds of years' worth of sacrifices to Zeus, all held together with clay and mixed with water from the river Alpheios. By the second century AD, when the traveler Pausanias described it, it was approximately 23 feet tall—but no trace of it has been found by the German archaeological teams. The exact location may yet be discovered.

Below: The Palaistra at Olympia was part of the buildings that formed the gymnasium, where athletes both trained and stayed during the games. Behind the colonnades were a series of rooms and halls. One in the southwest corner has been identified as being a dining room; three on the north side seem to have been a library.

The Vergina Tombs

The city states of classical Greece regarded their Macedonian neighbors to the north as little better than uncultivated barbarians. The great Macedonian king Philip II, father of Alexander the Great, made Macedon a significant power, gaining grudging respect. He defeated a coalition of Greek cities in battle in 338 BC. Philip's capital was the city of Pella, but the old capital had been a place called Aigai, the precise location of which had been lost since antiquity. It was known, however, that the royal house of Macedon had continued to bury its dead at Aigai. One possibility was the village of Vergina, outside which were a lot of ancient tombs. Many of these were far too old to be relevant and many were clearly not impressive enough; there were others of appropriate date and scale, but they had been robbed of their contents in the distant past. However, there was also the "Great Tumulus."

THE GREAT TUMULUS

This was a mound about 360 feet in diameter and was still, on average, 40 feet high. Earlier diggers had avoided it but the Greek archaeologist Manolis Andronikos made it the focus of his excavations. He began work on the tumulus itself in 1976, investigating the way it had been constructed; in the process most of the mound was stripped away, but this has now been recreated. The tombs that lay below it finally came to light in 1977. There were three. The first one, the earliest, had been robbed in antiquity but was decorated with accomplished wall paintings. The third tomb, the latest of the three, had not been robbed and produced both beautiful and valuable grave goods—but its impact was dwarfed by the second tomb, the middle one in terms of age. This was one of the most astonishing archaeological discoveries of recent years.

THE TREASURES OF THE SECOND TOMB

When the roof was opened it became obvious that the main chamber of the tomb was completely undisturbed. Bronze armor leaned against a wall and there were silver vessels on the floor. At the back of the chamber, facing the door, stood a marble sarcophagus. There were traces of wooden furniture; the wood had rotted away, but the ivory and gold inlays remained. More pieces of gold and ivory on the floor seemed to be all that was left of an elaborate shield, but the best was to come. Inside the marble sarcophagus was a magnificent gold larnax—a chest—weighing 24 lb, decorated with the starburst that was the symbol of the royal house of Macedon. It contained cremated remains, incompletely burned, which had originally been wrapped in a cloth woven from purple wool and gold thread; a wreath made from golden oak leaves had been placed on top.

A second chamber at the front was exposed. This had also contained furniture, gilded bronze armor and a beautiful gilded-silver case for a bow and arrows—and another gold larnax, also containing cremated remains wrapped in purple and gold cloth. Three gold disks were found in this antechamber, also decorated with the starburst of Macedon. The walls were decorated with paintings, and the style of both these and the finds within the tomb dated it to

the latter half of the fourth century BC. All the evidence pointed to it belonging to a senior figure in the Macedonian royal house. In all likelihood this would be the king himself, and the chances were that his remains lay in the larnax from the main chamber, the one with the starburst on its lid.

Given the dating, many felt that the only real candidate was Philip himself. The bones were those of a man who had been between 35 and 55 when he died, and Philip had been assassinated at 46. There was another possibility, Philip's other surviving son—another Philip—who had been murdered in 317 BC. The identity of the occupant is still disputed, but the bones did bear signs of weapon damage, notably a severe eye wound—one such as that known from historical sources to have been sustained by Philip II about 18 years before his death. The medical-forensic team at Manchester, England were asked to attempt a facial reconstruction, which served to emphasize the effects of this injury on the dead man's face. Comparing the Manchester reconstruction to known portraits of the king does seem to lend weight to the identification, and it is highly likely that the cremated remains from the "starburst" larnax are those of Philip II.

Opposite: Two of the Macedonian tombs which lay outside the village of Vergina contained thrones like this. One has been confidently dated to the 340s BC—earlier than Tomb 2 in the Great Tumulus, which may have belonged to Philip II.

Above: A map showing the location of Vergina.

Below: A bow and arrow case from the tomb at Vergina.

Shipwrecks in the Mediterranean

The Mediterranean has been a highway for trade for thousands of years. There is evidence of trading by the sea from the Bronze Age onwards, in the clearest possible form—wrecked ships and their cargoes.

The great Bronze Age civilizations of the eastern Mediterranean knew, traded with, and in some cases even had diplomatic relations with each other. The exchange of luxury goods is well documented and there was evidently a more everyday system of trade, especially of raw materials. Some of this trade will have gone by land, but a lot must have traveled by sea. In many cases it would have been quicker, easier, and more convenient, and probably safer. This maritime trade is illustrated in wall paintings from the Aegean island of Thera, and documented in records such as those from Egypt. The movement of goods across the region can be tracked using finds from archaeological sites on land, but it is most vividly illustrated in the remains of the ships themselves.

The weather in the Mediterranean can be deceptive, and —even today— ships can be surprisingly vulnerable. In addition there has always been the risk of piracy. More than 1000 pre-medieval wrecks are now known from the Mediterranean, and increasingly sophisticated equipment and techniques in underwater archaeology have made a significant contribution to increasing their numbers.

Ulu Burun

One of the earliest wrecks is that of Ulu Burun, which dates from the 14th century BC. It was found by one of the oldest, most un-technological methods—being seen by a Turkish sponge diver near Kas in southern Turkey in 1982. He reported what he had discovered and excavations were begun in 1984 by George Bass and Cemal Pulak. The wreck lies in about 150 feet of water at a point where the seabed shelves quite steeply, so excavating it has been a difficult task. The ship's journey has been deduced from the cargo that was found; it seems to have been following a standard counter-clockwise route, partly determined by prevailing winds,

from the Levant towards the Aegean past the south coast of Anatolia. Here it sank, but its journey would normally have taken it back down toward northern Africa and Egypt.

The cargo of the Ulu Burun ship was sensational. There were 350 large copper ingots from Cyprus, weighing about 10 tons, and another ton of tin ingots. Copper was the major constituent of bronze and, together with this proportion of tin, could have made an

Opposite: A mosaic showing a ship being unloaded, from Roman North Africa. The sea routes between North Africa and Rome were of vital importance, and appear to have been very busy.

Above: Details from one of the wall paintings in the buried Bronze Age town of Akrotiri on the island of Thera. These Bronze Age ships are rowed by many oarsmen, and appear to have been steered by a helmsman using a single large steering oar. This fresco was originally more than 20 feet long and ran as a continuous frieze above the doors and windows of one of the upper rooms in the town.

enormous quantity of tools, luxury objects, and weapons. There were also ingots of glass, ebony, logs from Egypt and ivory. There were ostrich shells and evidence of fruits and spices—pomegranates, figs, olives, almonds, and acorns. A hinged wooden writing tablet was found; the leaves would have been covered in wax on which notes could have been made and smoothed away but that has not survived, so we don't know what language was being used.

There was a lot of pottery. This included ten large jars, pithoi, one of which was packed with smaller pots, and about 150 amphorae. About 100 of these smaller jars contained yellow terebinthine resin, which would probably have been used to make perfume. Quite apart from the raw metal, there were also a lot of finished weapons. Like the pots, these came from different places on the ship's journey— the Aegean, Cyprus, the Levant. There were cylinder seals of different origins, too, and a scarab of Queen Nefertiti of Egypt, possibly part of a jeweler's accumulation of scrap. Over 700 agate beads were retrieved, as were some made from Baltic amber. There were more mundane tools: adzes and sickle blades, and weights for a balance. Even a pair of finger cymbals was discovered. A shrub, thorny burnet, had been used as packing around the cargo. Astonishingly, the ship was only 50 feet long. The Ulu Burun wreck is a testament to the cosmopolitan nature of Mediterranean trade. Some cargo may have been heading for a particular destination—one of the Mycenaean centers on mainland Greece has been suggested—but a lot seems to have been for trade en route.

The Ulu Burun ship is rare in being so early, but it is not unique. However, the majority of the wrecks found in the Mediterranean date from between 500 BC and AD 500. Like the Ulu Burun wreck, the Mahdia ship was discovered by sponge divers, this time off Tunisia in the early years of the 20th century. It dates to 70–90 BC.

ROMAN TRADE

As the Roman Empire grew, so did Rome's need for trade—for raw materials, food, and luxury goods. The Mahdia ship, 130 feet long, had another varied cargo and again it seems to have been traveling from east to west, probably from Greece toward Rome and central Italy. It carried 60 marble columns, column bases and capitals, lamps, anchors, rotary grain mills and many sculptures. While these and the columns came from Greece, many of the miscellaneous other finds came from all over the Mediterranean. This suggests that while transporting the columns and statues may have been the main purpose of the journey—they had been loaded before anything else—trade along the way had been equally important.

There are a lot of Roman wrecks, so many that there are enough to provide a plausible analysis of various international networks—commercial trade, taxation, the transport of the loot of empire (it has been suggested that the Mahdia sculptures were removed from Athens following the Roman sack of that city in 86 BC, for example). There certainly seems to have been a particularly significant increase in sea traffic between 200 BC and AD 200, and the range of items discovered has been very wide indeed. A Roman wreck off Taranto in southern Italy carried semi-finished sarcophagi destined for aristocratic burials, and many of the wrecked ships off southern France carried amphorae containing wine, olive oil, and pickled fish. The origin of some of these storage jars has even been traced to a particular estate near Cosa in Tuscany.

Evidence for trade continues to come to light. In 1999, for instance, nine Roman ships dating from between the second century BC and the fifth century AD were found in the silted-up harbor at Pisa. They are well preserved, and represent the largest group of Roman ships found together—to date.

Opposite above: Amphorae—jars of various sizes—were used to transport many kinds of cargo. They were frequently stamped with identifying marks which can sometimes be traced back to where they were manufactured, and possibly filled.

Opposite below: Nails from the Taranto wreck. Shipwrecks usually produce large numbers of nails and quantities of wood, often from the ship itself. Careful surveying can clarify exactly where they come from, and helps identify any that might have been part of the cargo.

Below: Objects recovered from the seabed have to be conserved carefully if they are not going to deteriorate. As with all archaeology, keeping accurate records and plans is essential when dealing with miscellaneous recovered artifacts. These are from the Taranto wreck.

Underwater Archaeology

Archaeology is not confined to the land, and working on underwater sites can include excavating submerged lakeside settlements or investigating deep wells and springs. But the most obvious underwater sites are sunken harbors or places like Alexandria, and shipwrecks.

The introduction of submersible survey craft has increased the pace of discovery in recent years; explorations in the Mediterranean, for example, have been finding wrecks at depths which could not previously be reached. Geophysical reconnaissance is just as useful under the sea as it is on land but some of the most important finds, like the Ulu Burun wreck, are still being made by local sponge divers.

Working underwater is difficult and expensive, and conservation problems can add to the difficulties. It may be necessary to shift a lot of sediment, and detailed drawings and records still have to be made. Bulky objects like cannons and large storage jars have to be lifted. Many useful aids have been developed in recent years, like the hoses used to remove silt and debris. It is worth it: shipwrecks provide an unrivaled picture of a specific moment, frozen in time, and the effort is matched by the rewards.

Right: A diver holds a ceramic vessel from the remains of a ship wrecked in 1025 AD in the Serce Liman Bay. Marine archaeologist Dr George Bass surmised that the ship carried a cargo of glass, and hence called it the "Glass Wreck."

The Etruscans

The Etruscans, who flourished in the north-western part of central Italy between about 700 and 400 BC, have long had a reputation for being "mysterious." They have also had a reputation for being obsessed with death, largely because a lot of what is known about them comes from their tombs. In fact their art—admittedly much of it from these tombs—bursts with life and vitality. Their reputation for being mysterious also partly stems from their language, which has long been popularly supposed to be both peculiar and unreadable. It can actually be read, but there is not much of it. This means that a disproportionate amount of written material from the ancient world concerning the Etruscans comes from their enemies, hardly impartial sources of information.

Etruria, the region the Etruscans inhabited, was roughly equivalent to modern Tuscany. There were independent city states, based around 12 places like Tarquinia and Cerveteri, which formed the "Etruscan League," a loose confederation. Not a lot is presently known about these cities, but they seem to have been well fortified; certainly they are often in good defensive positions, on hilltops. As time went on, the area of Etruscan influence in Italy expanded, and they undoubtedly also had good international contacts— grave goods come from all around the Mediterranean, particularly Greece, and some items in the earlier tombs come from Egypt. They were also in contact with the Phoenicians. There has always been much speculation about where the Etruscans themselves came from, starting in antiquity, but modern research has shown that their civilization developed relatively locally.

Though not much archaeological work has been done on Etruscan towns, the cemeteries have been known, investigated and—unfortunately—looted for very many years. This has not just led to the removal of objects made in precious metals and other, more exotic materials, but has also included beautiful Greek red- and black-figure vases, with which many tombs were well supplied. During the 1830s, for example, an estimated 3400 pots were "recovered" from tombs in a single year. Throughout the 19th century many ended up in the collections of European museums, which were in the early stages of their development.

Opposite: The extensive cemeteries at Cerveteri contain both rounded chamber tombs and rectangular structures. The chambers are cut from the rock, which is comparatively soft and easy to work. Mounds of earth then covered the tops. 18th and 19th-century travelers were impressed by these "cities of the dead."

Above: Burial niches in a columbarium.

Above inset: A map showing the location of the Cerveteri and Tarquinia.

ETRUSCAN CEMETERIES

Etruscan cemeteries are generally very obvious and frequently extensive, like that of Cerveteri. Society seems to have been strongly hierarchical, with a definite aristocratic or upper class, and this is reflected in burial practices. The tombs of the Etruscan "aristocracy" took different forms over time, with round tumuli being replaced by rows of rectangular edifices. The round chamber tombs at Cerveteri were originally carved out of the soft rock—a volcanic tufa—and were covered with mounds of earth; they can be as large as 130 feet in diameter. Inside, the rock-cut structure is rather like a house in appearance. The Tomb of the Reliefs at Cerveteri represents a banqueting room, for example, with things like drinking cups "hanging" from the wall. This tomb has a series of couches, complete with cushions, also carved from the rock; the bodies of the dead would have placed upon these.

Many tombs are also beautifully decorated with wall paintings. These frescoes celebrate the pleasures of life in a way that perhaps appears curious when associated with death, possibly one of the factors leading to the supposed "mysterious" nature of the Etruscans. It has been suggested that the frequent scenes of banqueting represent funeral feasts, though there has also been some speculation that the Etruscans could have generally envisaged the afterlife as a banquet. The Tomb of the Leopards at Tarquinia has some particularly

Opposite: A wall painting illustrating a harvest festival.

Above: A musician from the Tinclinio tomb at Tarquinia plays the lyre. Images of the natural world are common in tomb paintings, varying in size from the large leopards in the tomb that carries their name to the small birds that frequently appear in the backgrounds, as here.

beautiful examples. Here the diners recline while they are served with food and drink, a practice common in the eastern Mediterranean, while dancers move across the longer walls of the burial chamber. A musician plays an unusual double flute, an instrument that appears in paintings from different tombs as well. Other subjects for frescoes include athletic competitions. In Tarquinia's Tomb of the Augurs, two men engage in a wrestling match; beside them is a pile of metal bowls, possibly the prize, and they are watched by a judge or referee. Again this may represent a ceremony in honor of the deceased, in this case funeral games rather than feasting.

Women seem to have had a relatively liberated position among the Etruscans when compared to the Greeks or Romans. In tomb frescoes, such of those of the Tomb of the Leopards, they are shown dining with men, something simply not acceptable in the Greek world. Wives are also accorded an equal position with their husbands on the sarcophagi found in tombs.

As a method of dealing with the dead, cremation prevailed at some periods. Cremated remains were interred in columbaria, niches cut from the rock. Inhumation—burial—has had the greatest impact on later perception of the Etruscans, however, and the sarcophagi are an important factor. They are remarkable, topped with sculptures of the people whose bodies lie inside. As time passed, these figures became more and more realistic. The Etruscans do seem to have been interested in people as individuals, and many of these later figures seem to be approaching portraits, and not necessarily idealized or particularly flattering ones, either.

SARCOPHAGI AND GRAVE GOODS

The sarcophagi can be made in terracotta, the soft volcanic tufa of the region, or even in alabaster. They normally come in three main pieces: the coffin itself, often made in a single piece, a covering slab and a lid. The latter was often made in two halves and consisted of a life-size figure, or a couple, representing the deceased. The people are often shown reclining on cushions, as though taking part in one of the feasts so frequently portrayed on the walls of the tombs. Many of these have also ended up in the museums of Europe, as have a lot of the items found in the tombs, like the red and black figure vases.

Originally the tombs contained many imported goods, not just the Greek vases but artifacts in ivory and objects made with amber, all bearing testimony to the importance of trade. There is evidence, too, of Etruscan exports. Etruscan amphorae have been found in shipwrecks and Etruscan bronze vessels have even been found in some central European burials. Whether the Greek pots, though undoubtedly beautiful, were valued for their intrinsic qualities or for what they originally contained is still debated. There can be no doubt of their value today, though. Looting still continues and one anonymous 20th-century tomb robber claimed to have ransacked "about 4000" Etruscan tombs. Attempts at controlling the menace of grave robbing do not seem to have had much effect, and the international market in antiquities still has some shady corners.

Opposite: A reclining couple on an Etruscan sarcophagus from Cerveteri, c. 525–500 BC. The focus is on the heads of the people, rather than on the form of their bodies, which is somewhat stiff and comparatively unrealistic. At this date, however, there does not seem to be a great desire to reflect their individual appearance.

Above: The sarcophagus of Larthia Seianti, found in 1877 in a family tomb near Chiusi in northern Etruria. This dates from the second century BC, and looks much more like a real person than an idealized image.

Left: Frescoes from the Tomb of the Leopards at Tarquinia showing diners being served and entertained.

Reading Etruscan

It is widely supposed that Etruscan is one of the world's "lost" languages, one of the things that has lent Etruscan culture much of its romantic mystery. As it was unrelated to Latin, or to any other languages spoken in Italy, many ancient authors assumed that it must have an exotic foreign origin, and that therefore the same would be true of the people themselves. The Greek historian Herodotus was of this opinion, and it has proved difficult to dislodge. Etruscan civilization did, however, develop in Italy.

Another myth difficult to dislodge is that the Etruscan language is undeciphered. The Etruscan alphabet was adopted and modified from the Greek alphabet (the Greeks had done the same thing with the Phoenician alphabet) and, in actual fact, over 10,000 written items survive which can be read and understood. However, they are mostly brief and uninformative: "I belong to Thancvil Fulni," for example—simple statements of ownership or the names on sarcophagi. Out of those 10,000 items, only six are more than 50 words in length. However, recent discoveries have helped. Pyrgi was the harbor town for Cerveteri and three gold tablets were found there; they proved to be a brief Etruscan equivalent of the Rosetta Stone. They recorded a dedication to the Etruscan goddess Uni by someone called Thefarie Valianus; one is in Phoenician, but the other two are in Etruscan. Another significant contribution came from the discovery of an Etruscan book some 1200 words long. This was a religious calendar containing details of various rituals and ceremonies, and had been used to bind up an Etruscan "mummy"; it was found in Zagreb. The supposed mystery of the Etruscan language is not really a mystery at all.

Rome

The center of Roman power was Rome itself. Its origins are the subject of legend, and illustrious writers such as Livy and Virgil have told embellished stories of the beginnings of Rome. It is true that from small beginnings Rome quickly expanded into a city of around a million people, and the focus of a great empire, but much of the reliable information about the development of the city has been provided by archaeological evidence rather than the literature of the ancient world.

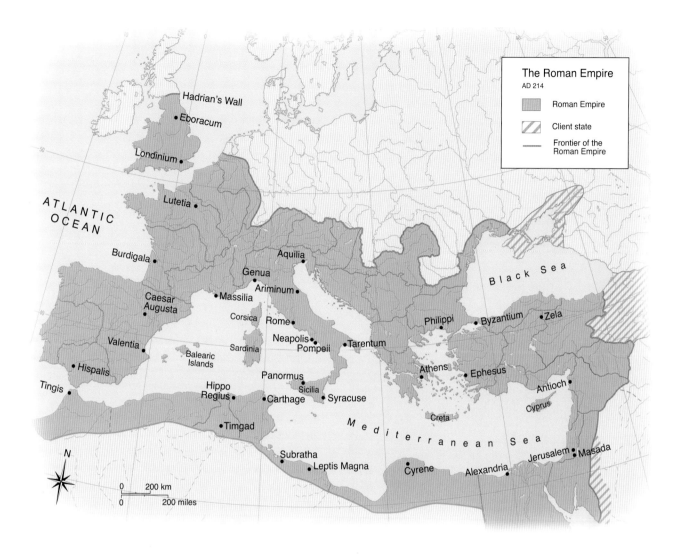

EARLY EVIDENCE

There was some early settlement on the site of the later city; traces of Iron Age huts and burials have been found, which date to between the ninth and seventh centuries BC. There may be more, and perhaps even earlier settlements in the area, but many of these are unlikely ever to be excavated because of the structures which lie above them. Rome, never entirely lost or forgotten, though buried in parts, is one of the most complex—and largest—archaeological sites in the world. Buildings which date back to the Roman Empire still stand in some places and have been used for different purposes, sometimes converted into ecclesiastical buildings. Others have been used as a source of ready-prepared building materials. There has been an increase in archaeological activity since the 1980s, but a lot of this is piecemeal because of the problems of working in a major modern city.

Opposite: The Pantheon was built by Hadrian in AD 118–125, and still stands today largely because of the strength of its construction. Despite its being so impressive and evidently important, no one actually knows what purpose it served. It may have been a temple to all the gods or it could just have been used as a ceremonial space.

Above: A map showing the extent of the Roman Empire in the second century, an area that stretched from Hadrian's Wall to Egypt and encompassed the Mediterranean coastline.

In the sixth century BC the Tarquinian kings began the process which turned Rome from little more than a village into the capital of the Roman Empire. A drain was constructed, the Cloaca Maxima, which made it possible to dry out some of the marshy areas. The early kings were replaced by the Republic (which lasted from 509 to 27 BC) and Rome began to expand its power and influence. Spectacular building projects were initiated by

THE COLOSSEUM

The largest amphitheater in the Roman Empire was the Colosseum in Rome, properly called the Flavian Amphitheater. It was begun by the Emperor Vespasian in AD 70 and completed and inaugurated by his son Titus ten years later. Building it used about 130,000 cubic yards of Travertine limestone, with 300 tons of iron clamps holding the stone blocks together. Huge amounts of brick and concrete (a combination of lime mortar and tufa aggregate which the Romans used to lay in courses rather than pour) were used in the vaults and ribs that supported the seating. It was the tallest building in the city.

At the core of the program of entertainments staged at the Colosseum were gladiatorial combats, displays and fights involving wild animals, and public executions. The latter were often staged as vivid

Left: A detail of the exterior of the Colosseum. It was the tallest building in ancient Rome, and must have been very impressive for both spectators and performers.

Below: A fragment of inscribed masonry with an example of Roman brickwork behind.

politicians keen to insure public support, and these were continued—on an increasingly excessive scale—by the earlier emperors. By the second century AD the Roman Empire stretched from Britain to Egypt, and from the Atlantic shore of Portugal to the farther southern reaches of the Black Sea.

Rome, as the capital city, was the recipient of much of the benefit. Resources—money, tribute, and treasure looted from subject nations, raw materials, foodstuffs—passed into the city. Unrest in Rome itself could have disastrous consequences for the emperors, and they were careful to try and keep the populace content. Great efforts were made to insure that most people were adequately fed, and entertainments and festivals were held that would keep them occupied. As a result there were some unusual imports: the need for exotic wild animals in the arena, for instance, generated a rather specialist industry connected to their supply and care. Entertainments like these were not confined to Rome; they were an essential part of Roman culture, and amphitheaters were built all over the empire.

reconstructions of the more gruesome myths and legends. Some Roman authors describe variations on these themes, such as Martial's account of female beast-fighters, but essentially the Colosseum was a theater of death.

INSIDE THE COLOSSEUM

Estimates of seating capacity vary, from 50,000 to about 78,000, and social status dictated where these spectators sat and what they wore. Though this may have changed over time, basically the poor, slaves, and women ended up at the very top, with other classes of society in the better seats below. The higher your social standing, the closer to the arena you were. The Emperor and the Vestal Virgins had special boxes opposite each other, and on this level would also be members of the senatorial class, wearing white togas with red borders. Some of the places still have the names of individual senators from the late Roman Empire carved on them. Above them came the knights (equites), while above

Above: The interior of the Colosseum. The middle three spectator zones had built-in stone seating, while the Emperor, Vestal Virgins and senators were at the bottom, closest to the action in the arena. At the top were the common people and slaves, whose view must have been poor. Below the surface of the Colosseum's arena was a network of tunnels and chambers, able to handle large numbers of both human and animal performers. The subterranean exit led straight to the Ludus Magnus, the main gladiatorial school.

them were ordinary citizens, the plebs, and all of these in togas as well.

There was a special place for boys, who would sit with their tutors; soldiers on leave had their own area too, as did scribes, foreign dignitaries, and some of the priesthoods. And right at the top, about 160 feet away from the arena and 130 feet above it, was a gallery for commoners—slaves, the poor, and women. This was either standing space, or had very steeply-raked

The Gladiators

Gladiatorial training schools were founded to service the demands of the Colosseum. The main one, the Ludus Magnus, was next to it on the eastern side. Part was revealed in 1937 for the first time but about half remains unexcavated, lying under the modern street and buildings. It had its own arena, ringed by seating for spectators: it could have held about 3000 observers. Gladiators could practice in front of their audience, and this gave their followers a chance to asses their abilities, their strengths and weaknesses, before fights in the Colosseum itself. The gladiators came from different backgrounds. Some might be prisoners of war or condemned criminals, and some might regard it as a profession—they could be slaves, freedmen or volunteers. The criminals and captured prisoners were generally considered expendable, but the freedmen or volunteers would have fought for their own profit as well as that of the "stable" to which they belonged. Though a good, well-trained gladiator was a valuable commodity, and thus likely to be relatively protected, the chance of actually surviving a career in the arena was small and no fighter was admitted to the arena until he had sworn away his life "willingly and freely." Gladiators specialized in different types of fighting, armor and weapons. The Retarius, for example, used only a net and a trident; the Thracian had a curved scimitar and a round shield; and both the Myrmillo and the Samnite were more heavily armed, with swords and large oblong shields. Others fought on horseback or from chariots, and many fights involved elaborate sets or plots.

The shows the gladiators appeared in were originally sponsored by individuals, but from the

reign of Domitian (AD 81–96) it was decreed that fights in Rome could only be given by the emperor. A day's program would generally be in three parts with the gladiatorial contests in the afternoon. The first part, in the morning, would usually be the wild-animal hunts, with executions held around noon. Shows could be relatively brief, but could also last for many days. Trajan is supposed to have marked his conquest of Dacia with an entertainment involving 11,000 animals and 10,000 gladiators which lasted over 123 days in AD 107.

Opposite: A mosaic showing gladiators. The Retarius has lost and kneels before his opponent; the umpire seems to be hovering in the background.

Above: Images of gladiators crop up everywhere. This one is on an oil lamp.

Left: A gladiator fights a lion in a mosaic. Beast fights generally took place in the morning, main gladiatorial combat in the afternoon.

wooden benches. Some groups were prohibited from attending at all—actors, ex-gladiators, and gravediggers.

Nowadays the buildings that underlie the arena itself are visible; originally they would have been overlaid by planking covered in sand. The arena, like the whole amphitheater, was the biggest in the Roman world, and could be used to stage elaborately extravagant spectacles. The first games apparently included a re-enactment of a sea battle and a display of swimming animals, but no one has been able to work out exactly how this was achieved—principally, how the arena could have been made watertight. There is some evidence for hydraulic lifting systems at either end of the underground network, though these could simply have supplied drinking water. Any rainwater which collected in the arena was led, via a system of drains, into a large channel and from there into the River Tiber.

Also below ground were the tunnels along which both human and animal performers would enter the arena. There was another tunnel at the eastern end connecting the Colosseum with the main gladiators' barracks, and there were other, separate ones, for the Vestal Virgins so they would not have to pass through the crowds to get to their boxes. The Colosseum was topped by a system of wooden masts and sails (or an immense awning—a velum) which, when rigged by sailors from the imperial fleet whose barracks were nearby, provided some shade or shelter for spectators below. Exactly how this worked has been the subject of much speculation, computer modeling, and attempts at partial reconstruction.

THE FORUM

To the majority of Roman citizens, the Roman Forum would have been the most important place in the city. It was a combination of marketplace, museum, law courts, administrative center and religious center—and was also a place to demonstrate wealth and influence by constructing impressive buildings.

It had been somewhere for political assemblies—and riots—and even public feasts. Under Julius Caesar and the emperors who followed him this slightly anarchic space was transformed into a monument to imperial authority. There were great temples, basilicas (columned halls), on the north and south sides, a new Senate House and triumphal arches. But it was still used by the people of Rome: the basilicas continued to be used for legal proceedings and lawsuits were often another form of public entertainment. Judements could be crowded. Not only were there a large number of judges, but the opposing parties would bring their supporters and there could also be many unconnected onlookers. There must have been moments of boredom: the paving in the aisles and on the front steps of the Basilica Julia is marked with game boards made by people who were spending time hanging around the

Above: A general view of the Roman Forum, which conveys some of the complexity of the site. Even after the central area was exposed at the end of the 19th century, it still remained a potentially confusing location. It was one of the most important places in the imperial city, a focus for much state ceremonial.

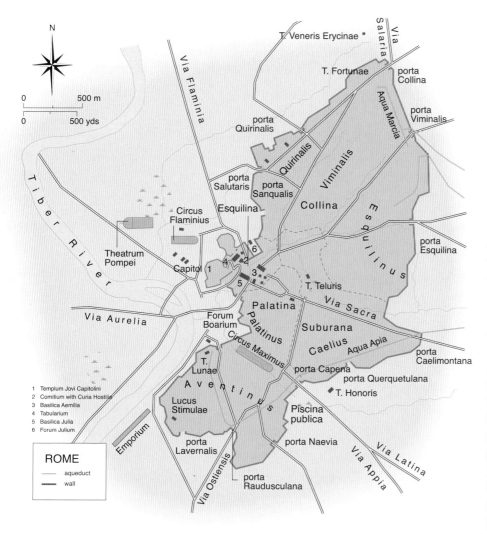

ROME

— aqueduct
▬ wall

1 Templum Jovi Capitolini
2 Comitium with Curia Hostilia
3 Basilica Aemilia
4 Tabularium
5 Basilica Julia
6 Forum Julium

courts. The Forum buildings also became the base for some parts of the administration, like the office of weights and measures. State funerals were held there, and temples were built to deceased emperors. In AD 283 there was a massive fire—fires had long been a serious problem in Rome—which necessitated major rebuilding.

As time went on the Forum was adapted to changing needs. The Senate House, for example, was converted into the church of St. Hadrian in AD 630; signs of this, in its turn, vanished almost completely in 1935–8 when restoration was carried out. The population of the city was very much reduced by the time it became a Christian church—it has been estimated that it fell from about a million to 10,000—and the immense buildings of the Forum soon fell into decay. Parts began to collapse and it must have become rather dangerous. In the 15th and 16th centuries the ruins were treated as a quarry that contained useful material for constructing the Rome of the Renaissance. A systematic approach to investigating the site began in the early years of the 19th century, but it was still patchy and haphazard until after 1870, when large parts of the central area were uncovered. More recently, in the 1980s, there has been a major program of research and conservation. It still remains a complex site.

Above: A plan of the city of Rome at the time of the Republic.

Left: A view of the Roman Forum.

FEEDING ROME

With the city's huge population, the majority of whom would often be poor and hungry, keeping supplies flowing was not just necessary. It was vital for keeping the peace.

Grains, oil, and wine were the staples of the Roman diet and most of the people would rely on these. Meat certainly wouldn't form a significant part of most people's diet. A huge quantity of these staples, grain particularly, would have been needed each year and the population depended on imports. By and large the system for moving foodstuffs into the city was relatively reliable; even so, there are documented instances of food shortages. When a shortage loomed, merchants tended to hoard supplies, which pushed prices up—at which point rioting was likely. There was another problem, too. Food cost money; and though some free food was distributed, people would need to work to pay for more. The state generated some jobs, notably in construction and allied trades, from the time of Augustus (31 BC–AD 14).

Above: Roman houses and warehouses at Ostia. Many had small windows which were a security measure.

OSTIA—ROME'S PORT

Most of Rome's imports came by water. The River Tiber was navigable for boats with a shallow draft for all of the distance from the coast to the center of the city. The town of Ostia at the mouth of the river acted as Rome's port, but its anchorage was poor and facilities were inadequate. Finally, in AD 42, the Emperor Claudius initiated the creation of an artificial harbor, canals connecting it with the Tiber and two moles, which partly sheltered the harbor from the sea. Over the years more work was done to improve the situation further.

Opposite below: Mosaic of a ship from Ostia. Import fleets, such as those of grain ships from Egypt, appear to have sent messenger ships ahead of them to announce their arrival. The timing of this was evidently completely unpredictable, which stresses the uncertain nature of maritime trade.

Above: These large storage jars, set into the ground, were used for holding grain at Ostia.

Right: Though most of the diet would have been based on grains, olive oil, and wine, other things would have played a part, and fish was essential. This was not so much because of a particular fondness for fish itself, but because of the importance of the fish sauce garum or liquamen. This was made from fermented fish and was used as a seasoning. It was, however, expensive; it was also very strong.

Ostia and Rome both had many warehouses, frequently multistory, and some were enormous. One, the Horrea Galbana, had 140 rooms on the ground floor alone. Many had raised floors, which helped to protect grain from moisture (and possibly from vermin, a little), and were very solidly built with walls often 3 feet thick. They also show a great concern with security: windows in outside walls were high up, narrow, and kept to a minimum, and traces have been found of elaborate locking systems for both external and internal doors. These doors were deliberately too narrow for large carts, indicating that most goods must have been moved by manpower—which would have required a lot of laborers.

The supply system was controlled by guilds. There were guilds for the merchants of various different commodities, guilds for those who hauled them, guilds for shippers, guilds for people connected to the construction of dockyard buildings. In Ostia many of these guilds seem to have been based in the Piazzale delle Corporazioni, a rectangular colonnaded building that had 61 small rooms opening off the colonnade. In front of each room there was a mosaic depicting the type of trade represented within.

MONTE TESTACCIO

One extraordinary testimony to the scale of consumption—and consequent waste—comes from an artificial hill. Monte Testaccio covers nearly 24,000 square yards and is over 115 feet tall—and is composed entirely of broken amphorae dating to between AD 140 and 250, mostly ones previously containing olive oil. It was not a random dump, however; it lay at the back of a ring of warehouses and had been built deliberately, with layers of larger and coarser pieces of pottery stabilized by packing with smaller shards. It had level terraces and retaining walls built of amphorae, and it appears that these were carried up the dump intact and smashed once they were in the right place. Everything had been sprinkled with powdered lime, presumably to reduce the smell. It is believed that the Romans did not re-use olive oil amphorae, in particular, because they could become contaminated by any rancid oil which was absorbed by the inner surface. Calculating the quantity of commodities required by a city the size of Rome is

largely a matter of educated guesswork, but it has been suggested that a year's supply of oil, assuming a population of about a million and several other factors, would be about 5.3 million gallons—or approximately 290,000 amphorae. The empties were also sometimes used in construction, as filler or as a component of concrete.

Keeping Rome supplied would have provided employment for very many people, both in or near the city itself and in the wider empire. A lot of studies have been done on food shortages and the consequent riots, but the extraordinary thing is that most of the time it actually worked.

Opposite: A mosaic of a servant in a kitchen from Pompeii. He seems to be carrying a plate of figs, but seafood features strongly.

Above: A street in Ostia showing several millstones.

Left: A maximum of a quarter of Rome's population qualified for free handouts of food, distributed as a form of state assistance. This fresco of the free distribution of bread comes from Pompeii.

IVNIVS

The Population of Rome

The population of Rome was very diverse, becoming more so as time went on. A high level of immigration from all over the empire helped to push population numbers up; some new arrivals would have been slaves or captives, of course, but many would just have been attracted to the great city. Despite the efforts to feed and entertain all these people, Rome must have been a difficult and at times thoroughly unpleasant city to live in. While Rome possessed areas of extreme wealth, it also had corresponding areas of slums.

The extremely poor seem to have lived rough; evidence from the last years of empire appears to show that they were living in tombs, under the awnings of the theater or in shacks around the city. This was doubtless true in earlier times as well, but such transient shelters do not leave much of a trace in the archaeological record of a city like Rome. At times mortality could be very high—the population was densely packed, leading to the spread of disease—and the poorest might end up in mass graves, or in mass cremations. The water supply could be somewhat arbitrary, and sanitary arrangements rather random, though more work and research remains to be done on this. There were some public latrines but drains were by no means universal; there seem to have been a lot of cesspits and it is thought that the contents could well have been used as fertilizer. Nor did Roman drains have traps, so gases like methane could easily escape from the sewers: this was undoubtedly smelly but it could also lead to explosions. In addition some drains had to be cleaned manually and those in low-lying areas could back up into the houses when the level of the Tiber rose. Vermin would have been a significant problem.

Though Rome was by a long way the biggest city of its time—in fact there were no cities of comparable size anywhere else until the 19th century—it acted as a model for others throughout the Roman Empire. Just as there were amphitheaters elsewhere, there were also city walls, temples, administrative buildings, law courts, and sophisticated roads, all of which were based on Roman originals. They became a unifying and defining factor, part of what made cities, and civilization, "Roman".

The Vestal Virgins

Vesta was the Roman goddess of the hearth, protector of the home; she became the protecting goddess of the whole Roman state. Her temple was located just behind the Forum. Unfortunately, the builders of the Renaissance treated this area as yet another quarry and the temple has been reduced to a mound of concrete surrounded by blocks of tufa. The temple had no statue of Vesta, but there was a sacred fire, which it was the duty of her handmaidens to keep alight. These handmaidens were the Vestal Virgins.

The Role of the Vestal Virgins

There were six Vestals, appointed by the chief priest: the emperor. Only girls between the ages of six and ten were eligible (they were likely to be virgins) and they had to serve for 30 years, after which point they could marry. A Vestal Virgin's property passed to the state instead of back to her family on her death, so rich families would try to keep their daughters off the list of candidates; appointment as a Vestal also meant that a girl could not become involved in any dynastic marriage with another wealthy family. The six Vestals traditionally wore old-fashioned dress and had complicated hairstyles of the kind most women wore only at marriage and, of course, they had to remain chaste during their term of service. In return they controlled their own property, which other women could not; they had right of way on the crowded streets, and could drive carriages in the city—a privilege reserved for them and the empress alone among women. The Vestals lived near their temple in a house which was lavishly rebuilt after the great fire of AD 64. This accommodation was not just for the Vestals themselves, but also for their numerous servants and slaves. The house was big enough for each of the six to have had a substantial apartment of her own, and it had its own gardens and suite of baths.

It may seem as though the Vestals had a better life than most Roman women, who were essentially male possessions. But their morals were a matter of general concern, and the consequences for slipping could be appalling. They could be buried alive for failing in their vow of chastity, as this transgression was generally supposed to be responsible for any

disasters that befell the state. For example, sloppy morals among the Vestals rather than military incompetence could be—and were—blamed for bringing about a defeat in battle.

Right: A statue of a Vestal Virgin from the Forum.

*Opposite: A wall painting from Pompeii showing either Flora or Primavera, the manifestation of spring. This fresco gives a better impression of the fluidity of women's dress than many statues.
Though the clothing of the Vestals was heavier and old-fashioned, it must still have had a certain elegance and grace.*

Hadrian's Villa

Owning a villa, or several, was an essential part of being a Roman of some social standing. Cicero had at least eight, and he was only fairly well off. Imperial villas were on a different scale, and one of the greatest is that of the Emperor Hadrian (who ruled from AD 117 to AD 138) at Tivoli, to the north-east of Rome.

The precise boundaries of the Villa—a complex of buildings—are difficult to establish but it was certainly immense. About twice the size of the city of Pompeii, it covered about half a square mile. The Italian state owns about half of the site; only part of this has been cleared and only a fraction of that has been excavated. Some restoration has been done but there are many inaccessible areas, such as most of the subterranean passages and corridors.

Exploration began early, in the 16th century, and later the famous artist Piranesi worked on a plan which was published after his death, in 1781. Modern work started at the end of the 19th century. The piecemeal nature of research has meant that, overall, Hadrian's Villa seems rather disjointed; however, parts of what remain are decidedly impressive and beautiful.

Much of the construction work on the Villa appears to have taken place between AD 118 and 125—written evidence of this is preserved within the ruins. In Roman brickworks some individual bricks were stamped with information about their origins before they were fired. Analyzing these "brickmarks"

is a pernickety, detailed job, but it has been done and the most common ones at the Villa date from 123 and 124.

The purpose of some of the specific buildings is unclear, but there was definitely a residential core to the Villa, surrounded by service buildings. At present it is thought that these were storerooms, warehouses, and workrooms, and that the Villa's slaves and servants would have slept elsewhere. There were cell-like offices and a library; imperial administration would continue here when the emperor was in residence. Shrines have been identified among the other ruins, and there were temples. There were also theaters, bath complexes, and garden "features" such as the Scenic Canal. There are colonnaded walkways, buttressed terraces which seem to have been planned—at least in part—to gain better views across the valleys around the Villa, and a largely interconnected underground network. Some buildings conform to a recognized Roman formula, some are reinterpretations of existing types, and some are completely radical and original. It is not surprising that Hadrian's Villa has influenced artists and architects for many years, and continues to do so today.

Opposite and above: Views of the gardens at Hadrian's Villa. Reflections in water were an essential part of the design of the Scenic Canal; the statues faced the water and seem to be contemplating it. The present sculptures are mostly modern copies as the originals are now under cover in the nearby Canal Block. The Canal Block, in a prime position, may have been intended for guests or high officials. Fragments of painting and mosaic have been found which also seem to imply privileged inhabitants.

Pompeii and Herculaneum

The massive volcanic eruption which took place in the area of the Bay of Naples on August 24, AD 79 destroyed, but also preserved, two extraordinary archaeological sites, Pompeii and Herculaneum.

When Vesuvius exploded on that August afternoon it was the beginning of what has been described as a long tragedy. It was not an instantaneous disaster, such as an earthquake, nor were there lava flows that would have destroyed everything in their path. Instead, over about 20 hours, both towns were buried in a layer of ash and other volcanic material, preserving a way of life: houses, shops, workplaces, theaters, administrative buildings, bathhouses and, often, the inhabitants. Estimates vary, but Pompeii probably had a population of about 20,000. Herculaneum appears to have been much smaller, a town of about 4000 people. It lay closer to Vesuvius than Pompeii, about 4.5 miles away, whereas Pompeii was at about 5.5 miles' distance. Astonishingly, there is an eyewitness account of what happened from the Roman writer Pliny the Younger who was staying with his uncle, Pliny the Elder, about 18 miles from Vesuvius across the bay of Naples at Misenum. His uncle, who had sailed in response to an appeal for help, was one of the casualties.

Opposite: The Forum at Pompeii, with Vesuvius looming in the background.

Above: A plan of the town of Pompeii.

Left: Guard dogs seem to have been common in Pompeii, and one is represented on this mosaic. The Latin, reading cave canem, *means "beware of the dog."*

In the early phases of the eruption, at least, it would have been possible for some of the people to get away. There have been attempts to calculate the number of victims but this is almost impossible: remains found during early digging on the site went unrecorded, parts of both towns have yet to be excavated (in Herculaneum's case, that's about 75 percent), and many people may have perished in the countryside. More information comes to light all the time. It used to be thought that most of the population of Herculaneum had escaped—for instance, refugees from there seem to have settled in Naples—but excavations starting in the 1980s showed otherwise: very many people had died at the seafront.

Dawn on August 26 would have revealed a landscape completely altered from that of two days earlier. Vesuvius' top had vanished and the coastline was different. Pompeii had been covered by ash and pumice deposits to a depth of about 16 feet. Some upper parts of buildings would probably have been visible, but otherwise the city had been effectively entombed.

Herculaneum had vanished utterly; it had been buried to a depth of about 65 feet by volcanic material. Some of this had hit the town in liquid form, surging into buildings, filling and burying them completely, to such an extent that digging at Herculaneum today has been described as being more like quarrying than excavating.

Above: Buildings in the town of Herculaneum survived to a much greater height than those in Pompeii because of the depth of burial and the speed with which it happened. Much wood was also preserved, instantly carbonized by the extreme temperatures in the pyroclastic surges.

POST-ERUPTION ACTIVITY

The wonderful level of preservation at both Pompeii and Herculaneum has led to the idea that they present the Roman world "frozen in time," that they are a sort of sealed time capsule from the past. However, this is not entirely so. The eruption itself changed things like the coastline and human activity since then has also had its effects. There is clear evidence from Pompeii that the site was disturbed in antiquity, even very soon after the eruption, by people possibly seeking family members or possessions, or just treasure hunting. Herculaneum was too deeply buried, but it too was disturbed in the 18th

century when well diggings uncovered ancient remains. This led to tunneling from the original well shaft, organized by the Prince d'Elbeuf who was looking for material he could used in a villa he hoped to build. Some of the items found were smuggled out of Italy. These excavations were expanded by the Bourbon rulers of Naples but they were dangerous and expensive, and attention shifted to the nearby site of Pompeii.

This had been rediscovered in the last years of the 16th century. The existence of Pompeii had not been forgotten—and the area where it lay was even known locally as "la cività," the city—but over the years its precise location slipped from memory until the cutting of a water channel exposed antiquities. Buildings started to be brought to light toward the end of the 18th century: the temple of Isis, the larger of the two theaters, the Triangular Forum, and a villa containing about 20 bodies which caused a sensation. The basic aim of this early excavation was the search for works of art or treasures in the form of gold and silver objects. By the 19th century the site had many visitors, starting a tradition which continues today, and systematic investigations began under the direction of Giuseppe Fiorelli. The emphasis today is on consolidating and documenting a lot of the previous work—much remains unpublished and therefore unstudied—and conserving the ruins, although some more meticulous new digging has taken place.

A PICTURE OF EVERYDAY LIFE

Despite all this post-eruption activity at both sites, they still do present a valuable picture of everyday life in a Roman town. At Herculaneum, engulfed by pyroclastic surges and volcanic mud, even wood has been preserved, generally carbonized in the high temperatures. Wooden structures at Pompeii can be recreated by the same plaster cast technique used on the bodies of the victims; there are casts, for example, of the wooden shutters used to close shop entrances at night. Even loaves of bread have been discovered; one from Herculaneum bears the initials A and M, which may have helped to distinguish it from lots of other loaves being baked in a general oven.

Some of the most fascinating parts of Pompeii are the backstreets, the areas of ordinary shops, taverns, and houses. Public buildings are preserved in other Roman towns, though not so well as in Pompeii and Herculaneum, but the more mundane buildings are almost unique in the Roman world. And some aspects of them—the level of graffiti, for example—are definitely unique. Without Pompeii we would not have known the extent to which electioneering slogans covered the walls, for example, and many other things.

Above: A counter from a food or wine shop on the Via di Terme in Pompeii. Storage jars—dolia—were set into the counters of shops like this. Their contents were not generally preserved, but would probably have been dry goods, perhaps nuts, or possibly fruit and vegetables.

Left: The street surface here in Pompeii was durable—though it must have been bumpy—but, even so, carts have worn it down. Caring for, and maybe providing, the pavements beside the streets seems to have been the responsibility of individuals: they often change between one property and the next. The streets themselves were certainly centrally maintained.

Shops and Workshops

When it comes to shops and workshops it is not generally possible to tell what they sold or manufactured, though this is clear in some cases. Bakeries and some cookshops are easy to recognize from the grain mills which would have been turned by donkeys, and in one case at least the donkeys were left behind when the owners—who locked the door behind them—fled. Food

and drink shops are numerous. One in Herculaneum still possesses a huge wooden rack, rather like a modern wine rack, above head height; this would have been used to store amphorae. The food and drink shops preserved in Pompeii had distinctive counters in an "L" shape, so that the person behind the counter could serve both customers inside the shop and passers-by on the street. There were similar establishments with the same arrangement at the front but with either accommodation or a larger room which would have contained seating at the back. Inscriptions describe some of these as being a hospitium, or inn, and describe the owner as a caupo or copo, the equivalent of a bar owner today, so this extra accommodation wasn't only for the owner's family. Some of these, like the recently excavated House of the Chaste Lovers, are decorated with wall paintings. In one customers are shown gaming, eating, and drinking, having their cups refilled; in another a wine delivery by donkey-drawn wagon is depicted.

Food

Food remains have been recovered, either carbonized like the bread or mineralized like some of the fruit stones and seeds recovered from Pompeii's drainage system (it was a closed system, not one that drained into the sea, and may have functioned like a soakaway). Among other things carbonized pomegranates have been found, and grape pips, cherry stones, and fig seeds have all been recovered. Bone fragments have been retrieved as well, so we know that the inhabitants of Pompeii and Herculaneum ate things like small birds and a lot of fish; seashells indicated the consumption of seafood such as scallops. The food market was at the northeast of the Forum and had a central pavilion with running water which was evidently used for cleaning fish: scales and bones were found here too. Supplies would have come into Pompeii from both the coast and the surrounding countryside, generally by cart and wagon. Ruts have been worn in the surface of the roads, and they would often have been muddy and difficult for pedestrians to use—the pavements at the side were raised above street level—leading to the provision of stepping stones going from one side to the other.

There is an extraordinary variety of houses in both towns. There is basic family accommodation behind or above shops, and large apartment buildings—one several stories high survives at Herculaneum, preserved to a greater height than anything at Pompeii because of the depth to which the town was buried. There are a great number of villas and more modest homes, and in some it is possible to make an informed guess at the profession of the resident. Medical tools such as scalpels, probes, and gynaecological instruments were found in one, and there were also pestles and mortars which would have been used to prepare drug treatments, so it is highly likely that the owner would have been a doctor. Plants would often have been used when treating the sick and research in Pompeiian gardens, using the plaster cast technique on the spaces left by roots, has shown that many potentially beneficial herbs were commonplace. The level of medical care is also demonstrated by the fact that some of the people found had well-set fractures, even if they had already got a degree of osteoporosis, although some people's bones had been poorly set.

Pompeii today is still under threat, as is Herculaneum. Pompeii particularly has to contend with many visitors, and there have been problems with vandalism and theft. There was a serious earthquake in 1980 which caused damage and, rising above both towns, there is still Vesuvius. It has been silent since 1944, but is undoubtedly still active.

Opposite above: A modern storeroom containing amphorae at Pompeii gives an impression of the scale of the archaeological treasures found at the site.

Opposite below: Ancient Roman grafitti are among the features that bring the site alive for visitors.

Below: A bakery, with millstones and even a large number of carbonized loaves of bread, was discovered in the commercial area of Pompeii.

The Victims

When and how the people of Pompeii and Herculaneum died depended on where they were. The initial explosion, at about 1.00 p.m. on August 24, sent a column of ash straight up into the air which eventually began to spread out, and ash and pumice began to fall on Pompeii. People either fled or took cover; some must have been hit by larger fragments. As the ash fall continued, progress through it would have become harder; it must have been rather like wading through excessively dusty ballbearings. Ash began building up and people who had taken shelter in buildings either found themselves trapped inside or moved to upper levels. Roofs and ceilings would have begun creaking ominously under the weight, and people moved closer to walls or under staircases. Some tried to scramble upward on the mounting pumice. Close to midnight there seems to have been a pause in the rain of ash, followed by a renewed, heavier fall.

Herculaneum, however, was about to be hit by a superheated pyroclastic cloud, the first of six pyroclastic surges and flows which affected the area. This traveled at speeds in excess of 60 miles an hour, and had a phenomenally high temperature. Above the town, as moisture in the soil began to overheat, mudflows began to form, but another pyroclastic surge hit the place first. People died immediately. Many of the inhabitants—about 250 have been found to date—had taken shelter in vaulted chambers, possibly boathouses, by the shore. These would have probably have protected them in an earthquake, but as it was they expired instantly. The place where

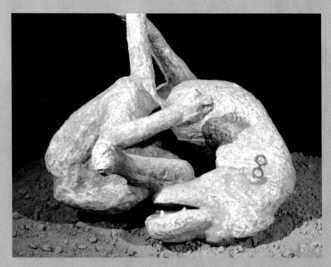

they died was then buried swiftly under the ash and boiling mud, preserving their skeletons, and we now know that they died from the effects of the heat rather than from asphyxiation.

In Pompeii many people had already been buried under ash deposits and collapsing houses. Those who were still alive early in the morning of August 25 were killed by more pyroclastic surges, and the effects of the intense heat can still be seen in the position of the bodies. Many look as though they are protecting themselves, but this is the so-called "pugilistic position" caused by extreme heat contracting the muscles. Debris from the surges surrounded the bodies and then there came two more, burying them even more deeply. Most of the people who died in the early stages were found inside buildings, but a lot of the victims of the pyroclastic surges were in open spaces, often streets. Many of them appear to have been trying to head south or east; they had evidently decided there was no point trying to sit out whatever was going on.

Opposite: Excavating the casts of the bodies of three children and two adults at Pompeii in 1961.

Above: Humans were not the only victims, of course, and the remains of animals are not uncommon. This watchdog was from the House of Vesonius Primus.

Left: Many of the Pompeiian victims of the eruption evidently tried to find shelter by walls or under staircases.

Giuseppe Fiorelli, who had been put in charge of excavations at Pompeii in 1860, devised a brilliant—if slightly disconcerting—way of dealing with the remains of the people. A body buried in the volcanic debris would gradually decay and leave a hollow space, like a cocoon, in the surrounding ash. These cavities were found, still containing skeletons, and Fiorelli decided to try and retain them, realizing they preserved the form of the dead Pompeiians. He simply had the cavities filled through a small opening with plaster of Paris, which created a cast. After the plaster had hardened the ash would be removed, and there would be an accurate body cast of one of the dead inhabitants of Pompeii. Since then this technique has also been used on cavities left by other things, such as wooden furniture, that have also decayed.

Systematic study of the human remains from Pompeii and Herculaneum has only really taken place in the last 25 to 30 years. Unfortunately the high temperature of the pyroclastic surges and flows was too high to permit the survival of DNA from those people who died in them, but plenty of work can still be done. It has been possible to determine some of the diseases people had, for example. Arthritis, injuries and tooth decay were all common but there were rarer conditions like Paget's disease and, surprisingly, 11 percent of the adults studied appear to have suffered from spina bifida. Tuberculosis and malaria seem to have been endemic. The study of one large group, who evidently tried to escape together, shows that nearly 20 per cent of them had brucellosis. This is caught from infected milk products, and similar food-borne diseases must have been relatively common at a time without efficient methods of keeping food fresh through the summer. Other people's remains show the effects of their work: one young man had been a fisherman, for instance. He had astonishing upper body strength, from hauling nets and net weights, and had worn down the teeth on the right side of his mouth by gripping the lines of the nets. More studies have shown what people ate or drank: sweetening wine with syrup of lead acetate was common (it was cheaper than honey) and this left its traces in the bones—and affected men more frequently than women. They evidently drank more wine.

The most affecting thing about the remains is how evocative they are, how they reflect individual lives—and deaths. A pregnant woman sought shelter in the chambers at Herculaneum, and died holding a small child up against her shoulder. Another woman in the Villa of the Mysteries just outside Pompeii had struggled to stay on top of a heap of ash which must have accumulated for hours before she gave up or was overwhelmed. An elderly man remained beside his money chest in the House of the Sailor in what must have been one of the strongest rooms of the building, but eventually the roof fell in and he was crushed. A group who were trying to escape did not get far, and were found just outside one of the gates. There are many other similar stories which can be reconstructed due to the level of preservation and the efforts of archaeologists.

Wall Paintings

Fragments of wall paintings have been found all over the Roman world; fresco was a popular form of decoration. In Pompeii and Herculaneum they are exceptionally well preserved, though there are many problems of conservation. Pompeii had been badly damaged by an earthquake in 62 AD and there is evidence that a great deal of work was either going on or was very recent; there must have been a need for redecoration. In one house painting even seems to have been interrupted by the eruption itself.

An artist, or artists, worked alongside a plasterer as the colors used had to be applied to the fine skim of plaster as it dried. This is what seem to have been happening in the House of the Painters at Work, a recent excavation, at precisely the moment the eruption began. Soft plaster was being laid ready for painting, but was pitted by stones from the ash fall before it could dry. There are marks left by scaffolding and a shelf which would have held paint pots; these were actually found on the floor. The pigments they contained were derived from mineral sources, except for the black which was of vegetable origin.

Similar paint pots have been found elsewhere—about 200 have been found in the sites buried by Vesuvius—and colormen's workshops have also been found. One of these contained nine mortars in which colors would have been ground and it has been possible to identify traces of the pigments they once held. Other places in the same area, just off the road to the Forum, also contained evidence of having been used by color merchants; one had blocks of orange ocher, for instance.

There was also a building which has been identified as an artists' workshop: this time, there was evidence not just of pigments but also of the tools of the trade—tiny mortars and pestles, mixing spoons, and the plumb lines which fresco painters used to transfer designs onto walls.

How the Frescoes were Painted

Once in a client's house, the team of artists—a highly skilled and well-paid painter who did the main panels, another who worked on the side panels, assistants to mix colors and prepare plaster—would have had to work quickly before the damp plaster dried, so designs are likely to have been finalized beforehand. A basic background wash went on first and then the more complicated parts of the decoration were sketched in, usually in pale yellow ocher. Once finished the painting would effectively become one with the plaster; the surface would become slightly leathery, at which point the wall painting could be polished to a high sheen. But the artists in the House of the Painters at Work never reached that stage. Their frescoes are unfinished; there is a half-completed yellow ocher sketch. This, combined with the pockmarked plaster, suggests the exact moment when they downed tools and ran.

Opposite: A mythological wall painting from the House of the Vetii. This was painted after the earthquake of AD 62 and is of exceptional quality; the artists must have been well paid for such work. The owners evidently had no qualms about paying for the restoration of their house.

Left: Not all the wall paintings were formal, depicting religious subjects or illustrating myths. many came from humbler settings, and reflected a more everyday outlook. This fresco shows a street seller with a customer.

The Baths

Public baths were an important feature of Roman towns, and Pompeii and Herculaneum were no different to others. The Suburban Baths at Herculaneum are probably the most impressive and best-preserved ones still in existence; even some of the carved woodwork has been found.

Anyone, however poor, could use the public baths, and entrance fees were kept to a minimum; they were a vital part of public hygiene as only the very wealthiest had their own bath suites. They became a social center: people met their friends, did business deals, exercised and even had excess body hair removed there (and there were frequent complaints about the noise coming from bathhouses). Men and women are not supposed to have met at the baths—there were either separate buildings for the sexes, or separate bathing times—but laws were regularly passed emphasizing this point, so there must have been some laxity.

Inside the bathhouse there were rooms of differing temperature, cold, warm, and hot—a frigidarium, tepidarium, and calderium—with hot and cold plunge baths. Clothes were stored in niches or hung on nails, and bathers generally started in the hottest room where they sweated out any dirt and impurities. They were then oiled and scraped down, and rinsed themselves off in a hot bath. They would then make their way to the frigidarium for a refreshing cold plunge.

Underfloor heating systems did become common over time, and there was also a certain amount of cavity-wall heating. The Forum Baths at Pompeii, a relatively new complex in AD 79, had this, but only in the hot room. The warm room, in the men's section at least, was heated by a charcoal brazier. The need to try and retain as much heat as possible meant that any windows were small, so these rooms would have been particularly gloomy. Exercise would generally take place near the baths, in an attached court known as a palaestra: running and wrestling were common sports. Bathhouses, as popular centers of activity, were also generally surrounded by shops and taverns.

There has been some speculation that bathhouses may have had another function... Some Roman authors fulminated against them without being completely clear about what exactly was upsetting them so much, but clues may come from bathhouses like Pompeii's Suburban Baths. The wall paintings here are extraordinarily sexually explicit, and wildly varied, even by Roman standards.

Opposite: This gorgeous wall deocoration of Neptune and Amphitrite comes from the Suburban Baths. The exceptional level of preservation of the decorations of Herculaneum's Suburban Baths gives a good impression of how colorful the rooms must have been.

Left: The Suburban Baths in Herculaneum have been very well preserved, and present a unique insight into what a Roman bathhouse was really like: details such as ceilings and full-height arches do not often survive elsewhere.

The Romans
in North Africa

Some of the most spectacular and well-preserved Roman cities are found on or near the coast of North Africa. Unlike many cities elsewhere in the Roman Empire they were not generally used as sources of building stone after the collapse of Roman rule, so much can still be seen above ground.

Large parts of North Africa were substantially under Roman control early in the first millennium AD. North Africa was very important to Rome; it was relatively close and controlling it consolidated Rome's overall hold on the Mediterranean. Even the Phoenician city of Carthage, which had been destroyed by the Romans in 146 BC after their victory over the Carthaginians in the Punic Wars, was eventually rebuilt as a Roman city. It has also has some dramatic remains. In addition, North Africa was an important source of raw materials and other resources, much evidence of which has been found in shipwrecks.

LEPTIS MAGNA

Leptis Magna, now in Libya, was one of the most important cities—in fact the Emperor Septimus Severus, who ruled between AD 193 and 211, was born there. Many of the remains of the city date to the early years AD; the theater was dated to AD 1–2, for instance. There was also a market, originally built in AD 8 but much expanded about thirty years later—a sign of the city's growth. A lot of work took place later. A set of baths are some of the most complete Roman buildings still in existence—sand protected most of the roof from damage and much of the vaulting still exists—and these were built at about the same time as Septimus Severus was in power. Leptis Magna certainly benefited from its link with the emperor, and acquired some large, "imperial" buildings as a result. One of these was a triumphal arch, but there was also a new forum.

Much of the building material for all of this construction came from the wider Roman Empire, like some of the marble which was from Asia Minor. However, there were significant quarries in North Africa, and rock from the Mons Claudianus quarry in the Egyptian Eastern Desert was so fine that it was reserved for imperial use. In fact it was even known as "imperial purple," it is a granodorite with a distinctive purplish cast. Keeping this remote quarry going must have been intensely demanding, both in terms of maintaining the workforce and transporting the end result. Olives seem to have been another significant export from the North African colonies, and there is evidence of large-scale olive processing at Leptis Magna. Olive oil was not just used for food and cooking; it could also be used for lighting and even for cleaning products. The sheer size of the operation at Leptis indicates that it was not purely for the use of the citizens.

Opposite: The market place at Leptis Magna was expanded very soon after it was first established, with the construction of porticoes around it. Two pavilions were also created inside the open courtyard.

Right: The stage and the area immediately behind it in Leptis Magna's theater.

TIMGAD

There are other cities. Timgad, now in Algeria, was essentially a military town, established by the Third Legion who were quartered nearby. North Africa, like other parts of the extended Roman Empire, was garrisoned; the Punic Wars were a not-so-distant fact, and several forts have been found and excavated. Timgad was carefully planned from the start, constructed on a strict grid, and like Leptis Magna it benefited from the region's association with Septimus Severus. During his reign a triumphal arch was erected here too, on the road from Lambaesis where the third legion was stationed.

SABRATHA

There is another notable city on the Libyan coast, Sabratha. This is also well preserved. Excavations here were begun by the Italians before the Second World War, and picked up again afterwards by Kathleen Kenyon, who excavated Jericho. Here evidence was found from the levels which lay beneath the Roman city—Sabratha had previously been a Punic settlement. The Roman city itself seems to have grown steadily in prosperity; old buildings were refurbished over time, and the use of expensive marble increased. The theater, which dates to the latter part of the second century AD, was one of the largest and most imposing in Roman Africa; now partly reconstructed, it conveys an excellent impression of the effect it would have had in its heyday. There is certainly no doubt about the wealth of Rome's North African colonies.

Above: A relief of two theatrical masks from the front of the stage in the theater of Sabratha.

Left: The temple of Isis at the edge of the sea in Sabratha. The cult of this Egyptian goddess—the wife of Osiris, ruler of the underworld—was popular all over the Roman world, not just in Africa.

The Near
and Middle East

Jericho

When the British archaeologist Kathleen Kenyon began excavating at Tell es-Sultan, the site of the ancient city of Jericho in the Jordan valley, her main aim was to excavate the biblical city, the Jericho of the Bronze and Iron Ages, the Jericho whose walls were brought down by Joshua's trumpets. But the most important things she discovered go back farther than that. Very much farther.

In the nineteenth century it was thought that agriculture had probably developed in the Nile valley about 4000 BC, and that it would have gone hand in hand with the development of pottery. The Neolithic – the term actually means "new stone" and comes from a new type of stone technology – had been associated with the invention of ceramics. From earlier excavations on the site, Kenyon knew that there were deep settlement layers beneath the Bronze Age city. Every time her own trenches went below that level she encountered underlying deposits which seemed to be Neolithic in date. These were substantial and appeared to cover the same area as the later Bronze Age town, about 30,000 sq. yards. However, she found no pottery in the early layers at all, though they were very deep. She was able to distinguish two phases of occupation and, because of the lack of pottery, called them Pre-Pottery Neolithic A and B, often referred to as PPNA and PPNB. The settlements she had found were evidently farming communities, despite their lack of ceramics.

EARLY DATES

Radiocarbon dating was just becoming available and Kenyon sent samples from Jericho's earliest levels to the pioneering laboratory at the University of Chicago run by Willard Libby. The results were shocking – the lab dated the samples to between the eighth and seventh millennia BC, well before the supposed "start" date of 4000 BC. Jericho had evidently been occupied by people cultivating grain for thousands of years before then, stretching back to between about 9000 and 7000 BC, and with an even earlier, non-farming, phase going back to about 12,000 BC. These dates were soon confirmed by readings from other early agricultural sites, and Kenyon's excavation had provided the first evidence for the period which saw the start of farming.

Before then, and for some time afterward, most humans were hunter-gatherers, living by hunting animals, fishing, and gathering wild foodstuffs, whether plants or shellfish, and moving around to exploit seasonal variations. The very lowest levels at Jericho, before the Neolithic ones, date back to 10,500 and the end of the Ice Age, and reveal a settled community which had grown up around a spring. The people belonged to what is known as the Natufian culture. Their round buildings were partly sunk into the ground and they had stored large amounts of barley and wheat, but these were still wild; it is possible to tell because domestication changes the form of the grains. The people may have

Opposite: The stone tower from the walls of the Pre-Pottery Neolithic settlement at Jericho. This was built of solid stone set in mud mortar and contained an internal staircase; work of such sophistication and size from such an early date was a considerable surprise. The tower is set into the inside of the settlement's wall. It would probably have been more likely to have been built on the outside if it had fulfilled a purely defensive role.

Above: The vast thickness of the deposits at Jericho bears witness to the sheer length of time the site has been occupied. The level of human settlements gradually rise over time in a site like this, as rubbish and the ruins of collapsed and abandoned mud-brick houses are built on by successive generations.

experimented with sowing the grain they had gathered, but we cannot tell. They must, however, have had a secure enough food supply in the area to enable them to have settled in one place for most of the year, at least.

The Pre-Pottery Neolithic communities, on the other hand, existed on a combination of farming and herding, with some hunting and gathering. Their crops included several forms of wheat, barley, and lentils, and domesticated goats appeared in the later, PPNB, phase. Work since the 1950s has shown that animal domestication had begun earlier elsewhere; though the people at Jericho had begun cultivating plants very early, they had adopted animal keeping later than some other communities, notably ones farther to the north.

THE WALLS

Despite this revolutionary evidence about the early date of farming, the buildings, and the things they contained, proved to be the most surprising. Firstly, there was the size. Construction on the scale discovered by the archaeologists was completely unprecedented for such an early date. The PPNA settlement had been surrounded by a large ditch cut into the bedrock as well as a wall over 12 feet high and approximatetly 9 feet thick. This massive construction had even been supplemented by the addition of a tower over 25 feet high, made of solid masonry with an interior staircase leading up to a flat roof. The purpose of this tower and the perimeter wall has been debated. Kenyon thought they were defensive but more recent theories have suggested that if they were, then they were protecting the village from flash floods and mudslides rather than hostile people. They were both certainly eventually buried in waterborne silt and gravel, and not rebuilt. The second astonishing fact about them is their sophistication; they were very well built indeed.

THE VILLAGE – AND THE DEAD

The area inside the walls covered a large area and could probably have housed about 500 people at any one time. The houses were built of stones or mud bricks, were often partly sunk into the ground like the earlier Natufian houses and, like them, were round. The next, PPNB, phase saw the construction of rectangular houses; houses from both periods had plaster floors, but the later houses' floors had been painted and polished.

The people of early Neolithic Jericho had lived with their dead, literally. Kenyon was only able to excavate about a tenth of the whole settlement, but she found 276 burials and all of them were associated with buildings. They were below floors, between walls, under other household structures and even within the tower. Very few were accompanied by artefacts but a lot of them, mostly adults, were not accompanied by their skulls; these had been interred separately.

Clusters of skulls which had been decorated came from PPNB levels. Seven were found in one pit, for example, and isolated ones also turned up in the houses and beneath the polished and painted house floors. Faces had been modeled in plaster over the actual bones, and a lot of the skulls used for this lacked their lower jaws, a possible indication that they had been disinterred for ceremonial decoration after several years' burial with the rest of the bones. Sometimes cowrie shells were inset for the eyes and there are traces of other decoration on the

plaster of one: it seems to have a painted mustache. Some of these skulls appear to have then been reburied while some were kept, presumably for display, in the house above the rest of the bones. Some of these heads are in good condition and even convey a vivid impression of a particular individual. Great care was evidently taken in preparing these skull portraits, and they may have been part of an ancestor cult. Since these discoveries at Jericho other plastered skulls have been found in contemporary sites elsewhere in the Levant and there are many examples of burials which have been revisited with the purpose of removing the head. Nowhere, however, have enough burials been found to account for all of the inhabitants of a particular site, so some form of selection was obviously involved.

Both Kenyon and her predecessors at Jericho also discovered large figures, almost life size, which had been made out of plaster. The faces of these figures bear some resemblance to the portrait skulls, and perhaps they too were part of an ancestor cult, or maybe they represented gods or goddesses. It is also noticeable that plaster was being used almost like pottery, anticipating the later use of clay.

Above: Plaster head, with inlaid eyes made from shells, which comes from seventh-millennium Jericho. Plaster statues like this bear a strong resemblance to the plastered portrait skulls that were found in the excavations and may well have played a similar part in any ancestor cult.

Kathleen Kenyon

Born in 1906, Kathleen Kenyon was to become one of the great archaeologists of the 20th century. She studied at Oxford in the 1920s and later worked at many sites, including Great Zimbabwe and the Roman city of Sabratha in north Africa. Closer to home, in Britain, she also worked with Mortimer Wheeler on Verulamium, the Roman city of St. Albans, just north of London. She also became the director of the Institute of Archaeology in London.

She began digging at the site of Jericho in 1952, and the large-scale excavations which she ran there until 1958 provided some of the first evidence for the early date at which farming began, as well as exposing an extraordinary walled settlement. She received a lot of honors and became Dame Kathleen Kenyon in 1973, five years before her death.

Below: Kathleen Kenyon and C. N. Goodman examining pieces of Roman pottery discovered at Verulamium (St. Albans). A nearly complete Roman theater was unearthed at the site. With the help of 30 workers, Kenyon and Goodman excavated part of the main outer wall and the complete entrance to the stage.

Catalhöyük

James Melaart, a British archaeologist, discovered the Turkish site of Catalhöyük in 1958. His excavations, which ended in 1965, demonstrated that the town he had found was both extremely large in extent—over 155,500 square yards—and entirely Neolithic. It had never been thought that settlements of this early date could be so large or so sophisticated. In 1993 Ian Hodder began excavating at the huge site again, leading an international research project.

Catalhöyük was founded in the middle of the Anatolian plateau about 7300 BC and occupied for about a thousand years, and provides evidence for everyday life and the importance of ritual more than 9000 years ago. The settlement mound still stands over 50 feet high; the town was packed with housing and must have had thousands of inhabitants.

The houses were essentially rectangular boxes, built next to each other without approaches at ground level, and were bordered on all four sides by others. Each one had a trapdoor in the roof and a staircase—a wooden ladder—against one wall. Generally they had one main room with a smaller one opening off it, and the larger room had a central area surrounded by low platforms. Both walls and floors were plastered, and the walls frequently had painted designs on them. One of the reasons why the settlement mound was so high was that old houses formed the foundations of new ones. The average life of a mud-brick house was about 70 years, and when one deteriorated its timber supports would be removed—they had originally come from some distance and would have been too valuable to discard—and the house pulled down into itself. The new house was then constructed on top, and the floor consolidated and plastered. Sometimes a new house wasn't built in the gap, and the inhabitants of neighboring houses would use the space as a rubbish dump.

Many human burials have been found beneath the floors. Some houses have many—one has 68—while others have none. The bodies often seem to have been specially prepared: in some cases the soft tissue had been removed, possibly by exposure, and some of the bones had been sprinkled with colors, usually red ocher. Because these aren't included in every house, it looks as though some buildings may have been particularly important, maybe to an extended family. Few of these burials were accompanied by any burial goods, but where these were included they were of significantly unusual origin: high-quality flint, copper, and seashells have all been found.

There is evidence of a rich ritual life at Catalhöyük. Some of the houses had sculptures on the walls or set into platforms, usually of a bull's head and horns which sometimes appear in multiple pairs. Clay figures were also found, often representing women. There is one particularly clear example in which a woman is depicted giving birth while seated in a chair supported by lions and, like the others, it probably expresses ideas of regeneration and fertility. These have led some people to regard Catalhöyük as an important site for evidence of the worship of a mother goddess.

Opposite: The painted walls of buildings at Catalhöyük are an almost unique survival, dating back over 8000 years. There were geometric shapes; less common are human figures, like these clustering around a massive animal, possibly a wild bull. Bulls seem to have had a special significance for the people of the town.

Right: A map showing the major settlements of the Near East in ancient times.

The Royal Tombs of Ur

Southern Mesopotamia, the land watered by the Tigris and Euphrates Rivers, has a long history of human occupation. Villages grew and became more sophisticated towns, bigger temples were constructed, and a form of early cuneiform writing made its appearance, developing out of simpler pictographic scripts.

GROWTH OF THE SUMERIAN CITIES

The beginning of the third millennium BC saw the growth of Sumerian city states. These depended on farming, using the water of the rivers for irrigation, and traded with their neighbors. Luxury materials, like the lapis lazuli that was so popular, came from farther away: that was originally from Afghanistan. Most of these exotic materials seem to have been destined for certain sectors of society, the elites, and each city state appears to have been ruled by a king who combined secular and religious authority. Though these states were independent, they had a lot of things in common such as styles of pottery, jewelry, and even the shape of the mud bricks used in buildings. Ur was one of these Sumerian city states, and later extended its rule over a wider area. The British archaeologist Leonard Woolley dug the site of Ur for 12 years from 1922. He explored its history from its earliest beginnings, a small farming village dating to about 7000 years ago, to its abandonment 5000 years later. His most famous finds date to its time as one of the most significant of the city states, in the middle of the third millennium BC.

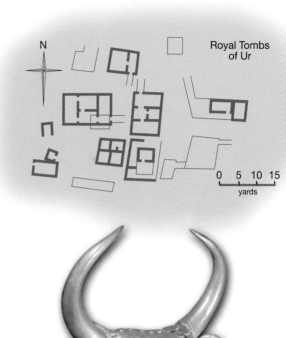

Sometime about 2600 BC the inhabitants of Ur began burying their dead in a cemetery which was to remain in use for almost 600 years. It lay near what would probably have been a sacred precinct, and Woolley was to excavate 2500 graves. Most of them belonged to

Opposite: Ur, seen here in a general view, was the site of a remarkable series of excavations undertaken by Leonard Woolley before the Second World War. Some of the most extraordinary archaeological finds came from the royal burials.

Above: An ornament of a bull, made in gold and silver.

Left: Court jewelry for Queen Pu-abi. Wigs were evidently worn over women's natural hair, and all the hair ornaments found have enabled their dimensions to be reconstructed. The queen's jewelry, in which she was interred, was very lavish and makes much use of gold, lapis lazuli, and carnelian.

ordinary people; bodies were buried simply, wrapped in matting and accompanied by a pot, maybe two. Others were wealthier and included some items made using luxury materials, imports from outside, and expensive items such as jewelry made from precious metals and lapis lazuli. And then there were the royal tombs.

There were only a few of these royal interments, 16 or 17, but they were very different from even the wealthiest of the others. These were chambers constructed below ground, often with vaulted roofs, and were entered from the surface down sloping ramps or through pits. Some of them had been robbed, often in antiquity, but still held many beautiful objects; others were intact. Their contents were spectacular. Inscriptions

in some of them may identify their occupants—there's a record of kings Meskalamdug and Akalamdug and a queen, Pu-abi—but there is still some doubt about their precise identity. Whatever their names, they seem to have all been members of a wealthy dynasty ruling between about 2600 and 2500 BC.

THE TREASURES

Woolley was an exceptionally careful excavator, especially for the 1920s, and his meticulous work in the royal tombs has made it possible for many of the pieces to be more clearly understood. Preservation conditions meant that parts of many items had decayed, like the wooden sounding-boxes of lyres, but it has been possible to

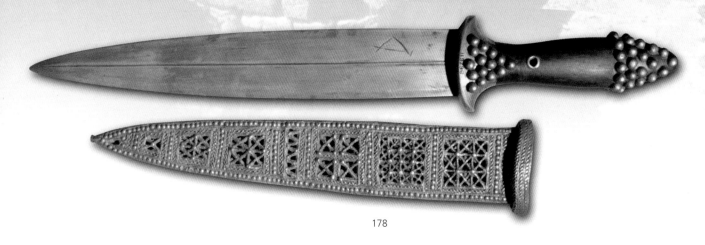

reconstruct many of them. Lyres regularly appear, reduced to their metal parts, stone and inlay in mother-of-pearl, and with some parts loose but still in place, and careful work was needed. Because of this it is now possible to see the original form of items like a gaming box, originally wood, which was covered in lapis and shell inlay. There was a wooden panel covered on both sides with scenes of war and celebration, made from lapis and shell, and there were two statues long known as the "ram in a thicket" figures, but which probably represented goats standing up against trees. They are made from gold, silver, lapis lazuli and shell on top of a wooden core and may have been part of a piece of furniture. Other items include armor and weapons—helmets, daggers, spears—as well as cups and other vessels. There are carved items, lamps, and other containers; jewelry including headdresses and necklaces of lapis lazuli, this time with carnelian and gold. There are toiletry kits and cosmetics containers. And there are also people. Not just the buried rulers, but many of their servants and retainers as well.

Human Sacrifice

Many court attendants accompanied the rulers of Ur into the afterlife, as did some animals. The remains of oxen were found, as were the wagons they had drawn—and the men who had driven them. There were guards wearing copper helmets and carrying spears, and there were the women of the court, ladies-in-waiting or concubines, with splendid jewelry. Most of these people lay outside the royal burial chambers themselves, but a few attendants were found inside; one king had three people with him, though there were many more outside, and a queen had two, found at the head and foot of her bier. It did look as though members of the royal family

went to their graves along with people from the royal household. One of the pits contained 68 women and six men, laid out in rows. This neat arrangement of bodies was something of a feature, and has prompted much speculation.

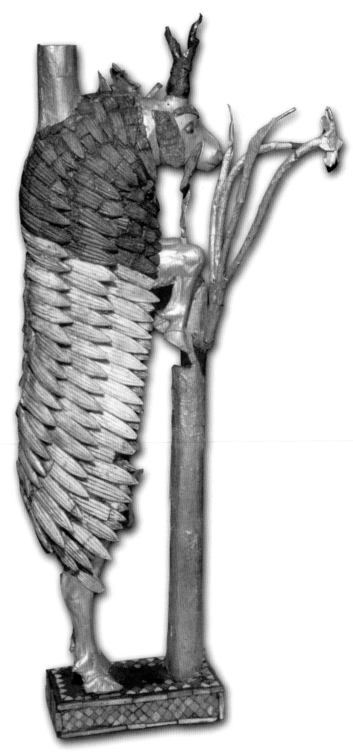

Opposite above: Ziggurats like this developed into quite a feature of Sumerian cities. This one, from Ur, was constructed about 2100, long after the royal tombs, though it may have covered an earlier one. It represented a stylized mountain, the home of the gods.

Opposite below: A gold dagger and its sheath from Ur; many weapons were found in the cemetery.

Right: The two small statues often referred to as the "ram in a thicket" actually appear to represent goats. An initial wooden carving was covered with precious materials, and they may have formed part of a piece of furniture.

The question of how all these people met their deaths was explored by Woolley, who noted that physical violence did not seem to have been employed. The bones had deteriorated too badly to have been much use in determining the cause of death but there were other clues. The elaborate headdresses worn by the women, for example, did not appear to have been disturbed by any blow to the head, or sudden fall such as might follow a stabbing. They also made it equally unlikely that the women had been killed outside the tomb and carried into it. The animals which dragged vehicles down must have been alive when they did so–traces of harness and other equipment remained, linking them—and it does seem as though all these sacrificial victims went into the pits alive.

There were no obvious traces of struggle and many of the bodies have been found in what appear to be deliberate positions: "decently composed," as Woolley put it. It may be that the people—and probably the animals too—were drugged in some way. It looks as though the tombs may have been filled in once the people had died, or perhaps when they were unconscious, and their bodies may have been arranged more neatly then, though something as heavy as a dead ox would have been difficult to maneuver. Sacrifices like these were confined to the royal tombs, and accompanying a ruler on the journey to the afterlife may even have been regarded as a privilege; a lot of attention and wealth was certainly expended on honoring the dead. Whatever the truth of the matter, the human sacrifices are an impressive demonstration of the power the rulers of Ur had over their subordinates.

Leonard Woolley

Leonard Woolley was one of the most careful, competent and skilled excavators of his time, and his approach to the complexities of a site like Ur was similarly cautious. He was born in 1880 and followed Sir Arthur Evans, the excavator of Knossos, at Oxford's Ashmolean Museum. He began working in the field, excavating in Nubia, and then worked on the Syrian site of Carchemish before the outbreak of the First World War. In 1921 he was appointed director of the excavations at Ur jointly by the British Museum and the University of Pennsylvania Museum, and dug there until 1934. Though he actually excavated a lot of the city, he is best known for the remarkable finds from the royal cemetery which was discovered during the first season in 1922, when some of his workers found gold and graves.

Typically, Woolley put off working in the area for four years until his teams of diggers could develop more technical expertise. Unfortunately, while his techniques may have been excellent, the notes he made of his excavations at the time are incomplete, making it difficult for the archaeologists of today to assess his conclusions.

Opposite above: The entrance to the ziggurat at Ur.

Opposite below:: The helmet of King Meskalamdug demonstrates the mastery of metalworking techniques in Ur; it is made of electrum, a mixture of gold and silver, and was shaped with great skill.

Below: A seal showing Gilgamesh and lions.

The Hittites

During the Late Bronze Age there were a number of significant powers, even empires, in the eastern Mediterranean and Middle East. Egypt left many remains behind it, as did most of the other great civilizations. The Hittites, on the contrary, were almost forgotten except for a few mentions in the Bible, where they were linked with the Levant.

Carved blocks of stone began turning up in Turkey during the 19th century; these were covered in what appeared to be a hieroglyphic script but one quite unlike Egyptian hieroglyphics. A German team began excavating at the Turkish site of Boghazkoy in 1906, and in 1912 Leonard Woolley started work at Carchemish in what is now Syria. Of the two sites, Boghazkoy proved to have been of more significance for the Hittites, however—it turned out to have been their capital, Hattusa.

Boghazkoy lies about 100 miles east of Ankara in central Anatolia. Its identification as Hattusa was confirmed in the many thousands of clay tablets that were found there in the remains of what had been several libraries or, more properly, archives. These documents also revealed something of the Hittites' history. Excavations at Hattusa continue to provide much information and have changed the way the Hittites, their vast empire and the whole history of the region is perceived. It used to be thought, for example, that the Hittites owed their success and their military advantage over their neighbors to iron tools, but it is now known that theirs was definitely a Late Bronze Age society, with iron playing a very minor part. In fact one of their major advantages would have been the three-man chariot they developed, an indicator of military strength particularly well depicted in a carved tablet from Carchemish.

Hattusa's location was demanding. It was relatively close to the mountain home of some of the Hittites' enemies, and had a difficult environment and terrain. According to Hittite histories, they had originally been based at the city of Kussara and had expanded from there to control most of Anatolia. Hattusa, however, was considered particularly holy—"the city of a thousand gods"—and the capital was moved. The location of Kussara is unknown, but the Hittites were certainly in Hattusa by 1680 BC; and it was to remain the Hittite capital for over 400 years until its destruction and abandonment sometime around 1185 BC at the end of the Late Bronze Age.

THE ROYAL ARCHIVES

The clay tablets found at Hattusa are astonishingly valuable archaeologically and historically. There are over 25,000 of them, and they seem to have been state archives. Not only do these documents provide a wealth of information about Hittite society and history (as they themselves saw it, of course), they also contain much information about other contemporary cultures. There are details of religion and state organization, and laws and punishments for various offences such as oathbreaking; the Hittite state appears to have been heavily controlled. There are tablets which talk of the foundation and early days of the Hittite state and, often most revealing, there are diplomatic records which can be of interest for events outside the Hittite empire. Some of these have been used to provide possible evidence for disturbances on the coast of north-western Turkey at the supposed time of the Trojan War, for example, and have even been used to correct what was previously thought to be historical fact. The great battle of Qadesh early in the 13th century BC between the Hittites and the Egyptians was thought to have been won by the latter, largely because the Egyptians said so. In actuality, it appears to have been won by the Hittites—and not just because they said so, but because they seem to have firmly established their control

Opposite: The lower part of Hattusa.

Right: The Lion Gate at Boghazkoy, the Hittite capital of Hattusa. This immense city was encircled by multiple rings of walls and one of its other gates is flanked by a beautiful relief of a figure.

over much of northern Levant and Syria after the date of the battle. A clay tablet of their version of the peace treaty following the battle of Qadesh actually exists: in fact a copy is displayed at the UN headquarters in New York.

The clay tablets also fascinated the archaeologists because of the mixture of languages used, and especially the Hittites' own language. The variety is testimony to the reach of the Hittite empire and the script used was cuneiform, a Mesopotamian tradition. The Hittite language turned out to belong to the Indo-European family of languages, a group including most European languages and a few others like Armenian, instead of being related to most other west-Asian tongues. There have been many attempts at explaining the origin and spread of languages and the confirmation of Hittite as the oldest Indo-European one, while important, has not helped clarify any potential population movements as the Hittites' own origins are obscure. Nonetheless, it does set them apart from most of their neighbors to the south and east.

The Hittites also used a hieroglyphic script, though not on documents like those from the archives. It was largely reserved for inscriptions on rock though it was also used on name seals that would have been used on personal documents. Deciphering hieroglyphics is exceptionally difficult, but happily the name seals had the same names in both hieroglyphics and cuneiform letters, making it possible to work out the meaning of the various hieroglyphic symbols.

THE CAPITAL CITY AND THE EMPIRE

Hattusa, as capital and royal seat of the Hittite empire, was a large city. It spread over more than 2 square miles

and incorporated many features of the landscape, like ridges, rock outcrops, and gorges. In many ways it was not the ideal site for a capital: it was remote and isolated, in rough terrain, and the harsh environment made it difficult to sustain. For about its first 250 years—the period before the Hittite empire reached its height, from about 1650 to 1400 BC—it was a smaller place, with the citadel as its focus. Here was the royal palace, and below that was what appears to have been a storage area and the city's main temple. These were surrounded by substantial fortifications.

The Hittite kingdom grew relatively gradually. King Hattusili I campaigned in northern Syria in the 17th century BC, heading southward to Aleppo and on toward the coast. Heading in the other direction, the next ruler, Mursili I, raided Babylon in 1595 BC. This early flurry of expansion was brought to an end by conflict within the ruling family, and almost seems to have set a pattern of alternating expansion and contraction.

Then Shuppiluliuma I began a series of conquests in 1345 BC, annexing much of northern Syria. Kings of many states signed treaties with him and vassal states seem to have retained some of their local characteristics. This period saw the height of the Hittite empire and between 1400 and 1185 BC Hattusa expanded dramatically. There was a lot of new construction: a great temple was built, as were some smaller ones and other buildings like huge grain stores and reservoirs for water. The royal palace was rebuilt, too. As yet not much is known about ordinary houses at Hattusa; most of the main part of the city is devoted to royal structures or major state facilities like the grain stores and temples. The construction of buildings permitting the storage of both food and water could have been undertaken because of a perceived threat from enemies, or as a response to difficult environmental conditions.

OTHER SITES OF THE HITTITE EMPIRE

There were, of course, many other Hittite sites. Yazilikaya, which appears to have been completed in the 13th century BC, is close to Hattusa and has been called a "rock sanctuary." There are many reliefs on the rock faces, carvings of Hittite gods and goddesses, and the sanctuary seems to have been created by King Tudhaliya IV as a memorial to his father. One of the rock chambers at Yazilikaya has slots in the walls and it has been suggested that these were designed to hold the cremated remains of members of the royal house, but there is no evidence of that having happened. So far, no Hittite royal burials have been found.

The Hittite towns excavated to date share some common features. They have large temples, substantial public buildings, are surrounded by a wall and rampart, and are entered through a monumental gate, or series of gates as at Hattusa, flanked by large figures. Alaca Höyük, also near to Hattusa, certainly fits this pattern, though it was relatively small. It had been developed on top of an earlier settlement, another frequently common factor. Carchemish, much further south, controlled a major ford over the Euphrates River and became important both strategically and commercially to the Hittites. Other towns—like Ortaköy just east of Hattusa and the frontier town of Masat—have provided more texts and archive material, and our knowledge of the Hittites and their empire keeps increasing.

THE END...

The Late Bronze Age saw many collapses across southwest Asia. The reasons for this are unclear, but it was certainly a period of severe disruption. Between 1200 and 1185 BC the Hittite sites all show evidence of destruction and desertion. In Hattusa there were fires in places such as the palace and temple area, and in some cases it looks as though the buildings might have been emptied of valuable and important material first. There is the likelihood that, once again, the empire had been affected by internal struggles in the royal family, and the normally tight control they exercised over their subjects may have broken down. There could also have been environmental factors—Hattusa was particularly vulnerable to environmental stress—and there is a text from the late period urgently requesting supplies of grain for the city. Whatever happened was conclusive enough to reduce the Hittites to a shadowy presence in the archaeological and historical record for over 3000 years.

Opposite above: A procession of figures from the Hittite sanctuary of Yazilikaya, an important religious center.

Opposite below: The extraordinary find of 25,000 clay writing tablets from archives in Hattusa, with more coming from other Hittite sites, has provided a unique insight into the organization of the Hittite state.

Below: The ruins of the great temple at Hattusa, and a city street.

Nineveh

During the Bronze Age a new power appeared in the north of Mesopotamia and began expanding westward. The Assyrians ruled they lands the conquered as occupiers rather than colonizers; when their empire began to decline after about 1200 BC they lost control of these areas and retreated to the heart of their empire, around Nineveh on the River Tigris. In the tenth century BC they began to push westward again and at its largest—in about 650 BC—the resurgent Assyrian Empire extended from Susa and Babylon in the south, near to the ancient coastline of the Persian Gulf, up to Anatolia, across to the Mediterranean and down into Egypt. Their occupation of Egypt did not last long and when Babylonia rose in defiance of their rule, the empire began to collapse once more.

EARLY EXCAVATIONS

During the 1840s, French and British diplomatic staff began exploring Mesopotamia and soon began uncovering the remains of Assyrian palaces from the latter imperial phase. Excavations at what was later revealed to be Nineveh were started in 1842 by the French consul Paul Emile Botta, but he found the results disappointing and moved to another site, Khorsabad, which was more productive.

Meanwhile Nimrud was being explored by the British diplomatic agent Austen Henry Layard. He found three great palaces there, and then moved to the site abandoned by the French where he discovered two more. His excavation methods were primitive, practically nonexistent by today's standards, and he was mainly concerned with recovering spectacular objects, having little interest in anything else. In his quest to find the things he was interested in, he and his diggers actually did a lot of damage—he "excavated" by tunneling around the walls of rooms in the palaces, creating nearly two of tunnels in the process. Among the things that didn't really catch his attention were the palace archives: the thousands of clay tablets his expedition found were literally shoveled up into baskets and dispatched to London. Work had already begun on deciphering cuneiform and the scholars there were able to read the tablets and identify the site of Layard's two palaces as Nineveh, the traditional seat of Assyrian rulers.

Huge walls protected Assyrian palaces, walls with impressive gateways. Inside these were separate blocks of rooms and passageways running around internal courtyards. Large statues of winged bulls with human heads, some as much as 12 feet tall, flanked the main doorways. There were ceremonial rooms, like the throne room or those connected to religious practices, but there were also domestic quarters, workshops, and extensive stores within the palace walls. Many of the palace buildings were highly decorated, often with alabaster panels depicting the ruler and his triumphs.

These, and the massive door statues, were the most sought-after objects for both Layard and his French counterpart Botta, and a lot of them were retrieved. Layard stated that he had found about one-and-a-half miles of reliefs at Nineveh.

CLAY TABLETS

In their own way, however, the clay tablets that Layard largely ignored were just as significant as the more obvious finds when it came to understanding the past, in fact probably more so. Assyrian rulers put together libraries of cuneiform tablets, recording the various historical and religious traditions of Mesopotamia going back centuries, and there were also the more factual palace archives and down-to-earth items dealing with everyday life. The discovery of the libraries resulted in bilingual dictionaries being developed and thus enabled the decipherment of Sumerian, which had also been written in a cuneiform script.

The early forays into Mesopotamian archaeology by French and British teams provided the Louvre and the British Museum with some of their most impressive objects, remnants of a civilization previously known only through the Bible. There have been many excavations since, notably in the first half of the 20th century. Overall, the early excavations in Mesopotamia resulted in the discovery of an almost entirely unknown culture, and inspired many of the next generation of archaeologists. Recent wars in the area have placed many sites, and their artifacts, in peril.

Opposite: A relief from Assurbanipal's palace, showing enemies—these are Elamites— surrendering following their defeat by the victorious king. One of the Elamites seems to be about to touch his forehead to the ground in submission.

Right: A cuneiform tablet from Nineveh. Many of these were found, and a lot were administrative, historical, or economic; this one is none of these. It is actually a medical text, describing methods of treating a persistent cough.

Persepolis

During the sixth century BC, the Persians created one of the greatest empires the world has ever seen, running, at its maximum extent, from the Turkish coast of the Aegean into Central Asia and down to the Gulf of Oman. Egypt became part of the Persian Empire, as did northern Thrace, which meant that the Persians threatened Greece directly. The Greeks defeated the Persian king Xerxes in the 470s, but the empire continued to exist until Alexander the Great's conquest of it between 333 and 323 BC. Much is known about the Persian Empire from the historical record, but much of that comes from Greek sources—their enemies—and archaeology has proved invaluable, especially for discovering archives of tablets and uncovering the signs of everyday life.

Persian expansion had begun under Cyrus, between 559 and 530 BC. His successor Cambyses added Egypt but was killed during a messy attempted coup; Darius succeeded him in 522 BC under apparently doubtful circumstances, and had to crush a rebellion. He began consolidating his empire and also started constructing a new and impressive imperial city that was completed by his heirs. The Greeks called this city Persepolis, by which name it continues to be known today, and it is one of the most remarkable survivals of this great empire. Like many of the most imposing remains of the ancient world, it was never completely forgotten in the centuries that followed. It remained visible, exposed to the weather and the view of passing travelers, and many of those returned to Europe with drawings and descriptions of the ruins.

PERSEPOLIS

From the start Persepolis was designed to impress; it was a ceremonial capital and royal residence. Originally it had been surrounded by mud-brick walls, but these are long vanished; a lot of other parts are much better preserved and some have been reassembled and restored. The main part of the city was constructed on a gigantic stone platform, nearly 50 feet higher than the plain on which it was built; it covered about 155,000 square yards. This main platform was reached by an appropriately large and imposing double staircase, and on top were vast buildings, some atop platforms of their own, also accessed by large staircases.

Opposite: The palace of Darius at Persepolis, the city which he founded. It was constructed on an immense artificial platform which rises some 50 feet above the surrounding landscape. Further platforms were even constructed on top for specific buildings.

Above: The ruins of Persepolis. The large sculpture of a bull—its horns have broken off—represents one of the key animals used in Persian art and architecture. The others are the lion and an imaginary beast, the griffin.

Left: A relief from Persepolis showing Darius.

The buildings on top of the platform included palaces built by both Darius and his successor Xerxes, a gigantic audience hall—the Apadana—and a building known as the Treasury. There were also more mundane structures, such as stables and storerooms, but the overall effect must have been one of levels rising upon levels, of vast colonnaded halls, ceremonial gateways and imposing staircases. The Apadana, an enormous pillared hall, had colonnaded porches on three of the four walls. The columns are almost like Greek ones, except for the fact that the capitals—the tops—represent great animals, which would have given the impression that the roof beams were held up by giant lions, bulls, or griffins. Like many of the remains at Persepolis, those of the Apadana are marked by standing pillars, restored in their original positions.

As with Assyrian palaces, many doorways in Persepolis were guarded by huge statues of winged bulls, and there were many relief carvings that also owe a lot to Assyrian artistic traditions. Many of these showed the king and the people of the court, government officials, or soldiers in the imperial armies. The stairs leading to the Apadana were decorated with reliefs, especially with the figures of notably tall soldiers but also with other people bearing tribute or gifts. These seem to represent the inhabitants of various parts of the Persian Empire and are carved so that the figures appear to be climbing the stairs.

At its height, Persepolis must have been impressive, but its end was sudden. It was occupied by Alexander the Great in 330 BC and was deliberately destroyed by fire, apparently after a night of drinking, and possibly in revenge for Xerxes' burning of Athens 150 years earlier. It did, however, resurface as a symbol of power, albeit temporarily: in the 20th century the Shah of Iran used it as an evocation of the past to bolster and legitimize his rule.

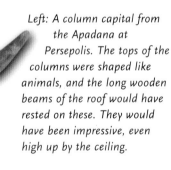

Left: A column capital from the Apadana at Persepolis. The tops of the columns were shaped like animals, and the long wooden beams of the roof would have rested on these. They would have been impressive, even high up by the ceiling.

Opposite: The staircase leading to the Apadana, decorated with relief carvings of people bringing gifts or tribute.

Above: The Palace of Darius in Persepolis.

ROYAL TOMBS AND SHRINES

Darius didn't confine himself to building Persepolis. He also built the first of the royal tombs at Naqsh-i Rustam near to the city. Like the others that followed, it was carved into the rock of a cliff face. The entrances to these royal tombs were elaborate, framed with reliefs of multiple pillars, and with further carvings above the entrance depicting the king. Darius is shown worshiping at a fire altar, standing on a platform supported by figures depicting the peoples of his empire.

Behistun is farther north, in western Iran. It is an important sacred site, located in a pass in the Zagros mountains, and an inscription here justifies Darius's accession to the throne after the civil war, describing his attempts to end it. This is accompanied by a relief of Darius receiving his defeated opponents, but the inscription is what really matters, and not just for its content. The same words were carved in three different languages—Old Persian, Akkadian and Elamite—which permitted their translation and played a vital role in the understanding of cuneiform. It provided a vital key for Akkadian, a much older tongue, which permitted archaeologists to understand much more about earlier civilizations.

Organizing an Empire

An immense imperial site like Persepolis inevitably raises questions about the culture that produced it and, as a result of Darius's reforms and consolidation, the Persian Empire was certainly effective. Despite its size, it was comparatively flexible in some areas; there was a lot of tolerance for local customs and religions, though there was a centralized administration and an imperial army. Darius, who ruled between 522 and 486 BC, divided the empire up into provinces, known as satrapies, and appointed Persian aristocrats as their governors. Agricultural land was divided up—some went in return for military service—and taxes were paid in silver. There was an elaborate network of roads across the empire, with lodging houses and checkpoints, and couriers were used. The system was so good that a fast courier could go between Susa in Babylonia near the Persian Gulf and the city of Sardis, in what is now western Turkey, in a week—a distance of approximately 1500 miles. The techniques which the Persian rulers developed for controling their enormous empire have provided a model for others.

The Dead Sea Scrolls

Some of the most famous archaeological treasures found in the 20th century, the Dead Sea Scrolls were found by accident, though the story may well have grown in the telling. The amazing discovery was made by Muhammad adh-Dibh, a young shepherd belonging to the Ta'amireh tribe of Bedouin, which ranged through the wilderness lying between Bethlehem and the Dead Sea. He was looking for an animal which had gone missing among the cliffs overlooking the Dead Sea's north-western shore in the winter of 1946–7.

While scanning the rocks, Muhammad adh-Dibh noticed a strange opening high up on the face of a cliff and threw a speculative stone into it. Instead of hearing it fall against rock, he heard a rather metallic noise so he tried again and this time had no doubt: his stone had hit pottery. He made his way to the cave mouth, peered in—and saw wide necked, lidded jars standing in rows. He returned in the company of friends and they squeezed through the small entrance and began investigating the jars, hoping they would contain gold. What they actually found inside the jars were bundles of rags containing folds of smooth brown leather. These turned out to be scrolls covered in writing.

Eventually some of the scrolls found their way to Bethlehem and into the hands of dealers in antiquities; the exact circumstances are hard to establish. From the dealers they passed into the ownership of assorted collectors, including the Orthodox archbishop of Jerusalem, who bought several items, including a huge leather scroll of the

Book of Isaiah. Some visiting scholars saw his purchases and recognized the importance of the material.

A systematic search of the area of the original find was launched and further discoveries were made. In the end the whole find was a substantial collection of documents, mostly written on leather scrolls although some were on papyrus. They had been tightly rolled up in linen and placed in their pottery jars, and had then been deposited in several caves. The jars were found to contain fragments, and sometimes large portions, of almost all the books of the Hebrew Bible but there was also other material including what appears to be a rule book for a religious community, dubbed the "Manual of Discipline." In 1952 a copper scroll in two halves was also found in a cave. All of the finds gave the impression of having been hidden for safekeeping.

The wider area of the Dead Sea had also been surveyed by archaeologists, and this revealed the site of Khirbat Qumran. It is also on the western side of the

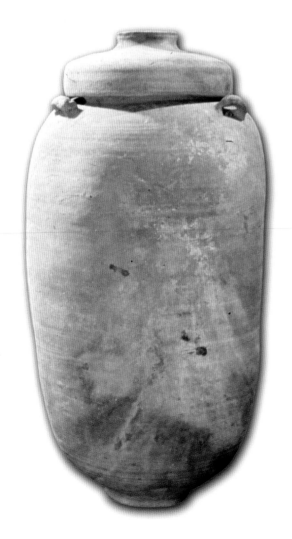

Opposite: The cliffs which overlook the north western shore of the Dead Sea are riddled with caves like the cave of the Dead Sea Scrolls, but most are lower down. The initial find in one of the caves here prompted further investigations which found a lot more material.

Above: Part of the Isaiah scroll, one of the first things found, which was bought by the Orthodox archbishop of Jerusalem. The leather scroll is over 20 feet long and is the oldest version of the Book of Isaiah in existence.

Left: A lot of the scrolls were rolled and wrapped up in linen, and then placed in jars for safekeeping. Some of these had been broken in rock falls, but many were still intact.

Dead Sea, close to some of the caves where scrolls were found. Excavations there showed that it had been abandoned twice, once in AD 31 following an earthquake and again in AD 68, when Roman persecution is likely to have made life very difficult in the circumstances of the First Jewish Revolt, which was going on at the time. Qumran seems to have been an Essene settlement, a type of Jewish monastic community. A scriptorium, a building where texts were copied, was found at Qumran and one of the main tasks in Essene communities was the copying of religious texts. The Essenes also lived by a specific set of somewhat austere rules.

In AD 66 the First Jewish Revolt had begun; this was crushed by the Roman army, with only the fortress of Masada holding out until AD 73 or 74. In crushing the insurgency the Romans sacked Jerusalem and looted the temple, taking any treasure they found back to Rome; an Essene community would have found it necessary to hide their most precious possessions, their sacred books and other vital texts, as the defenders of Masada also did. None of the Dead Sea Scrolls is more recent than the First Jewish Revolt, so they are highly likely to have been an Essene cache, whether they had originated in Qumran or not.

Above: Fragments of a scroll. Not everything was as well-preserved or extensive as the great scroll of the Book of Isaiah; much was fragmentary and had to be carefully reconstructed.

THE COPPER SCROLL

When the Copper Scroll was found in two parts in 1952, it could not be opened; it was too badly corroded. Fragments of writing could just be deciphered, however, etched into the soft metal, and they seemed to refer to deposits of treasure. The scroll had clearly been intended to last. When it was eventually carefully opened it was found to consist of a list of treasures and ostensibly clear descriptions of where they had been hidden.

Unlike the rest of the Dead Sea Scrolls in its content as well as the material it was made from, the Copper Scroll contains no possible Essene material or biblical texts. In addition, it had been rather roughly written, probably not by a professional scribe. Many experts believe it records the hiding places of treasure removed from the temple in Jerusalem just before the Roman attack in AD 67—but not one item has been found although lots of people have searched using the scroll as a guide. The dating matches the period of the First Jewish Revolt, but most people today also believe that the Copper Scroll is not entirely what it seems, and that some sort of code was actually used.

Masada

The isolated plateau which towers above the deserts of the western shores of the Dead Sea is one of the most dramatic archaeological sites in the Middle East. This rock, Masada, is important for both its archaeology and its place in the history of the region.

In the early 1960s the site was excavated by the Israeli
archaeologist Yigael Yadin. It was an exceptionally difficult
place on which to organize a major dig; both the terrain and
the environment were problematic and the excavation was
enormous. Many members of the huge teams of diggers
were international volunteers and Yadin's military experience
proved invaluable; the Masada dig has been described as a
"triumph of logistics."

HEROD'S PALACE

Masada's obvious natural defences had attracted the
attention of King Herod sometime between 36 and 30 BC.
He strengthened them and built a fortified palace on the top,
as well as adding immense water cisterns which would
contain water for his palaces and gardens and provide
essential supplies during any siege, which later came about.
There were other buildings vital to the running of a royal
palace, like the bathhouses and gardens, and a second
palace, known as the Summer Palace, was also constructed.
This was situated on the northern tip of the plateau and rises
up in tiers on three terraces; it has a fantastic view, as do
many points on the summit. Yadin's excavation did reveal
more than was already known about Herod's buildings at
the site, but it had a greater significance than that for the
state of Israel. At the time the state had not been in existence
for long and Masada provided a focal point for a sense of
national identity because of its slightly later history.

It had been the site of a last stand by Jewish opponents
to Roman rule at the end of the First Jewish Revolt, which
had been recorded by the historian Josephus. By AD 73 the
Revolt, which had begun six years before, was almost over.
Jerusalem had been sacked in AD 67 and the fortress of
Masada became the last remaining Jewish stronghold. There
were 967 defenders, women and children as well as men,
and they were initially able to withstand the attempts to take
the rock made by the Roman Army's Tenth Legion. The
Romans encircled Masada with a series of small forts
connected by a wall, thus preventing both the delivery of
supplies to the fortress and the possibility of a break-out by
its defenders. The remains of these can still be seen; there

*Opposite: The view of the surrounding country as seen from the
ruins of Herod's palace at Masada. The height of the plateau was
one of Masada's major assets; huge artificial water cisterns ensured
supplies, initially for Herod's palace and gardens and then for the
defenders during the Roman army's siege.*

Right: Ruins on the plateau of Masada.

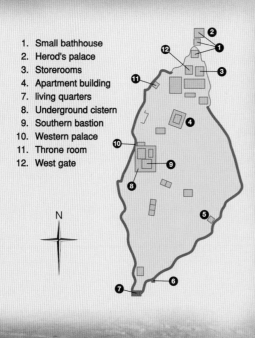

1. Small bathhouse
2. Herod's palace
3. Storerooms
4. Apartment building
7. living quarters
8. Underground cistern
9. Southern bastion
10. Western palace
11. Throne room
12. West gate

were a total of eight siege forts and the wall was over nearly 2 miles long, a measure of how seriously the Roman Empire took this small group of Jewish militants. The daunting logistics involved were also a sign of the empire's desire to quash any serious resistance in areas under its control. In the end the Romans built a huge siege ramp up to the fortress as any other form of direct assault was impossible; this immense earthwork remains today and still affords the easiest access. Masada fell to the Romans and, according to Josephus, the surviving defenders committed suicide rather than live and become captives and slaves of Rome. The theme of resistance to overwhelming odds had a resonance for the Jewish community both in Israel and elsewhere, especially at the time of the dig.

THE 1963—5 EXCAVATIONS

The 1963—5 excavations found plenty of evidence from this phase of Masada's occupation, quite apart from all the Roman remains on the flat land surrounding the rock. There were two ritual baths on the plateau and a synagogue, beneath the floor of which were two religious scrolls. These had been buried just before the fall of Masada, and their situation was reminiscent of the hiding of the Dead Sea Scrolls, which had probably been taken from Qumran to their hiding places at about the same date.

An especially intriguing find was that of 11 pieces of pottery which had personal names on them. These inscriptions could, of course, simply have recorded the ownership of the vessels and there is no archaeological indication that they might represent anything else. However, Josephus gives a detailed account of the last stand and the suicide of the defenders, stating that the men killed their families, that ten of the surviving men were then selected—by lot—to kill the rest of the garrison, and that one man was chosen, also by lot, to kill the others before killing himself. Inevitably, there have been suggestions that these pottery sherds are a relic of the terrible ending of the First Jewish Revolt. While some interpretations of the excavations at Masada support the account of the last days given by Josephus, others do not —and the site is still controversial.

Left: Masada, with the mountains behind it. The Romans' great siege ramp was built toward the northern end of the plateau, on the same side as the mountains.

Above: A plan of the settlement at Masada.

Africa

Olduvai Gorge

Olduvai Gorge in Tanzania is a part of the Great Rift Valley in East Africa. It is a canyon 30 miles long and up to 300 feet deep, and the geological conditions which prevail there are ideal for the preservation of ancient remains. It is now one of the best-known archaeological sites in the world and has become a major African tourist attraction, all because of a chance discovery in 1959.

Mary and Louis Leakey had been working in Olduvai for some time, having worked their way down the rift valley from Kenya where they had made several important finds connected to early hominid activity. They had also found plenty of early stone tools and animal bones at Olduvai but, as in Kenya, physical remains—human fossils—had eluded them.

On July 17, 1959, Mary set off to explore a part of the gorge which had been affected by erosion after the rains earlier in the year. She was alone, except for two dogs, as Louis was in bed with flu. When she reached the place she intended to survey she noticed "plenty of material" lying on the surface: stone artifacts and animal bones. Then, sticking out of the side, she spotted something else. It looked suspiciously like a hominid bone, part of the mastoid process, the bony projection below the ear. It was, however, very thick and solid. She investigated further, gently brushing some earth away, and saw two large teeth still in place; they were definitely hominid. She rushed back to camp to tell Louis what she had found, and he immediately went to investigate despite his illness.

Over 400 fragments of bone were eventually recovered, and Mary was able to reconstruct the skull she had found. It proved to be that of an australopithecine, a heavily built adult, and the lava layers between which the fossils were found could be dated. The bones proved to be an astonishing 1.79 million years old. Hominids had been living in East Africa, by a lake in Olduvai Gorge, much longer than anyone thought possible.

This completely shattered the views then current that humankind was of East Asian or even European origin, and the pace of investigation increased all over the world. Even though many other, older, discoveries have been made since then, at Olduvai and elsewhere—and though each one is potentially capable of altering our understanding of our past—Olduvai remains important. Africa is still the only continent on which the very oldest hominid fossils have been found.

WHAT ARE AUSTRALOPITHECINES?

The information which makes up the human family tree is both patchy and changing as new discoveries are made and argued about. Australopithecines, however, do not appear to have been our direct ancestors. They did walk on two legs, though they had relatively small brains. The two sexes seem to have been quite different in size, with males up to 4 feet 7 inches tall and females nearly four feet (47 inches is the tallest

so far). Studies of primate behavior have been used to suggest how australopithecines might have behaved, and it seems safe to suggest that they would have eaten a variety of foodstuffs. Some archaeologists believe that they had the ability to make simple tools out of stones—the oldest tools date to before the earliest currently known remains of our own genus, Homo—but there is no evidence that they used fire, buried their dead, or constructed shelters. There may, however, have been some form of vocal communication—though what form that might have taken remains a matter of conjectures

Opposite: Olduvai Gorge in northern Tanzania is part of the Great Rift Valley. The geological conditions are perfect for preservation, and some of the most important archaeological finds in the world have come from here.

Below: An australopithecine skull, dating to between 3 and 1 million years ago. The ridge on top of the skull is quite marked.

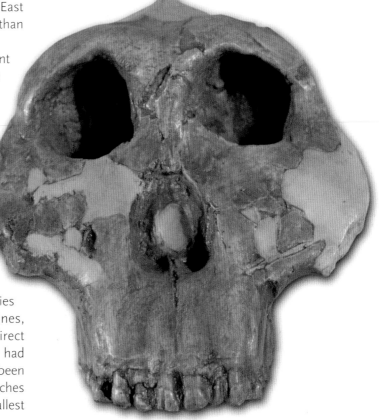

The Pyramids

There is no doubt that the pyramids of Egypt form one of the most powerful examples of the ingenuity, skills and expertise of people who lived a very long time ago, and they have been objects of awe for thousands of years.

From the reign of the Third-Dynasty King Djoser in the middle of the third millennium BC until the end of the Old Kingdom hundreds of years later, all Egyptian rulers were interred in huge stone structures. These were mostly situated on the western side of the Nile valley and within reach of the city of Memphis, near modern Cairo. Almost nothing survives of Memphis as its abandoned buildings were used as a quarry for Cairo, but the pyramids are a testament to the importance of the city.

SAQQARA

Saqqara has been described as the main cemetery for Memphis, and it was there that King Djoser built his step-shaped pyramid, the oldest stone building in the world, which inaugurated the practice of royal pyramid-building. Djoser's pyramid is in six steps and contained something like 430,500 cubic yards of clay and stone; it is nearly 200 feet high. During its construction there were evidently changes of plan, and it shows that the builders possessed great technical skill. The body of the king was interred in a chamber under the pyramid, actually below ground level, and a network of rooms and tunnels were created. There is a complex of buildings still associated with it, such as a temple for regular offerings to the king's spirit or ka. The buildings and the pyramid are surrounded by an enclosure and there is a unique feature to this: a sed festival court. After thirty years the king had to perform a ritualized race during his sed festival to demonstrate that he was still fit and energetic enough to rule, and there are reliefs showing Djoser doing just that, running between two markers. The whole construction is a testament not just to the undoubted skill and ability of the architect—his name appears to

Opposite: The step pyramid of King Djoser at Saqqara. The stepped stages might have represented a stairway to be used for reaching heaven, something described in texts found in the nearby pyramid of King Unas.

Above: The Bent Pyramid at Dashur gets its name from the change in angle half way up. It was built by the first king of the Fourth Dynasty, Snefru, the father of Khufu who constructed the Great Pyramid at Giza. It is thought that the changes were made because subsidence had become a problem; the pyramid was, however, finished and still retains much of its limestone casing.

Below: The pyramids of Niuserre and Neferikare at Abu Sir.

have been Imhotep—and the workers, but also to the economic and organizational power of the Egyptian state, even in this very early phase.

There are other pyramids at Saqqara, and surrounding them are other tombs, those of nobles. Though these may well have been constructed at the same time as the pyramids with which they were associated, they would not have been used until such time as their owners died. These tombs were beautifully decorated with scenes in painted relief, and one of the most notable is that of Nefer. Some of the carvings show scenes of everyday life: vegetables being planted, ships sailing on the Nile, papyrus being cut and harvested. One of the oldest mummies yet found was discovered in Nefer's tomb in the 1940s; a pit had been cut into the floor of the tomb to contain the mummified body. This may have been that of Nefer himself though it could also be someone called Waty, who seems to have been a friend. Even though the process of mummification was

Below: Excavations by an American team at Giza. Archaeological digs there in the 1920s discovered the remains of Queen Hetepheres' funerary equipment, and in 1954 the Egyptian archaeologist Kamal el-Mallakh found the remains of one of King Khufu's funerary boats close to the Great Pyramid.

not completely mastered at this stage, some 4500 years ago, the body was almost intact.

GIZA

Giza is home to the most famous of the pyramids, built by rulers of the 4th Dynasty. King Snefru (2575–2551 BC) had built his elsewhere, but his son Khufu (Cheops), grandson Khafre, and great-grandson Menkaure built theirs together at Giza, creating a remarkable monument which became one of the wonders of the ancient world.

Khufu's pyramid, known as the Great Pyramid, is the largest of the three. It has been stripped of the limestone casing that once covered it, and would originally have been about 9 feet taller than it is today, about 450 feet. It has been calculated that nearly 2.5 million blocks went into its construction, and these had an average weight of 2.3 tons. There are at least three chambers inside, plus corridors and two "ventilation" shafts which probably had a ritual rather than purely practical use.

In May 1954 the Egyptian archaeologist Kamal el-Mallakh was carrying out clearance work to one side of the Great Pyramid when his workmen found a pit covered by immense limestone blocks. The pit itself turned out to be 100 feet long, 16 feet deep and

contained an extraordinary survivor—a dismantled boat in more than 1000 pieces which had been made in cedar. It was carefully studied and researched, and when it was reassembled it was found to be 140 feet long. There are another four pits around the pyramid, three empty and one still sealed, and it is presumed that these also contained (and the sealed one may still contain) similar boats. The reconstructed boat did seem to have been used, and may have been the means of bringing the king's funeral cortege across the river to his pyramid.

Most pyramids have been thoroughly emptied of their contents by tomb robbers, and Khufu's is no exception. However, in 1925 an American expedition led by George Reisner was exploring the area around the base and discovered a shaft grave, consisting of a vertical shaft 100 feet deep leading into a chamber. This contained the funerary equipment of Hetepheres, Khufu's mother, and included a beautifully made sedan chair in gilded wood, a bed, two chairs decorated with carvings of papyrus, and a leather case for walking sticks. There was a sarcophagus in the shaft but it had been empty, and though an alabaster container was found to have contained the queen's internal organs—removed during mummification—there was no other trace of her body. It may be that her tomb had been robbed in

antiquity, a theory possibly borne out by the damage sustained to some of the furniture.

Khafre's pyramid is the most complete and appears bigger than Khufu's because it was built on slightly higher ground. The funerary complex associated with it is particularly impressive—it includes the Sphinx—and his valley temple, built of reddish granite from Aswan on a quay at the edge of the Nile valley, is quite distinctive. Menkaure's pyramid is much smaller—about half the size of those of his father and grandfather—and it has been suggested that constructing the two enormous ones may have put too much strain on the country's resources.

How Were the Pyramids Built?

There is no doubt that building the pyramids would have been an intensive and expensive process. The Greek historian Herodotus, writing many centuries later, said that slave labor had been used, but that is now thought unlikely. It is more probable that work was confined to the inundation period of the year, the three months or so when the flooding waters of the Nile made it impossible for people to work on the land.

The site had to be carefully chosen. It had to be on the west side of the river, associated with the dead and

the underworld. It had to be high enough to avoid any danger from the Nile's regular floods, though it also had to be close enough to the river because that was how some of the stone would arrive at the site. It also had to be solid ground, so solid that it could take the immense weight without subsiding at all. Once the location had been determined, the base would have to be leveled off accurately after the alignment had been determined. Each side had to face one of the main compass points, and it is probable that north was established by taking a reading on a specific star. The base, of course, had to be perfectly square. Then construction work could begin.

The precise method by which pyramids were raised is actually not known, and there has been some contention about potential methods. Herodotus stated that levers were used to raise the blocks from one level to the next and ramps have also been suggested. These could have run straight out from the pyramid under construction, though that seems unlikely as such a ramp would have had to become enormous to allow blocks to be hauled

up to the very top, and no trace of such a structure has been found. Another possibility is that a ramp wound around the sides, rising with the layers, and that it was dismantled as construction work was finished.

THE SPHINX

Part of Khafre's funerary complex, the Sphinx is the earliest of Egypt's many colossal statues. It seems to have been wearing a uraeus, the representation of a rearing cobra that kings wore on the forehead as part of the royal headdress, so it is probable that it represents Khafre himself. It was carved from a natural limestone outcrop next to the king's valley temple, and the head is formed of much better quality stone than the body, which is softer and has been badly eroded. About a thousand years after Khafre's death the 18th Dynasty ruler Tuthmosis IV restored the Sphinx and added the carved stone which stands between its paws. Made from

part of the mortuary temple, it records a dream in which Tuthmosis was promised the throne if he repaired the body of the Sphinx and cleared the sand away.

Opposite above: A step pyramid which is situated in the desert outside Cairo. The pyramids at Giza are famous all over the world but there are over 100 pyramids in Egypt.

Opposite below: The three main pyramids at Giza. Khafre's is in the middle, with some of the facing stone still present at the top, while those of his father Khufu and son Menkaure lie to either side. Menkaure's is much smaller, and it has been suggested that this may be because of the investment—in time, labor, and resources—devoted to the other two. It may also have been down to a change in religious emphasis.

Below: The Sphinx forms part of the funerary monuments connected to Khafre's pyramid at Giza.

Amarna

In the middle of the New Kingdom, religious authority—the most profound power in the Egyptian state—was challenged by the king, Akhenaten, who ruled between 1353 and 1335 BC. He created a religious revolution, replacing the whole pantheon of Egyptian gods with one god, Aten, the divine solar disk. A temple to Aten was constructed at Thebes, in the temple complex at Karnak, but it was torn down after Akhenaten's death when his successors reverted to the old religion, and determined efforts were made to remove any trace of both him and his cult from the records. Thebes was, after all, the center for the worship of Amun.

Akhenaten moved the capital of Egypt away from Thebes and established a new city at Amarna many miles to the north in Middle Egypt. Known as Akhetaten, the city was occupied for only twenty years, being abandoned after Akhenaten's death. It was rediscovered in the nineteenth century and has been the subject of serious archaeological investigations since the 1890s. Never substantially built over, it is almost the only Egyptian city to have been so intensively studied.

Amarna has provided a picture of ordered urban life. The population has been estimated at between 20,000 and 50,000, and research has shown that the surrounding area could easily have supported a city of some 45,000 people. There is a gradual variation in house sizes—there are no major gaps, like an absence of medium-sized houses, for example—indicating a society with a smooth gradation between rich and poor, rather than one with sharp differences. There was one, however: between the royal family and the people; that difference remained. Many things have been found at Amarna, from details of everyday life (judging by the heaps of domestic refuse, rubbish must have been a problem) to a great artistic treasure and invaluable archives.

THE WORKSHOP OF THUTMOSE

The German archaeologist Ludwig Borchart dug at Amarna from 1908 to 1914. He concentrated on the south of the city, mainly on the large private houses in that area. In 1912 he was working on a house that seemed to have belonged to the royal sculptor Thutmose—other sculptors had also lived and had their workshops in the district—where he found a variety of unfinished and trial pieces. Among them was what has since become one of the most famous items of Egyptian art, an astonishingly realistic, and rather modern, portrait bust of Akhenaten's wife Nefertiti. It is made of limestone, painted realistically, and stands almost 20 inches tall. It is now in a museum in Berlin.

Nothing like this had been found before; the realism is untypical of Egyptian art, flying against all the conventions which governed artistic expression. This is true of much of the art from the Amarna period, as the time of Akhenaten's rule is known. Even more unconventional was the way in which Akhenaten had himself and his family shown in other pieces. Ancient Egyptian artists usually depicted the body according to a strict set of rules; pharaohs, particularly, were shown as perfect physical specimens, young and fit. Akhenaten, on the other hand, is shown with what may be more realism—he has a long face with full lips, an extremely

Opposite: This relief of Akhenaten, his wife Nefertiti worshiping the aten. The sun shines down on the royal couple, its rays depicted as lines ending in a hand of blessing.

Left: Akhenaten's distinctive features make statues of him easy to identify. Shown in a manner which may have reflected reality, his portrayal is a complete contrast to the standards of Egyptian art and emphasizes the radical changes of his reign.

long neck, and an oddly shaped body with a marked paunch. He and his family were also depicted in scenes which were much more informal than was previously the norm—these were unthinkable before his reign, and were not seen again after his death.

THE AMARNA LETTERS

Amarna wasn't just the center for the new religion, but was also the new administrative capital of Egypt. Akhenaten's political relationships were not only confined to areas under direct Egyptian control, but extended outside the Egyptian empire to the other great powers of the Late Bronze Age. A remarkable discovery, made by some of the local people in 1887, has thrown unexpected light on this. The villagers were digging at Amarna, possibly for decayed mud bricks which could be used as fertilizer, when they came upon a cache of small clay tablets. They were inscribed with an unfamiliar script and were not particularly well received by the dealers in antiquities to whom they were taken; in fact some of them, probably as many as 150, were thrown away.

Archaeologists, however, had the opposite reaction. The people had evidently stumbled on the remains of the "House of the Letters of Pharaoh," the royal archives, and the clay tablets were diplomatic records, foreign correspondence. More have turned up since, usually in excavations. At the time, Akkadian was the lingua franca, rather like English is today, and most of the tablets were written in that language using a cuneiform script. The tablets throw a valuable and rare light on the relationships Egypt had with its neighbors,

and on the relationships these peoples had with each other. Without the Amarna letters, for example, the interactions between the small city states of Canaan would be unknown.

One of the major subjects discussed in the letters is the exchange of gifts between rulers, and it is obvious that a huge quantity of luxury goods, really precious items, must have been in circulation. Only a minority of these have since surfaced in the archaeological record. Letters like these came from rulers of equal standing: the kings of the Hittite empire, Assyria, Babylonia. The wealthiest ruler was the king of Egypt and the letters often ask directly for gifts. However, the majority of the letters are from rulers in the Levant who owed formal allegiance to the pharaoh. They were expected to send tribute to Egypt, useful things like good-looking girls and glass, and to quarter Egyptian troops in their territories. Such a window into the past is a rare discovery.

Left: Three of the Amarna letters, clay tablets sent to Akhenaten by Rib-Addi of Byblos. He was hoping to gain Egyptian support against his enemies.

The Rosetta Stone

The discovery of the Rosetta Stone was a direct consequence of the struggle between Napoleon and Britain. Napoleon's invasion of Egypt in 1798, and its continuing occupation, was challenged by Nelson's navy in the Mediterranean. Egyptian ports were strengthened and a large slab of black basalt was uncovered during work at Rashid (called Rosetta by the Europeans). The discovery itself wasn't particularly strange; what was unusual was that the slab was covered in writing, in three separate scripts. Like many other things, the stone eventually became a prize of war and was sent to Britain, arriving in Portsmouth in 1802. It was dispatched to the British Museum in London, where it can still be seen.

The three texts were in Egyptian hieroglyphics, a cursive version of the heiroglyphic script known as Demotic, and Greek. Of these, only the Greek could be understood, but that meant that the Rosetta Stone could be used as a key to deciphering the other two. There had been several previous attempts at breaking the code of hieroglyphics, but the breakthrough finally came due to a combination of the Rosetta Stone and the brilliant French scholar Jean François Champollion, who was to die aged only 42 in 1832. It had already been proposed that the names of kings and queens were probably the symbols that appeared inside cartouches (oval rings) and Champollion was able to use these royal names as the start. From interpreting those symbols he was able to gradually decipher the rest of the inscription, working on the basis that the Egyptian language had been written in a combination of both ideographic and phonetic script. He and his successors were then able to compare their translations of hieroglyphics, both those and others, with equivalents in Coptic, the modern descendant of the Ancient Egyptian language. Other texts are more informative and interesting; others were also useful for deciphering the language; but the Rosetta Stone remains central because of the role it played in increasing our understanding.

Opposite above: The painted limestone bust of Nefertiti, Akhenaten's queen, which is one of the masterpieces of Egyptian art. It was found at Amarna in 1912 by a German expedition in what appears to have been the studio of Thutmose, the royal sculptor.

Left: The Rosetta Stone, clearly showing the three scripts: hieroglyphics at the top, Demotic in the middle, and Greek at the bottom.

Tutankhamun and the Valley of the Kings

The finding of the tomb of Tutankhamun, one of the most magnificent discoveries in archaeology, was no accident but the result of hard work and systematic searching.

CARTER'S LAST CHANCE

Howard Carter, a British archaeologist, had long felt that Tutankhamun's tomb lay in the Valley of the Kings, somewhere near that of Rameses VI in a relatively small triangle of ground which appeared to be the only remaining possibility. Tutankhamun had been a relatively unimportant pharaoh, reigning only ten years and dying young, but his resting place had never been found. With financial support and help from Lord Carnarvon, with whom he had worked since 1907, he began excavating in the valley in 1917. By 1921–2, however, nothing had been found and Carnarvon wanted to call off the search. Carter persuaded him to back one last attempt, and began what should have been his final season there on November 1, 1922. He decided to look again at some work that had been done in the first season which had only revealed the foundations of a few workmen's huts—and three days later his diggers discovered the first of a series of rock-cut steps.

These were eventually cleared down to the

level of a door, which Carter's workmen partly exposed; it was closed, sealed, and marked with the symbols of the royal necropolis. Carter did not go straight ahead as Carnarvon, his partner and backer, was back in Britain: he was contacted immediately and arrived just over two weeks later. The door was finally cleared and the excavators passed into the passage behind. This had been completely filled with rubble. Both the door and the passage showed signs of having been resealed and refilled, and a few broken items were found as the infill was cleared: there had obviously been some plundering. On November 26 Carter and Carnarvon reached a second sealed doorway, again with seals recognizable as those of the both the royal necropolis and Tutankhamun. And again it looked as though the door had been sealed and resealed. Carter made a tiny breach in the door, tested the hole with a rod and found a void behind, then checked for bad air with a candle flame; it was fine. He widened the hole, inserted the candle, and peered in. In his own words: "At first I could see nothing... but presently, as my eyes grew accustomed to the light, details of the room within emerged slowly from the mist, strange animals, statues, and everywhere the glint of gold." He was so stunned that he couldn't speak, and Carnarvon had to ask if he could see anything. "Yes," Carter replied, "wonderful things."

Opposite: Tutankhamun and his wife Ankhesenamun, from a small gilded shrine, which was found still standing on its silver-covered sled in the antechamber.

Above: The goddess Nekhbet was represented by the vulture; she was the goddess of Upper Egypt.

Right: The solid part of an ostrich feather fan from the tomb; the feathers themselves have long since disappeared.

WONDERFUL THINGS

Though tomb robbers may have entered the tomb, they had evidently removed little, or had left so much behind that their depredations made little difference. Carter and Carnarvon were looking into an antechamber which has been described very accurately as "looking like an exotic Ancient Egyptian junk shop." Though the tomb was comparatively small, it was packed with all sorts of things: items of furniture like beds, chests, and couches, two life-size statues of the king guarding another door, even a dismantled chariot.

Carter began to excavate the tomb systematically, taking his time as it was so full of treasures. The time when Tutankhamun ruled, toward the end of the 18th

Dynasty just after the rule of Akhenaten, was a "golden age" for Egyptian workmanship. Not only had the craftsmen and artists developed their skills and range of expertise, they also had access to an enormous range of high-quality materials. Some came from the lands forming the Egyptian empire and some from farther away like Afghanistan and equatorial Africa. The range of goods the tomb contained reflected this; most were exquisite. There were thrones, a beautiful golden shrine guarded by four goddesses (called a canopic chest, this would have held the jars containing the king's internal organs, removed during mummification), weapons, musical instruments, wine and food ... everything Tutankhamun would need in the afterlife, including a wide range of beautiful jewelry.

One of the biggest surprises came from the burial chamber itself, but Carnarvon was not there to see it as he had died in April 1923. When the door to this was opened, Carter was confronted by a wall of gold. It was part of the outermost one of four shrines, nested within one another, which surrounded the sarcophagus. Within that was the coffin—or, rather, were the coffins: there were three, again nested in each other like a giant Russian doll. The lid of the first one was lifted in 1925, revealing the second coffin, also of gilded wood with details picked out in faience, lapis lazuli, and obsidian. The third coffin was of solid gold, approximately 1 inch thick. It was partly covered with a layer of hardened unguents, and Carter had to use a careful combination of hammers, solvents, and heat to free it. When it was eventually lifted there was another surprise: the king's mummy had been fitted with a magnificent and beautiful mask covering his head and shoulders.

The splendor of the tomb is overwhelming, and yet this was a small tomb of a minor ruler. The wealth that would have been contained in a larger tomb, one for someone who had ruled for longer like Tutankhamun and Akhenaten's predecessor Amenhotep III, or the powerful Rameses II, is almost unimaginable. However, their tombs did not survive intact; Tutankhamun's did, largely, and the quality of the items found within it is of the highest order.

WHO WAS TUTANKHAMUN?

The unguents that had been poured over Tutankhamun's gold coffin, and which had made it hard to remove, had damaged his body badly. Even though it was undisturbed, it had been

Howard Carter and Lord Carnarvon

By the time he discovered the tomb of Tutankhamun in 1922, the British archaeologist Howard Carter had already spent many years working on sites in Egypt. Born in 1873, he arrived in the country in 1891 and began training under Flinders Petrie, a great Egyptologist, and received a thorough grounding in excavation methods. He worked on digs for the Egypt Exploration Fund and eventually joined the Egyptian government's Antiquities Service as a chief inspector. Carter resigned in 1905—he could be prickly, especially with people he regarded as fools, and had apparently had a dispute with some tourists—and earned a precarious living as a freelancer. His partnership with George Herbert, Lord Carnarvon began in 1907.

Carnarvon was wealthy, wintering in Egypt for the sake of his health, and was a keen amateur Egyptologist. He needed Carter's professional help with his excavations and they began working together, discovering a series of tombs of noblemen on the west bank of the Nile opposite Thebes until the First World War. Carnarvon was granted a permit to dig in the Valley of the Kings in 1917; Carter was convinced that the lost tomb of Tutankhamun could be found, and five years later they made their major discovery.

Work continued at the tomb until 1928, overshadowed by Carnarvon's death from pneumonia following a septic mosquito bite in April 1923. Carter himself died in 1939, having become one of the most famous archaeologists in the world.

Below: Howard Carter supervising carpenters preparing to re-seal Tutankhamun's tomb.

Opposite: The gold mask from Tutankhamun's mummy, one of the most famous archaeological finds in the world. It is inlaid with lapis lazuli, carnelian, turquoise and glass paste, and weighs about 24 pounds.

reduced to little more than "bone and ashes" as a result. No examination of the body has been able to determine a definite cause of death, but it could establish his age: Tutankhamun had been only 18 or 19 when he died.

He had been born in Amarna, Akhenaten's capital city, and his original name of Tutankhaten reflected Akhenaten's new, heretical religion. His precise parentage is unknown; Akhenaten could have been his half-brother or even his father. Some people see a likeness between Tutankhamun's face and that shown on Akhenaten's statues, but tests are not possible as Akhenaten's mummy has not been found. A mysterious tomb had been found in 1907, containing a mummy which was originally thought to be that of Akhenaten but which is now believed to probably be that of his relative and sometime co-ruler Smenkhare. There are strong physical similarities between that mummy and Tutankhamun's, however, so there may be a familial link.

Whatever his parentage, he was to be Akhenaten's successor as pharaoh following the death of Smenkhare and came to the throne as a child of under 10. He was 'protected' by a group of powerful officials, notably Ay and Horemheb who were, successively, to rule Egypt after his death. With Tutankhamun's accession to the

throne, Egypt was returned to the old religion and the capital moved back to Thebes.

Tutankhamun was married to Ankhesenamun, one of Akhenaten's daughters, who appears regularly on objects from the tomb, often sharing in her husband's leisure activities. One of the most pathetic finds recovered by Carter was a simple wooden box. It contained two small wooden coffins, and inside each was the small body of a still-born girl. One was of seven months' gestation, the other of five, and an attempt had been made at embalming the older one. She, at least, may have suffered from a congenital condition, Sprengel's deformity, which is characterized by spina bifida and scoliosis. There is no clue to their identity, but they are likely to have been Tutankhamun and Ankhesenamun's premature daughters.

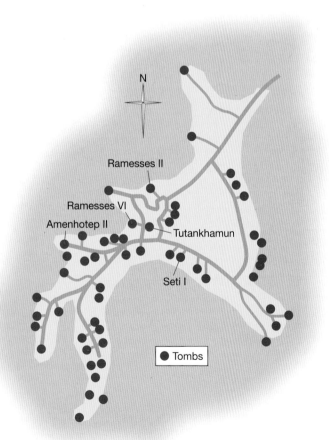

Left: A plan of the Valley of the Kings.

Above: The relatively remote location of the Valley of the Kings, well away from inhabited areas in the time of the New Kingdom when it was established, may well have been intended to provide some protection for the tombs located within it, but it may have had other, symbolic advantages.

THE VALLEY OF THE KINGS

Throughout the time of the New Kingdom, except for the reign of Akhenaten, Thebes was an important center for both the state religion and the state administration. Rulers were based there, and the precipitous Valley of the Kings on the western side of the Nile became an obvious place for them to be buried. Most of the royal tombs were constructed in the eastern valley, though there are a few in the remoter western part. One of the reasons that made the site so attractive may have been its distance from the settlements by the river, which might have been hoped to deter tomb robbers. However, all the tombs—except for that of Tutankhamun, which had been raided and resealed—were looted in antiquity.

The tombs basically follow the same layout, though they become more complicated over time. Steps lead to a series of descending corridors, then to an antechamber and a burial chamber; attempts were always made to hide the entrances. Inside they were beautifully decorated. Amenhotep II's burial chamber is painted with a blue and gold starry ceiling and the decoration is at its most complete in that of Seti I.

Below: Anubis, the god of embalming, tending a mummy. The people who oversaw the preparation of a body for the afterlife had priestly titles and followed rituals going back to the days of the Old Kingdom; eviscerating the corpse and wrapping it would have been done by more menial employees. This fresco comes from the tomb of Sennedjem at Deir el-Medina, the craftsmen's village relatively close to the Valley of the Kings. It housed the most talented craftspeople in Egypt from the 18th to the 20th Dynasties.

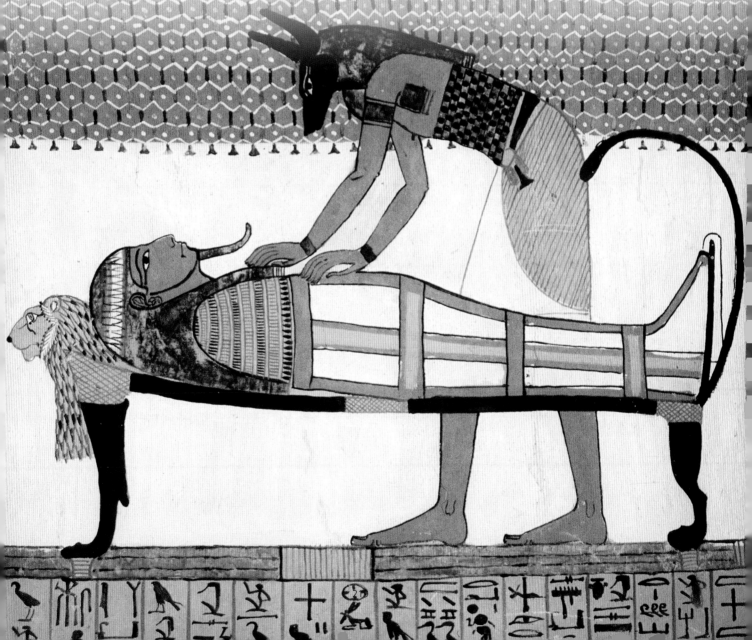

It sometimes seems as though there can be little still to be discovered in the Valley of the Kings, but some work continues. A cache of royal mummies was found at Deir el-Bahri, and more were discovered in a side chamber in the tomb of Amenhotep II. Like the ones from Deir el-Bahri, they had been collected together and seem to have been rewrapped, presumably after their original burials had been disturbed by thieves. The mummies of some rulers, however, are still missing; they include Tuthmosis I, Hatshepsut, Akhenaten, and Tutankhamun's successors Ay and Horemheb. There may be a third cache.

KV5

Close to the tomb of Tutankhamun and opposite that of Rameses II, the American archaeologist Kent Weeks has been working in a tomb known as KV5 (Kings' Valley 5). It was originally found in 1825, but had not been thoroughly explored. Howard Carter investigated it again in 1902 but only briefly; he reburied the entrance thinking the tomb had little importance. Weeks, the director of the Theban Mapping Project, relocated it in 1985–6.

The first part was damaged by, among other things, a broken sewer and pressure from tourist coaches, but despite this the tomb is proving to be valuable and surprising. There was a royal cartouche, that of Rameses II, above the door and it is possible it may be the resting place of Rameses' sons, many of whom predeceased him (he was about 90 when he died). This seems likely as damaged reliefs show Rameses leading his sons into the presence of funerary deities. Children of pharaohs could be buried in the Valley of the Kings, as could queens, though they were more often interred in their own valley, the nearby Valley of the Queens. It quickly became clear that the tomb Weeks was investigating was enormous—the whole complex structure may contain more than 150 chambers and corridors, and most of these have not yet been cleared. The first human remains turned up in 1997, and it will be interesting to see how much more is found in this major excavation.

Left: The tombs were not only decorated with pictures of the gods. We can learn much about everyday life from studying the paintings. This shows a scene of a harvest offering.

The Temples of Egypt

Religion was central to the stability of Ancient Egypt and there were a vast number of gods and goddesses. Some, such as Amun, the king of the gods; Osiris, the god of the dead and the afterlife; and Hathor, the mother, goddess of love and the sky (among other things), had larger roles and greater importance than other, more specific deities like Tayet, the goddess of weaving. The key to prosperity was the relationship with the gods, and specifically the relationship between the pharaoh and the gods. As absolute monarchs, the kings of Egypt formed a link between humanity and the gods, and they derived their power directly from them. It was the duty of a king to both build temples and make sure that offerings were made in them.

There were two basic kinds of temple: those dedicated to particular gods, and mortuary temples where ceremonies connected to a deceased ruler would be performed. Usually the only people permitted to enter a temple were the priests and the ruler; ordinary mortals were only allowed into outer areas, and then only for significant festivals. Most of the temples which still stand today were built during the New Kingdom, between about 1540 and 1075 BC. Older structures would be covered by newer ones as kings fulfilled their duty to construct temples and some, especially those close to centers like Cairo, were later used for building stone after being abandoned.

KARNAK AND LUXOR

The great temple complex at Karnak and the temple at Luxor are nearly two miles apart on the east bank of the Nile. Thebes, where they were built, was the most important city in Upper Egypt, and effectively the capital of the whole country for most of the New Kingdom, and the two temples were linked by an avenue of sphinxes.

Karnak's main sanctuary is dedicated to the worship of Amun, who became nationally important in the New Kingdom, though he started as a purely local god. Successive kings contributed to the complex of temples and the overall picture can be as hard to understand as it is undoubtedly impressive. Originally a canal connected the temples to the Nile, and there was a small landing stage near the entrance. One interesting survival is a mud-brick ramp at the back of the First Pylon which was probably built by one of the later kings, Nectanebo I, who ruled in the fourth century BC. This ramp gives an

Opposite: The gods and goddesses of Ancient Egypt could be shown in a variety of forms. At Karnak, for example, the god Amun often appears as a sphinx with a ram's head. The temples of Karnak and Luxor, which lies south, were linked by a processional route lined with sphinxes.

Right: The Hypostyle Hall of the great temple of Amun at Karnak, which was built by the 19th Dynasty ruler Seti I (c. 1290–1979 BC). The immense columns would have supported a roof, with a little light filtering down through clerestory windows.

Below: Karnak, reflected in the water of the sacred lake of the complex. This symbolized the primordial water and would have been used by the priests for ritual ablutions.

insight into the way the pylon was constructed, and was presumably supposed to be removed after the monument was complete.

Luxor was also dedicated to Amun, as well as to his wife and son, Mut and Khonsu. It was essentially designed as a focus for an annual festival in which images of the gods were taken between there and Karnak, and there are reliefs depicting this procession. The temple was cleared in the nineteenth century, by which time a village and a mosque had been built on top of the debris; the mosque survives but the village was moved.

ABU SIMBEL

One of the most famous rescues in archaeology came in the 1960s with the rescue of certain temples threatened by the construction of the Aswan High Dam. The lake behind it, now known as Lake Nasser, would have drowned many monuments in Lower Nubia had extreme measures not been taken. UNESCO responded to appeals from the Egyptian and Sudanese governments and 50 countries provided money or expertise, or both, in order to save many of the archaeological remains. Anything that could not be moved—like mud-brick fortresses—was carefully excavated and the results recorded in detail. The most daunting task was moving the great temples of Abu Simbel, built by one of the most powerful of the New Kingdom pharaohs, Rameses II.

There are two temples. The larger one is dedicated to Amun and other gods, including the deified Rameses, and the smaller to Hathor and Rameses' favorite wife

Nefertari. These had been cleared by the early explorer and Egyptologist Giovanni Belzoni in 1817; there was little to excite him—he was mainly looking for treasure or other things that could be transported to Europe—but the temples are spectacular in themselves. It was eventually decided to dismantle the temples carefully, separating them into carefully marked and sorted blocks, and reassemble them close to their original site but on much higher ground. The water of the lake was already rising as the work began and a protective coffer dam had to be constructed around the temples. The cuts were made as inconspicuously as they could be, and it is almost impossible to see where they were made today. The saving of these temples, which would otherwise have been completely lost beneath many feet of water, was a major success—and they were not the only ones that were relocated.

concept of maat, the correct order of things, and this may have been the reason why cartouches containing her name were erased. It looks as though she originally intended her tomb and her mortuary temple to have been linked by means of a passage starting near the entrance to her tomb in the Valley of the Kings. However, the builders struck bad rock and had to turn back, looping the passage round toward where they started.

A large number of royal mummies were found near Deir el-Bahri. The area also contains a lot of earlier shaft graves, dating to the Middle Kingdom. In 1881 Emile Brugsch, the assistant to the Director of Antiquities Gaston Maspero, was led to one of these by some of the local inhabitants who had been making an income from what they had found. Inside were forty royal mummies, including those of prominent pharaohs like Rameses II. They had been reburied here, secretly, during the 21st Dynasty, following the robbing of their actual tombs in the Valley of the Kings. The villagers had come across them in the 1870s, about ten years earlier.

Opposite: The interior of Nefertari's temple at Abu Simbel, emphasizing the darkness which would have been such a feature of most Egyptian temples.

Left: Hatshepsut's mortuary temple of Deir el-Bahri on the west side of the Nile. The Valley of the Kings lies behind the cliffs.

Below: Rameses II's temple at Abu Simbel, in its reconstructed position above Lake Nasser.

DEIR EL-BAHRI

Mortuary temples were necessary. The ka, the spirit of a person, was intimately tied to the physical body and required sustenance even after the individual had died. When it came to pharaohs, offerings for the owner's ka would be made every day in a splendid mortuary temple. Old Kingdom kings, interred in pyramids, had theirs close to the pyramid itself. In the New Kingdom, when rulers were buried in the Valley of the Kings opposite the city of Thebes, mortuary temples were separated from the tombs in the valley itself by steep cliffs. The temples were built at the foot of these cliffs, just beyond the cultivation limit.

One of the most remarkable is the female pharaoh Hatshepsut's temple at Deir el-Bahri. Hatshepsut must also have been remarkable: she ruled Egypt for 20 years, some of it jointly with her stepson Tuthmosis III. It used to be thought that he had removed her name from inscriptions after her death, and that he had probably removed her too, but it now seems more likely that their joint reign was successful. Her presence and prominence ran contrary to the Ancient Egyptian

Great Zimbabwe

Great Zimbabwe is one of the most powerful archaeological sites in the world. It has inspired myths and exotic stories about its origins, been used to bolster a wide variety of political views, and has also been an inspiration for many black Africans. A carved bird found there appears on the flag of the modern state of Zimbabwe, which took its name from the site when it achieved independence from the British in 1980.

Shona-speaking Zimbabweans use the word "zimbabwe" to identify the house and court belonging to a chief, which traditionally comprised a series of stone enclosures built on a hill. Great Zimbabwe is exceptional, both for its size and for its significance. Like many archaeological sites, it has been more widely known to the outside world since the 19th century, but its character and history have only recently come to be understood.

The site on which Great Zimbabwe was constructed, near Masvingo in modern Zimbabwe, was originally occupied by people who did not make use of stone between about AD 500 and 900; they were Early Iron Age farmers. The ancestors of the present-day Shona people arrived in the area and began construction about 1270 and the site flourished, becoming truly enormous, until about 1450. Great Zimbabwe

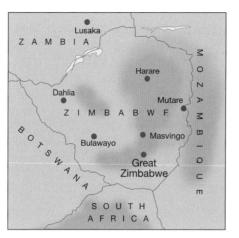

became the center of a Shona empire stretching from the northern parts of South Africa up to the River Zambesi, and running from what is now western Mozambique to eastern Botswana. The state was in contact with trading cities on the east African coast and ceramics from China and Persia, as well as a piece of southwest Asian glass, have been found in excavations. A coin minted in Kilwa in Tanzania was also recovered.

There were many natural advantages to the site of Great Zimbabwe which enabled it to grow into a city of—it has been estimated—about 18,000 people, controlling a large empire. One of the major ones came from its situation on the Zimbabwe plateau. This provided ideal conditions for cattle-farming as the plateau's height means that it is not infested by tsetse flies; cattle could also have grazed on lower areas nearby during the dry season. The climate was suitable for many crops, too,

such as beans, millet, sorghum and vegetables, and the plateau's natural resources included valuable materials—copper, iron, tin, and gold—as well as building stone from the granite outcrops. The soil was good, providing abundant grazing, and there was also water. An internal network seems to have been in operation, trading in copper, iron, salt, and other goods including soapstone and also gold and ivory. This would have brought Great Zimbabwe into contact with the coastal trading towns and thus have resulted in the import of glazed ceramics, glass beads, and fabrics including both cotton and silk. Cowrie shells have also been found. The coastal settlements and Great Zimbabwe both flourished at the same time, and also declined at the same time, suggesting that the link between them was strong. There would also have been trade in less exotic and unusual items, such as grain, foodstuffs, and cattle.

THE CITY

Great Zimbabwe's social organization was based on a clear hierarchy and the site essentially falls into three distinct areas reflecting this. The whole site is commanded by a large precipitous granite hill, one of two major areas with stone ruins; the other is on the opposite slope of the valley below. Between and around these areas was an extensive urban settlement which was made up of smaller buildings, huts constructed in clay, wood and thatch. This was where the ordinary people lived.

Opposite: The wall of the Great Enclosure, now believed to have been a pre-marriage initiation school. Substantial parts of the wall are still over 30 feet high.

Above: The ruins of the Great Enclosure include a conical tower about 27 feet high standing inside the main wall.

Left: A map showing the location of Great Zimbabwe.

Opposite: The approach to the Great Enclosure.

Above: The entrance stairs to the Hill Ruins, which included royal buildings as well as some which seem to have had a religious purpose. High officials would also have lived here; "commoners" lived in the area around this hill and the stone ruins in the valley.

The ruins on Zimbabwe Hill are a collection of stone-walled enclosures and have been collectively called the Hill Ruin, the Complex, or even the Acropolis. This is where the king, some members of the royal family and important state officials would have lived; it also housed buildings of ritual or religious significance.

The cluster of structures in the valley is dominated by the extraordinary Great Enclosure, the largest structure remaining at Great Zimbabwe. It has been estimated that the outer wall alone contains over 900,000 stone blocks. This beautifully built granite wall is 800 feet long, and up to 15 feet thick and over 30 feet high. It was evidently constructed in several stages and the top of one length of it is decorated by an open double chevron design which runs for over 275 feet. Within this enclosure there is a unique tower in the form of a upward-tapering cone made of solid dry-stone masonry. This is about 18 feet in diameter and over 30 feet high; it is thought to represent a grain bin, a likely symbol for one of the most important royal functions—keeping the people fed. There are also other enclosures within the main wall, as well as a series of platforms, and the Great Enclosure has recently been interpreted as a pre-marriage initiation school. Other buildings in the valley include grain storage bins and a complex thought to have been for the royal wives.

THE BIRDS OF GREAT ZIMBABWE

Many of the entrances to the ruined buildings at Great Zimbabwe have slots in them which would have held posts, maybe of wood but also of stone. Some of these posts have survived, and seven soapstone posts topped with carved birds were found up in the Hill Ruin, in the area of the palace. Their exact original location is unknown, but they may have stood in a religious center. In Shona tradition, birds carry messages to the ancestors, whose spirits are thought to fly freely—and the spirits of former kings are believed to be particularly concerned with problems facing society as a whole, rather than the individual concerns of their descendants. They could also intercede with God on behalf of the people and the birds found at Great Zimbabwe may well be symbols of royal ancestors, or represent messengers from them. An eighth bird was discovered in a small enclosure in the valley area, lying against a symbolic grain store. It is thought that this enclosure was originally a sanctuary, possibly near to an area where royal wives would have given birth, and the bird could well have had protective qualities. This bird is the one depicted on the Zimbabwean flag.

The birds are not accurate portraits of any particular species; in fact they combine avian and human characteristics. Most seem to have toes rather than claws or talons and the legs are more human- than bird-like; one even seems to have lips. They are about 12 inches tall and sit on top of posts about 3 feet high. Nothing like these birds has been found elsewhere.

DECLINE

The main structures in the two areas with stone ruins were clearly designed to impress, and impress they do. Not only are they deliberately monumental, they also imply the expenditure of a significant amount of resources in their construction, principally labor and time as well as wealth. However, Great Zimbabwe was eventually abandoned, and though it was briefly reoccupied it never attained the same scale and brilliance.

The simultaneous decline in the trading towns of the east African coast may signify a common cause, and there have been some suggestions that a drop in gold prices might have been responsible. Great Zimbabwe was also likely to have been vulnerable to environmental deterioration; such a high population would have placed heavy demands on a wide surrounding area, and that may also have been a factor. The Shona capital moved away to Khami in western Zimbabwe. Shona tradition remembered Great Zimbabwe, though, and other "zimbabwes" continued to be built as the underlying culture persisted in some places—but none were as imposing as Great Zimbabwe.

INTERPRETING GREAT ZIMBABWE

Romantic accounts of Great Zimbabwe spread in the latter half of the nineteenth century, when the ruins were linked to the Queen of Sheba. Similarly exotic theories of its beginnings still cling to the place despite archaeological investigations that have clearly and unequivocally established both the site's date and its undoubtedly local and African origin. Many of these theories have arisen from a belief in some quarters that such sophisticated constructions had to have been created by people from outside what was seen as "darkest Africa." Arabs or Phoenicians have been suggested as possible builders or designers, and some colonialists still adhere to the view that the city could not have been created by Africans without outside help or influence despite evidence to the contrary.

Since 1929—30 and the first serious archaeological excavations at Great Zimbabwe by Gertrude Caton-Thompson these "migratory" or "diffusionist" views have been shown to be false. She ended her 1931 report into the dig there by stating, quite clearly, that she had found nothing whatsoever to suggest that Great Zimbabwe was anything other than medieval in date and local in origin. Nor has anything been found by researchers since, and significant influence from other areas is just not part of Great Zimbabwe's development. It was a great achievement, and it is a sophisticated site—and it is also undoubtedly African.

Asia
and the Pacific

The Indus Valley Civilization

John Marshall was the director of the Archaeological Survey of India in the 1920s, and in 1924 he announced that traces of a "new" civilization had been discovered two years earlier in what was then north-west India and is now Pakistan. Strange seals had been found before then, engraved in an unknown script, but Marshall and his team were excavating cities. These, Mohenjo-daro and Harappa, were the first traces of a major Bronze Age civilization, dating to between 2600 and 1900 BC.

Now it is known that the "Indus Valley Civilization", as it is generally called, covered an enormous area. There were five major cities, as well as villages, towns, and smaller farming settlements. Mohenjo-daro, one of the main cities, is the most intensively explored and studied Indus Valley site.

MOHENJO-DARO

Recent work at the site of Mohenjo-daro has suggested that, overall, the city probably covered an extensive area—240,000 square yards—and about 10 percent of this has been excavated. The main area, the large citadel mound, was constructed on a platform and stands some 30 feet above the surrounding flood plain. It was enclosed by a wall, possibly to further protect it from flood waters. Most of the buildings at Mohenjo-daro, as at other Indus sites, were built using baked brick. There are other common factors, too, including the fact that standard units of measurement appear to have been in use across the region.

There were some prominent buildings in the citadel area of Mohenjo-daro, including one known as the Great Bath. This seems to have been an important feature and may have had a ritual purpose, perhaps being used for purification. The Bath itself measures about 32 feet by 23 feet and is approximately 8 feet deep; the usual fired bricks were set in bitumen here for waterproofing. It was surrounded by a colonnade and a complex of small rooms. Next to it was a huge ventilated granary, 165 feet long, and there are also the remains of a pillared hall.

The lower town, which could have had 100,000 inhabitants, was also set above the level of the flood plain, though it was unfortified. It was laid out in a grid pattern and houses were grouped around their own courtyards; they were often several stories high. Most striking, perhaps, is the fact that almost all of them had bathrooms and a well of their own, and were also connected to the city's sewage system—there was a complicated network of drains.

WHO RULED THE INDUS VALLEY CIVILIZATION?

The level of uniformity is striking, especially across such a wide area. Many people have assumed that such a situation had to be the result of dominance by an elite, probably a rather rigid one, but there is little archaeological evidence for this. There are no elite residences, better than everyone else's; there is no sign of any concentration of wealth; there is no apparent investment in lavish burials of particular individuals with a lot of grave goods. There is some evidence that there may have been some sort of priestly authority, but at present the Indus Valley Civilization seems refreshingly egalitarian, especially when contrasted with some contemporary ones, such as the Sumerian city of Ur with its elaborate royal burials and sacrifices.

THE INDUS SCRIPT

Even before Marshall's announcement, seals bearing mysterious writing had been turning up in the area; in fact, details of the first one studied were published in 1873. There are now nearly 3000 inscriptions, coming not just from the Indus Valley but also from farther afield, where they have been found in sites belonging to other civilizations. There are inscriptions on all sorts of things as well as seal stones and their impressions, from bracelets to axes and ladles; it was definitely a literate civilization. The script is made up of about 220 simple signs and almost 200 composite ones—and nobody today can read them.

No bilingual inscription, no key, has ever been found so the Indus script cannot be compared to another, known, language. No inscription is longer than 26 signs: too short to allow the identification of recurring patterns. For the moment, pending further discoveries, the Indus Valley Civilization remains firmly prehistoric.

Opposite: Part of the city of Mohenjo-daro, the most intensively studied site belonging to the Indus Valley Civilization. It flourished in the Bronze Age, probably mainly between 2500 and 2000 BC.

Below: A seal bearing the figure of a bull and an inscription in the script used throughout the Indus Valley Civilization.

Frozen Tombs
of the Altai

Open steppe lands run for over 4350 miles across Asia, from the Carpathian Mountains of Romania to Mongolia. To the north lie great forests, and south of the steppes are deserts, seas like the Black Sea and the Caspian, and high mountain ranges. The steppes are ideally suited to a wide-ranging, nomadic lifestyle, with people following flocks of animals for huge distances; armies that came out of the east across the steppes have often been a threat to more settled neighboring communities.

Ancient writers described nomadic people of the steppes and mountains, but hard evidence for the richness of early nomadic culture in the region came from some astonishing archaeological discoveries made in the Altai mountains of southern Siberia.

In the 19th century a local historian began collecting antiquities, some of which had been removed from burial mounds in the High Altai. These mounds, which are often called barrows, are essentially large piles of earth heaped with a lot of stones, and two of these were roughly excavated in 1865. Serious work, however, began in the 1920s when the Russian archaeologist Sergei Rudenko excavated a large one, part of a group of five big mounds and nine smaller ones. The ground beneath the mound was frozen, and this proved to be true of others at the site, which was called Pazyryk—a word just meaning "burial mound." Rudenko's digs in the 1920s were followed by further ones at the site at the end of the 1940s, and a series of remarkable finds emerged, dating to between about 600 and 400 BC.

The barrow mounds had all been built in approximately the same way. A pit between 13 and 23 feet deep had been dug, sometime between spring and early fall as the ground freezes solid in winter. A chamber made of larch logs was created in the pit and grave goods were put in, articles that the dead person would need in the afterlife—clothes, carpets, small tables, food and drink, even multi-stringed harps. There was also the coffin, made from a large hollowed-out larch trunk, which contained the bodies, generally of a man and a woman. The chamber was roofed with larch logs and then the pit was covered with layers of birch bark and twigs, followed by more logs and stones, up to ground level. Horses were killed and buried outside the chamber. Then the mound was constructed on top.

Not long after burial the ground beneath the mound began to freeze. The stones of the barrow were piled loosely, insulating the ground below and preventing it from heating up in summer, but

Opposite: A detail from a saddle cover in felt showing a griffin attacking an ibex. Attached to the ends of the saddle cover are large round pendants, also made from felt, trimmed with long horsehair which had been dyed deep red.

Above: The knotted pile carpet found at Pazyryk is the world's most ancient example of a tradition which continues today. Horsemen and elks march around the borders in bands alternating with geometric patterns; the elk face in one direction, and the men and horses the other. Though it was found in southern Siberia it was probably made in Persia.

Below: Pazyryk is in the Altai Mountains in Siberian Russia near the borders with China, Kazakhstan, and Mongolia.

allowing frost to penetrate it in winter. Water would also have seeped through, and this froze before it could rot any of the organic material inside the barrow. In the harsh climate of the High Altai the burials remained frozen for well over 2000 years, undisturbed except unfortunately —by ancient grave robbers. Fortunately, they didn't take everything.

THE FROZEN CHIEF AND HIS TATTOOS

Most items in the burials were decorated in some way, and that included the people. Barrow 2 was still solidly frozen. As a result it was largely intact and the discoveries which the excavators made in 1948 were remarkable. The burial chamber was lined with wall hangings in felt, and the grave goods included clothing and other textiles, gold and silver ornaments, mirrors, and wooden furniture. The decorated coffin was made from the usual hollowed-out tree trunk and inside it were the bodies of a man and a woman who had been wrapped in a woolen rug; there were also pieces of linen. The man's body was surprising, not because it was particularly well preserved—it wasn't; some parts had deteriorated and the robbers had also damaged it—but because of his amazingly well-preserved animal tattoos.

These designs covered his arms from shoulder to wrist, and his right leg; his left leg had been too badly damaged for the excavators to tell whether tattoos had decorated it also. There were also smaller tattoos on his chest. The patterns included real animals, such as the large fish on his leg, mountain goats and deer, but also imaginary ones like a griffin and a strange creature with horns and a feline tail. The tattooing appeared to have been done using a pricking technique, and had been carried out when the man was much younger and slimmer; he was probably in his 60s when he died and had put on weight after the tattoos had been completed. They could have been done as a mark of manhood or possibly to signify that he was of high social status, or perhaps both.

THE HORSES

The horse burials which accompanied every tomb had generally been ignored by the grave robbers. There were between seven and fourteen horses with each tomb and one, Barrow 5, included a cart or ceremonial carriage which had been partly dismantled. This four-wheeled wagon had been given a felt canopy decorated with appliqué swans. Some of the bodies of the horses from this mound were preserved, as were items of their

Above: A horseman from one of the wall hangings found at Pazyryk, in Barrow 5 which was notable for the preservation of some of the horses which accompanied the burials. The people who interred their dead at Pazyryk were nomadic pastoralists, probably moving with huge flocks of sheep. Horses seem to have played a special part in their culture.

Left: The tattoo of imaginary and real animals from one of the arms of the "frozen chief." These appear to have been done by pricking the skin and introducing a black color of some kind. They were done when he was young—he was in his 60s when he died—and may have marked his high social position.

equipment; there were bridles, saddles, and even horse blankets in felt and woven fabric, some of which had probably been very precious, like the beautiful Chinese silk used for one of the blankets. Horses would have had immense importance in nomadic society and their burial with the bodies of evidently important people underlines the significance of both the humans and the animals.

LEATHER AND FABULOUS FABRICS

A lot of leather survived in the burials. Thick leather was used to make bridle straps, for example, and finer material was used in delicate appliqué work. The leather-work is impressive but the textiles from the tombs are sensational. They include imported material from both China and Persia, illustrating the wide contacts of these nomadic people. Some of the silk embroidery found is the oldest yet discovered, and an astonishing pile carpet is also the earliest surviving example. Their colors are so well preserved that it is difficult to appreciate their age.

Some of the clothing and textiles were of more local manufacture. A lot of wool was used, to produce felted fabric as well as woven serges. This serge was used to make items as diverse as the upholstery for saddles, the soles of a woman's bootees, and strips which went into a coverlet. The bootees themselves are made of soft leather and have a flaring top which would have gone partway up the shin. They are heavily embroidered with beads and thread wrapped in metal, among other things—even on the soles—and cannot have been used in everyday wear. There were soft and coarse linen-like fabrics, and men's shirts had been woven in Siberian hemp fibers. Decorative trims had been woven or sometimes braided, and there were beautiful multi-colored felt saddle blankets ornamented with tassels. Without the frozen conditions much of this material would have vanished from the archaeological record, and there would have been no trace of the richness and sophistication of nomadic life about 2,500 years ago. Their international contacts would have been unknown.

UKOK

More finds are coming to light. In 1993 another tomb was discovered in the High Altai close to the Chinese border. This was also frozen, but had not been looted. Archaeological techniques were also more sophisticated than those of the 1920s and 1940s, and the excavator, Natalya Polosmak, was able to dig the barrow with regard to scientific advances. The frozen tomb contained

Above: Women praying at an altar, a detail from a piece of Persian fabric found at Pazyryk. It had been used to make panels on a coverlet; strips of Middle Eastern fabrics were alternated with strips of locally made serge.

the body of a tattooed woman aged about 25. She was lying in a log coffin and had been buried with leather items, textiles and a meal of horsemeat and mutton laid out on wooden dishes. She was wearing a headdress made out of hair and felt decorated with a design of gold-covered cats, a woolen dress and a silk blouse with maroon-colored piping; the silk of her shirt appears to have come from India. She also wore felt boots. Outside her burial chamber were the bodies of six horses; each had been killed by a blow to the head. Their felt saddle covers were preserved, as were parts of their reddish manes.

There are others, too. In 1995 the body of a man was discovered in Siberia. He had been buried about 3000 years ago, well before the people of Pazyryk, but had also been tattooed, this time with an elk design. He had too been buried with his horse.

The Lost Cities of the Silk Road

The land between China and Iran, and in places from there to the Mediterranean, was largely bleak, inhospitable, and dangerous. East of Iran there were deserts and mountains, terrible climatic conditions, and the ever-present threat of bandits. Nonetheless, one of the great trade routes of the world between East and West flourished here. Towns and settlements grew up at oases; states—some extensive, some ephemeral—developed by controlling trade along the way. Known as the Silk Road, this trading route was in fact a series of ancient routes, not "roads" as such; nor was silk the only commodity traded along it.

While the existence of the Silk Road had been known for many years—knowledge of it had never entirely faded and Marco Polo had traveled along parts of it—its physical traces and evidence of many of the settlements along its length only began to appear in the rest of the world in the 19th century, some as a result of what has been called "archaeological looting." By the Bronze Age, or even earlier, settlements had evolved in the region around oases. Some silk dating to about 4000 years ago was found in northern Afghanistan, so goods must have been transported west from China even then (silk was unique to China for very many years and production techniques were a closely guarded secret). About 2000 years ago, trade between China and the lands to its west developed to an enormous extent and nomads began to move with the trade. Some raided, some settled, some founded kingdoms, but despite all the political changes trade itself continued to flourish. This all contributed to a multicultural variety, characteristic of many places on the Silk Road until the spread of Islam.

THE TRADING ROUTES

The network of routes spread westward from China, fanning out in two main directions after the oasis of Dunhuang in the Gobi desert. Travelers passed through the Jade Gate toward the Taklamakan Desert and took one of two main routes west, one running south of the desert and one running north. The southern branch went north of the mountains of Tibet, between them and the Taklamakan, following a trail of oases until it bent northward at the desert's end and reached the town of Kashgar. Toward the western end of this route, between Khotan and Yarkand, another trading route ran south to India through the Karakoram pass. The northern Silk Road went across the desert from near Dunhuang to Hami and Turfan and, like the southern one, passed through oasis towns until it too reached Kashgar. This town, not

surprisingly, developed into the great market of the Silk Road. From Kashgar the route passed west over the Pamirs and split again, one branch passing through Samarkand and Bukhara and the other going farther south via Afghanistan. The two met again at Merv, and the Silk Road continued across Iran toward the ports of the Mediterranean. There were other, more minor, variations and routes which linked up with it as well.

Opposite: The "Three Immortals" caves near Kashgar. Cave temples are a common feature along the Silk Road; many were beautifully decorated and would probably have received offerings from travelers.

Below: A beacon tower in Xinkiang, near Guici caves.

Bottom: A caravan of camels in the Gobi Desert. Camels were used on the Silk Road, but so were other pack animals such as donkeys.

THE SILK ROAD, C.112 BC–AC 100

- trade route under Roman control
- trade route under Persian control
- trade route under Kushan control
- trade route under Chinese control
- trade route under Indian control
- trade route under no particular control

Rome
Byzantium
Tomi
Sardis
Trapezus
(Trebizond)
Edessa
Antioch
Alexandria
Damascus
Tyre
Petra
Dura-Europos
Tabriz
Aela
Palmyra
Ecbatana
Seleucia
Ctesiphon
Babylon
Hecatompylos
Bukhara
Tashkent
Susa
Charax
Merv
Samarkand
Kokand
Kashgar
Kumul (Ha-mi)
Lin-tzu
Herat
Kerman
Yarkand
Lou-lan
Persepolis
Kabul
Khotan
Miran
Cherchen
Tun-huang
Lanchow
Kaifeng
Yang-ti
Ormuz
Taxila
Lo-yang
Chian-ling
Omana
Pattala
Ch'eng-tu
Ch'ang-sha
Lhasa
Pataliputra

Egypt

N

0   300 km
0   300 miles

TRAVELING THE ROUTE

Few merchants or caravans would travel the whole of the Silk Road, a return journey of about 9300 miles. Pack animals, which included horses, donkeys, and bullocks as well as camels (and occasionally yaks), were exchanged for fresh ones at oasis staging posts. A single animal would have been unlikely to survive the journey and many died, even so. Roman merchants did not go all the way to China, nor did Chinese ones visit Rome: trade was controlled by middlemen and many items were also traded along the way. Silk certainly traveled the whole distance—it was much prized in Rome and the desire to possess it despite its vast cost was blamed for ruining the economy. Other luxury goods such as furs, ceramics, lacquer, and cinnamon bark also left China, and ivory, amber, precious metals and stones, wool and linen textiles, and glass were taken eastward. Ideas also spread along the route, notably Buddhism. Missionaries and pilgrims began to use the trading routes from India to China, taking with them their sacred books and examples of Buddhist art. Others, Nestorian Christianity and Manichaeism, also spread as their disciples moved eastward to avoid persecution.

Left: The ruins of Gaochan west of Turfan, on the northern side of the Taklamakan Desert. Turfan itself is an oasis which stands in a huge natural depression. It is surrounded by bleak hills and deserts, but the oasis towns of the Turfan Depression apparently once supplied produce like grapes and melons to the imperial court of China; irrigation systems transported meltwater via underground channels. Some of these oasis towns survived while others did not.

A Precarious Existence

The oasis towns surrounding the Taklamakan Desert were crucial to the survival of the link between China and states to the west. Despite their importance, little was known of them until relatively recent times. Life in the towns could be insecure. Nomad raiders threatened some, but the main danger came from the environment. These settlements had grown up where mountain ranges edged down to the Taklamakan—which had an evil reputation; the name translates as "go in and you won't come out"—and were largely dependent on water from run-off and mountain streams. This water was diverted into elaborate irrigation systems allowing the cultivation of both food and grazing for animals. If these systems were not maintained for any reason the desert would return. The town of Niya, on the southern route, seems to have been destroyed like this when the Chinese briefly lost control of the Silk Road at the end of the third century AD. Rivers could also change course, become silted up, or even dry up completely; changing climatic conditions meant that the flow was decreasing. Over time, the pattern of trade began to change and the rise of Islam to the west altered everything as it spread eastward; many statues and wall paintings were destroyed and temples, monasteries, and Buddhist stupas were abandoned. China shut itself off from contact with the West under the Ming Dynasty

(1368–1644) and the Silk Road was abandoned. The most significant of the oasis towns survived provided they possessed adequate water supplies, but most vanished under the sand. Other cities and towns which lay along the route were abandoned once the essential reason for their existence had gone.

Below: The Diamond Sutra, important not only for its text but for the fact that it is the world's earliest known printed book.

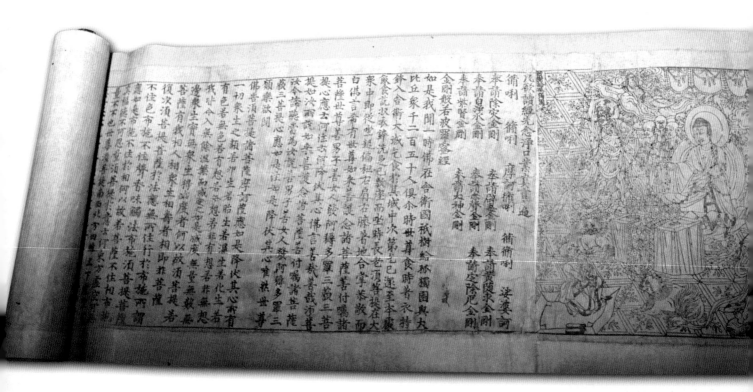

Legends persisted, however, and there were even a few finds which appeared in the 19th century. These inevitably attracted European explorers and adventurers who retrieved manuscripts and some antiquities. Some were fakes, but one of the manuscripts proved to be one of the oldest written works to survive and had done so because of the extreme dryness of the region. There were also reports of cities buried in the sand.

EXPLORER-ARCHAEOLOGISTS

This scattering of finds and reports brought the area to the attention of European archaeologists at a time when archaeology and exploration often went hand in hand. In 1895 the Swedish explorer Sven Hedin was one of the first to investigate some of the sites, in highly dangerous conditions: he was also aware that he was not qualified to conduct proper excavations, but knew that his reports would inspire others. On his next expedition, in 1899, he found the remains of the ancient Chinese garrison town of Loulan at the eastern end of the Taklamakan. At about the same time, at the other end of the desert, Aurel Stein had begun the first of his three archaeological expeditions. A controversial figure, he removed huge quantities of manuscripts and works of art from Chinese Central Asia and, as a result, is often regarded as little more than a looter by the Chinese. But he was not alone in this. As different national archaeological expeditions continued, artifacts were recovered and taken out of the country in a frenzy of competitive "collecting." Wall paintings were even hacked from temples and some of these, which ended up in Berlin, were destroyed during the Second World War. Stein's collection went to the British Museum in London.

FINDS FROM THE DESERT

Excavating in the Taklamakan, even on its edges, was exceptionally difficult. Local laborers could be hired at nearby oases but they were often reluctant to go into the desert and the conditions were appalling, even in winter which was the only possible time to dig. Nevertheless, Stein found many remains; the conditions for preservation were excellent. Mud bricks had been used for many buildings, but wood also remained—as did many more manuscripts. Some of these were evidently Buddhist but some were in Chinese, and one of those gave him a date for his first Taklamakan site at Dandan-uilik. It was a petition for the recovery of a donkey, and it had a definite Chinese date on it that corresponded to AD 781. He also found traces of the old irrigation systems and of the orchards they had watered; the town had also had avenues of poplar trees and their trunks remained, broken and half-buried in the sand.

Opposite above: Buddhist temples were carved into the rock at the Bezeklik oasis near Turfan. These caves were once covered with beautiful wall paintings, but many were removed and taken to Berlin by Albert von Le Coq, a German orientalist and explorer, where they were destroyed in the Second World War. Many of those remaining have been defaced over the years by local Muslims because they depict humans, contrary to the teachings of Islam.

Below: The ruins of Jiaohe, also known as Yarkhoto, close to Turfan. This ruined city is almost surrounded by two deep gorges, giving it a high level of natural protection; and though the ruins date from the early part of the first millennium AD, occupation goes back a lot farther. Fortified towns like this would have helped to protect the trade and merchants on the Silk Road.

Stein's most notorious finds came from the caves at Dunhuang, near where the two halves of the Silk Road split to go round the Taklamakan. Here are the Caves of a Thousand Buddhas, still impressive with more than 400 temples carved into the rock face and filled with wall paintings and sculptures. It was a very rich site because of its location: offerings would be made both in anticipation of a difficult journey and in thanks for a successful one. The whole complex is said to date from AD 366 and was never abandoned. However, the existence of parts of it had been forgotten and Stein heard that the guardian of the caves, a priest called Wang Yuan-lu, had found a huge cache of manuscripts in a sealed room. He met Wang in 1907 and eventually persuaded him to let him see the room containing the texts. It was small, but heaped with manuscripts piled more than 9 feet high. The exact circumstances of the agreement are obscure but Stein eventually managed to obtain a quantity of these from Wang, as well as paintings and silken banners. The most famous item in his haul was the Diamond Sutra, important not for its text but for the fact that it is the world's earliest-known printed book. It bears the name of the man who commissioned and distributed it (the world's first publisher) and also has a date on it which is the equivalent of May 11, 868. Not all the manuscripts Stein retrieved were religious, though. There is an invitation to a "strike-ball" match and a template for a letter which could be used as a model by someone who had to apologize to his host for drunken behavior, as well as a potential letter of reproach to be used in reply by the host.

Left: Three Buddhist scribes on a fresco from "Ming-oi". An enormous quantity of manuscripts has been retrieved from many sites on the Silk Road. Many are religious, and a lot of those are Buddhist. The Diamond Sutra, the world's oldest printed book, was found on the Silk Road at Dunhuang.

"Ming-oi" means "a thousand rooms" and is applied to many temple complexes. The frescoes come from one near Shikchin, on the northern side of the Taklamakan, which has come to be known by the general term.

The Mummies of the Silk Road

The climatic conditions that prevailed along the two Taklamakan arms of the Silk Road were not just ideal for preserving manuscripts, fabric and wood—they were also perfect for preserving people. Early excavations had found mummified remains, but they had not had a way of preserving or transporting them. This has now changed and there are, to date, about 300 known mummies from this area of western China, and they date from as long ago as 2000–1800 BC to the first centuries AD. Unlike mummies from Egypt or Peru, those from the Silk Road were preserved accidentally, not as the result of intervention, and the quality of some of them outshines anything deliberately undertaken elsewhere.

Because preservation was accidental, it was not a result of a single culture or way of burial. Mummies have been found in brick-lined chambers, in shallow pits, in deeper pits covered with layers of reeds ... in a wide variety of places. The oldest ones are very simply dressed in basic wraps of fabric—their clothes are equally well preserved—but after about 1000 BC people were much more fully clothed. There are shirts, skirts, cloaks, pants, dresses, leather shoes,

headdresses and hats (including feathered caps, and one man who had been buried with ten caps), and even woolen stockings. One woman wears a leather mitten—her other hand is bare—and many have evidence of facial decoration, either painted or tattooed. The fabrics are sophisticated; felts are common and the woven fabrics exhibit a high level of skill, especially the complicated twill plaids that have been found with some. The colors have also survived well; one plaid is a delicate check of light brown, light blue, and white, and one woman—dating to about 1000 BC—wears a long dress in a rich deep red. Some of the dyes and techniques used are mysterious, but so are the people.

The faces of the mummies have really given rise to the problem. They are definitely not Chinese, not of the physical type which is so characteristic of east Asia. Their hair is not characteristic either, being much lighter in color, sometimes auburn or reddish, and the male bodies tend to have rather more facial hair than is usually present farther east. In fact, they look rather Caucasian, with their very round eye sockets and high-bridged noses.

Left: Fragments of silk from "Ming-oi." Fabric often survives well in the dry conditions of the Silk Road sites, testifying to the material that gave these great trade routes their collective name.

Above: A detail of one of the mummies of the Silk Road.

Some support for this comes from the history of languages. Not all the manuscripts found along the Silk Road were in Chinese or Indian tongues; some were in the local languages. One of these was Khotanese, which seems to have been related to the Iranian group of languages. Another is Tokharian, which comes from the northern branch of the Silk Road where most of the mummies have been found. No complete documents in Tokharian have been found, but there are some words and personal names in other texts which have enabled linguists to determine that it fell into the Indo-European family of languages, coming from the same common ancestor as most of the European languages of today, as well as some others such as Armenian. It is not related to Chinese.

The Chinese also recorded their encounters with some of the people of Central Asia when they began to have prolonged contact with them in about the second century BC. What astonished the Han Chinese was how hairy the men were, and they also

Above: Embroidery from the caves at Dunhuang. Though this dates to between the third and fifth centuries AD, the colors are still bright and clear. The archaeologist and collector Aurel Stein found a lot of fabric at Dunhuang, ranging from huge lengths evidently designed to hang as banners from the tops of cliffs to much smaller pieces.

noted that the people had "reddish-white" or "white" skin, another Caucasian feature.

Much work is being done on this, but one thing should be noted: it is still possible to occasionally encounter people in modern Silk Road cities like Urumchi who conform to Caucasian physical characteristics, even though they and their families come from completely local backgrounds for generations. The whole area is one that can certainly be described as a melting pot, something no doubt encouraged by the long trading links and rich mix of cultures established along the network of the Silk Road.

The Terracotta Army

In March 1974, local people near Xian in China's Shaanxi province were digging a series of wells in the hope of improving their water supply in this heavily cultivated area. Instead of finding water, they uncovered a jumble of terracotta figures, the first indication of what has come to be known as the "eighth wonder of the world." They had accidentally discovered the army that was still guarding the tomb of China's First Emperor, Qin Shi Huangdi, and the archaeologists were called in.

The First Emperor, King Zheng, took his title—and his role—in 221 BC, effectively unifying China following the chaotic time known as the "Warring States" period which had lasted for over 200 years. From his capital at Xianyang he initiated sweeping reforms, imposing uniform standards of law, currency, administrative organization, and writing as well as in other matters. This drive for standardization extended, for example, to the gauge of wheeled vehicles. At his instigation, about 300,000 laborers worked on the Great Wall, to protect China from the nomadic tribes to the north, and a new palace was also built. He ordered the construction of a magnificent tomb, the building of which, according to historical sources, required about 700,000 workers.

The clay figures the peasants had found were part of this. They came from a huge mortuary complex and formed a guard on the tomb of the First Emperor himself, which lies under a huge burial mound nearby. This terracotta army had been stationed in battle formation in a series of three immense pits to the east of this mound (there is a fourth pit, but it contains no clay figures). The statistics are extraordinary. Altogether the creation of the pits alone would have necessitated the removal of about 4.23 tons of earth, as they cover a combined area of about 30,000 square yards. These pits were paved with fired clay bricks—there are about a quarter of a million of those—and they were roofed with a huge quantity of wood, much of it cypress and pine. Then there are the life-size models of the soldiers. At present it is estimated that there are about 7000 of them; there are also 600 horses. These pits are only a part of the whole; in its entirety the tomb of the First Emperor must have taken an immense amount of time and cost a vast amount, in terms of both manpower and money. It is highly likely that the chronicles were right, and that hundreds of thousands of people were involved, possibly over as long as ten years.

Opposite: Ranks of soldiers, hollow from abdomen height. Seen more closely, the difference between them becomes more obvious.

Right: The terracotta army reflects the composition of a real army of the time and is not simply made up of private soldiers. This figure represents a commanding officer or general, but the one depicting the army's commander-in-chief is not present.

THE FIGURES

When it comes to the terracotta soldiers themselves, we actually know the names of some of the craftsmen involved, as hidden away beneath the long coats or under the armpits of the figures are the signatures of 85 different sculptors. They used local clay, which was strong enough to make large pieces, and fired it at a high temperature thus giving the terracotta a rather gray surface. The potters must have been technically very skilled as they had obviously managed to achieve a consistent and accurate firing temperature: the statues are still hard despite being buried for about 2200 years. After firing the figures were painted, and traces of this

remain. There seem to have been two basic color schemes in the biggest pit, Pit 1, for instance: one group had green cloaks, dark blue pants and black shoes, laced in red. Their armor was also black but with white rivets, gold buttons, and purple cords.

Most impressive, perhaps, is the fact that every single soldier is unique. The bodies are standardized, but the faces are individual. Each statue is solid from the abdomen down and hollow above; the weight is supported by the legs. Some parts, like the head and forearms, were attached separately. So far, excavators have not discovered any identical faces; this level of portraiture is unique. It has been suggested that the figures reflect the ethnic mix of the First Emperor's realm, celebrating its unification, and this seems to be borne out by some ethnic features and the percentage of figures on which they appear. Quite apart from that, each face has been given character and expression— some look decidedly disgruntled, others are attentive or patient— and there are 25 different types of beard represented, which match the age, apparent character, basic face shape, and military post of the individual figures. Most of the soldiers are muscular, many are tall: it is an army of fit and healthy men, ready for battle.

THE ARMY

The composition of the different pits varies, and a lot has been learned from them about the organization of the First Emperor's armies. Pit 1 is large and contained the majority of the figures, most

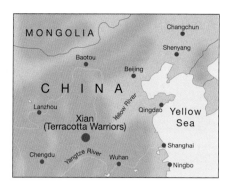

of them foot soldiers. They have no helmets—only officers wore those—but most of them wear armor. There are six chariots in this pit, two of which seem to represent command vehicles. Among the soldiers are archers, ordinary bowmen as well as crossbowmen, and three squads of unarmored infantry. From historical records it is known that Qin soldiers were renowned for their ferocity, and soldiers equipped and dressed in this way would certainly have been expected to take the initiative: they are attack troops, not defenders. They were also highly disciplined, the records attest—possibly because any soldier who failed to obey orders risked decapitation.

Pit 2 contained a wider variety of soldiers, and a lot of evidence for the fact that all the soldiers were originally armed comes from it; a huge quantity of arrowheads were found, just from the trial excavation. Here there are thought to be about 1400 figures and 80 chariots. There are armored archers, spearmen, armored cavalry, armored infantry, and even two commanders or generals. One stands in a command chariot and one with the infantry; they both wear distinctive coats of mail.

Pit 3 had collapsed onto its contents, causing considerable damage; however, it does appear that the soldiers in this pit represented the command unit. Of the 68 soldiers, many are officers; there are also four horses and a chariot, but the figure of the commander-in-chief is absent. The soldiers who make up his guards are exceptionally tall, with an average height of 6 feet 3 in compared to an average height for Pit 1 of 5 feet 11 in. The commander of the infantry vanguard from Pit 2 is the only figure that is taller, at 6 feet 5 in. Here the soldiers are all deployed to protect the commander, confirming that the figures are indeed drawn up in battle formation. Their armour came in two types: lighter mail, ideal for moving quickly, and a heavier variety that would have been better for close combat. Some of their weapons had a ceremonial function rather than a

Above: A map showing the location of the the find at Xian.

Left: There are many figures of archers, placed to use both ordinary bows and crossbows. Despite the looting shortly after the First Emperor's death, many arrowheads have been found, as have crossbow triggers.

Whether he is undisturbed or not is unknown; other areas of the tomb complex were certainly looted and damaged during the rebellions that broke out following the emperor's death in 210 BC.

The First Emperor's burial mound lies about 1 mile away from the pits containing his army. It is immense, an artificial mountain standing about 165 feet high. There are records of what it contained—rivers of mercury reproducing the courses of the great rivers of China, the emperor's finest furniture, the tomb itself encased in bronze. The tomb was booby trapped to deter robbers, with crossbows tensioned and placed appropriately. These records also state that those of the emperor's concubines who had not produced sons were killed to accompany him, and that the workers involved in fitting out the tomb were executed. Pits containing the bodies of many men have been found, and some of them seem to have indeed been executed, so this part of the historical record could well be accurate. Perhaps the rest is, too.

However, these historical records also state that the tomb was plundered only a few years after the burial of the First Emperor, who had died aged 49 or 50 in 221 BC. Most of the weapons of the terracotta soldiers were removed and a bronze bell decorated in silver and gold which dates to the right period—and which may well have come from the tomb itself—was found near by; it may have been abandoned loot. Until archaeologists do enter the mound there is no way of knowing for sure.

practical one, appropriate to their role with the commander-in-chief's guard.

THE FIRST EMPEROR'S TOMB

The pits containing the soldiers, spectacular though they are, are only part of Qin Shi Huangdi's immense funerary complex. Many other finds have been made—a half-size copy of a royal chariot complete with driver and four horses; burials of real horses; mass burials of men, possibly forced laborers; possible sacrificial temples intended for offerings of food and drink. However, the First Emperor's tomb itself has not been excavated; the archaeologists are deliberately holding back.

Right and above: Much has been learned about the real Qin armies from the terracotta army: details of even about incidental things like the scarves worn around the neck. It has been suggested that these scarves would have been important for soldiers posted to the colder parts of the realm, but they may simply have been worn like that to prevent the armour chafing.

Angkor

Trade was a major factor in the development of South-east Asia, especially maritime trade. From about 500 BC there are marked signs of social change and a series of wealthy kingdoms arose.

The period between 500 BC and 500 AD, known locally as the Bronze-Iron Age, is marked by the spread of metalworking. Bronze had been used much earlier, notably in Vietnam, but this period saw its use—and that of iron—expand. Competition for trade fueled contacts and exchange. During the last four centuries BC, seasonal sailing around the Bay of Bengal became much more regular. Coastal communities were linked by trade all the way from India to Indonesia and on into the Gulf of Thailand, and belief systems spread along with the trade goods, beliefs like Buddhism and Hinduism.

ANGKOR

Like many others in South-east Asia, the first large-scale civilization in Cambodia developed out of earlier, Bronze-Iron Age chiefdoms. Angkor itself is the modern name given to a massive complex of temples and cities in north-west Cambodia. It was ideally situated for communications, with easy river transport and plentiful supplies of fresh water (and fish), and was constructed

Opposite: Inside one of the courtyards of Angkor Wat. This enormous temple-mausoleum is the largest religious structure known, and was built during the reign of Suryavarman II, between AD 1113 and 1150. Transporting the building material would have been a major task, and the network of canals at Angkor may well have played an important part.

Above: A general view of part of Angkor Wat. The densely forested surroundings can make working on the enormous site of Angkor difficult.

by successive kings from three dynasties over a period of about 600 years. It was the center of a small state in the seventh and eighth centuries AD, and in AD 802 its ruler, Jayavarman II, had himself consecrated as supreme ruler on earth. His dynasty lasted for 200 years and saw a lot of construction at Angkor. Ordinary buildings were made from wood, whereas temples were constructed in stone and brick; they therefore survive where residential buildings do not, which can give the impression that the site mainly consists of temples. Sometimes these bear witness to the existence of forgotten structures. Indravarman, for example, built a new religious center dominated by shrines to his ancestors, but the inscriptions also describe a royal palace.

There has also been some recent excavation but working at Angkor can be problematic. The site is vast—the ruins cover an area of about 100 square miles. and are both difficult and dangerous to survey—and aerial reconnaissance has been vital. Some high-resolution radar studies have been done which have highlighted the presence of a network of canals around the city and temple complex. These canals irrigated fields and may also have been used to transport building materials for the temples. There also seem to be traces of a city on the site which predate Angkor, but more work needs to be done.

ANGKOR WAT

The many temples were often constructed to reflect the form of the home of the Hindu gods, Mount Meru, and

Above: Excavation and restoration in progress at Angkor Thom, a project sponsored by Cambodian UNESCO.

were not just designed for worship; they would also have held the cremated remains of the rulers. By far the biggest of these is Angkor Wat, built by Suryavarman who reigned between AD 1113 and 1150; it is, in fact, one of the largest religious monuments in existence. Sandstone was used to build this, Suryavarman's great temple-mausoleum, and the surface was covered in reliefs. Some of these relate to the Hindu religion, but many show the king and his court. The temple was also, apparently, once covered in fine gold.

ANGKOR THOM

This huge walled and moated city was built by the ruler Jayavarman VII, one of the successors of Suryavarman. It was dominated by a central temple-mausoleum called the Bayon. There is actually a written record of Angkor Thom at its height from a Chinese diplomat who stayed there in 1296, and his descriptions have been borne out by recent archaeological digs. Within the city walls there was a large population, including many staff and slaves for the palace, and there seems to have been a strong Chinese presence, probably largely traders. There were many canals, pools, roads, and houses.

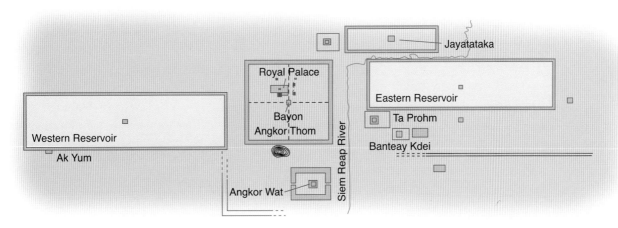

One of the notable features of Angkor are the frequently large and rectangular reservoirs, and it is not known precisely what purpose they served. They may have been practical, helping in some way with irrigation by providing water for the rice fields between the city and the Great Lake, which lay to the south. They may have been symbolic, serving some sort of ritual function and possibly representing the ocean surrounding the home of the gods in the Hindu religion. They may have had other purposes, and could always have been multi-

functional. Like so much in archaeology, these possibilities remain both controversial and up for debate.

Opposite: A huge head from the Bayon, Jayavarman VII's temple in Angkor Thom.

Below: Angkor Wat is decorated by beautiful reliefs. This one, a meeting of opposing armies, is thought to be derived from the great Hindu epic, the Mahabharata.

Above: A plan showing the layout of the complex at Angkor.

Australian Rock Art

Australia is in many ways a unique place and one of the ways in which it differs from everywhere else is in the nature of human occupation. Until the first European settlers arrived in the 18th century, it was populated exclusively by hunter-gatherers, and those hunter-gatherers had been there for many thousands of years. One of the most dazzling testimonies to the richness of their society is the rock art, found in many places across Australia and also spanning many thousands of years.

Some areas of the country have been carefully studied and one of these is in Kakadu National Park in the Northern Territory. Because of the sheer profusion of the archaeological remains and the beauty and complexity of the art, the archaeology at Kakadu has been likened to that from the Paleolithic in southwest France.

Humans initially spread across Australia when it was still joined to New Guinea. Sea levels were much lower—a lot of water was locked up in ice—and the journey across the sea that separated this landmass from Asia would have been possible. Dating the earliest occupation of Australia is controversial, as are the very early dates obtained for some sites. However, people spread quickly across the land; there are sites from all over Australia dating to 40,000–35,000 BP (before present) and some archaeologists and scientists believe these could be—and may already have been—pushed back a further 20,000 years to about 60,000–55,000 years ago. The explosion in Australian archaeology is comparatively recent; until just over 40 years ago, human settlement was thought to only date back some 10,000 years.

One problem in trying to establish when people first reached Australia is that sea levels rose quite dramatically, separating Australia from New Guinea and Tasmania and drowning coastal regions; much evidence must be under water. Despite this, the pace of discovery continues, pushing back dates and prompting heated arguments. One globally significant find which does not relate to the date for early occupation was that of the

cremated remains of a woman at Lake Mungo. She had been deliberately cremated about 25,000 years ago—the earliest known cremation in the world.

How Old is the Art?

Rock art is notoriously difficult to date, but some was certainly present in the Australia of the Ice Age. Fragments of ocher have been found in very old levels at some sites and these can be used to provide a date. They suggest that some of the art is at least 20,000 years old, maybe as old as 50,000 years. Once again, these figures are disputed.

At some archaeological sites occupation deposits can be used to provide a "not after" date for paintings and engravings. These deposits, which can be dated, have built up against the decorated rocks, so the art must be older than the archaeological deposits which cover it. One of these sites is the Early Man rock shelter in Queensland, where the occupation layers obscuring engravings were dated to 13,000 BP.

Advances in technology are also helping with dates and, as with those for cave paintings in the European Paleolithic, some are coming from the materials used to create the paintings, like the ocher from early occupation levels. A small sample of pigment was found in which human blood had been used as a binder: that dated to about 10,700 years ago.

Opposite: A fish painting from Anbangbang in Kakadu National Park, one of the most thoroughly studied sites.

Above: Examples of rock art are found in many places but the Kadadu National Park is one of the most important sites.

Left: Rock art from Ewaninga near Alice Springs. People had moved throughout Australia, even into its apparently forbidding heart, very early in the history of its occupation. There are dates for sites here which go back 30,000 years.

Another date came from some red pigment found in Queensland: 24,600 years ago.

In South Australia "desert varnish" forms on exposed rock; this chemical crust has microscopic organic material trapped within it, and that can be dated. In some places it has formed over rock engravings, and hence a minimum possible age can be given to the designs underlying the varnish. The oldest dates obtained by this method go back over 40,000 years, but some of these dates are, again, controversial. No one doubts that these sites are very old and the art some of the most ancient, but the question is how old. However old they may actually turn out to be, these older works come in a variety of different forms often pecked into the rock: lines of geometric forms, circles and animal tracks. Some are found in caves, notably at Konalda cave and others in the Mount Gambier area, and some are in the open air.

While most of the earliest art is geometric and abstract, more recent rock art is increasingly representational, with images of spiritual beings, people, animals, and plants. Arnhem Land in the north has some spectacular examples, and sites in the Kakadu National Park have been studied closely, providing an all-round context for the area's beautiful paintings.

WORKING IN THE KAKADU NATIONAL PARK

A large research project in Kakadu, an area noted for its magnificent rock art, was carried out in the 1980s by Rhys Jones of the Australian National University, and working closely with the local Aboriginal community was essential to its success. The people had powerful ties to the area and some of the specific sites and were also, legally, their owners. They wanted to insure that the archaeologists did not do anything to bring about any ritual—or more practical—danger: that they did not, for example, stray into any places which the community perceived as being ritually perilous. They were also very keen that one site should be finished before the next one was begun and that everything should be returned to its original appearance once digging was over. The archaeological team was accompanied by senior members of the various

Right: Rock shelters, like this one on the King Edward River near Kimberley in western Australia, were places where groups could camp temporarily. They were often visited repeatedly, sometimes over thousands of years, and are frequently decorated.

Aboriginal groups concerned and other people from the communities worked with them in the field laboratory.

ANBANGBANG

One of the most important sites investigated was the Anbangbang rock shelter. This enormous shelter showed promising signs of significant levels of occupation, even on initial inspection. Indeed, when it came to actual excavation, the upper levels contained a lot of organic material, usually rare in Australia but preserved here because of specific environmental conditions. Humans had begun occupying the site thousands of years earlier, probably well before 10,000 years ago and certainly before 6000 years ago. About then—6000 BP—the density of organic remains and tools increased significantly, and this happened again about 1000 years ago. Stone tools are generally the only artifacts to survive in Australian sites, which inevitably leads to them being given a certain emphasis, but at Anbangbang there were many others, mostly dating to the last millennium. There were bone implements and some had been hafted, probably onto fishing spears—they had traces of resin on them, used to make them stick to a handle. The excavators also even found wooden tools. There were traces of plant material, some of which had probably come from the nearby Anbangbang lagoon, and waterlilies seem to have been particularly popular. Evidence was found of over 50 species of fish and animals. These were doubtless hunted for food: the bones showed signs of butchering, so they were definitely the object of human exploitation. Anbangbang may have been a base camp used in the wet season, and

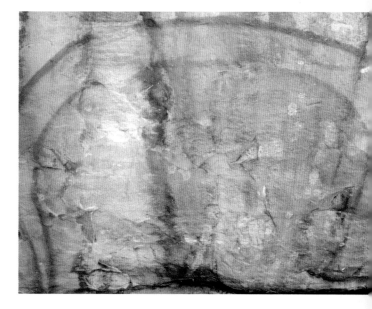

at the start of the dry season, by a group of about 25 people. Another rock shelter at Lindner produced coloring materials, small pieces of ocher that had been ground and shaped into facets with use. These occur throughout the occupation layers and may have come from some with very early dates—one of 53,000 BP has even been suggested.

CHALOUPKA'S DATING THEORY

Another means of dating the paintings has been suggested for the art from the Northern Territory, though it can be applied in other areas in a modified form. George Chaloupka has put forward the idea that changes in the types of animals represented on the rock were a reflection of reality, and that they can be used as a means of determining the possible earliest date for a painting. For example, the rises in sea levels and other environmental changes would have caused changes in the animal and plant species present in an area, and this fact can help establish when the paintings were made. According to this theory early paintings, coinciding with the height of the last period of glaciation, would be those containing land animals rather than marine creatures,

Opposite: A single figure from Anbangbang.

Above: A Rainbow Serpent from Ubirr in the Kakadu National Park.

Left: Not all rock art is representational; there are many symbols. These, interpreted as nature symbols, come from Kuyunba in the Northern Territory.

and might include some representations of ones which are now extinct. One painting, from a site beyond the boundary of the park, depicts a strange creature which has been tentatively identified as an animal now only known from fossil remains, called Palorchestes. After the rise in sea level, about 6000–7000 years ago, animals like the saltwater crocodile and the barramundi (giant perch) appear in paintings and the smaller marsupials—which would have moved farther inland—vanish. When freshwater wetlands developed about 1000 years ago there was another major environmental change, also reflected in the rock art. So, through time, depictions of terrestrial marsupials and food plants like yams are replaced by those of turtles and fish. Animals like these may reflect the painters' everyday reality, but there are other forms.

TERRITORIES AND TRADE— OR EXCHANGE

Rock art can also be used to say something about the way the land was used by different groups. The earliest art— the abstract and geometrical forms—was generally uniform across immense areas, whereas later work, often elaborately painted using many colors, shows marked regional differences. It has been suggested that this marks different regional identities, and there certainly appears to be some evidence for more base camps and cemeteries in more recent periods. People do seem to have become less mobile.

Trade, or ritual exchange, was important. The stone with which tools were made can be traced back to the places it came from, and much work has been done on the quarries for the distinctive greenstone which comes from south-eastern Australia; this was shaped into rough forms on site but was finished elsewhere. It was evidently traded over wide areas. Most traded items, unfortunately, do not survive in the archaeological record. However, from historical records it is known that pituri, a narcotic plant known as native tobacco which grows in central Australia and Queensland, was traded over very long distances, and the same was true of pearl shell from the northwest coast. Other items were also definitely exchanged—ocher, foodstuffs, the resin for attaching stone points to wooden handles—and this was an important part of Aboriginal life. There were established meeting places for ritual gift exchange and this must have fullfilled a useful purpose, probably in ritual as well as social terms.

Easter Island

Easter Island, with its dramatic statues, has posed more questions for archaeologists and historians than it has provided answers. The mystery of the enigmatic statues, together with the origins and fate of the society that produced them, has fascinated people for years and continues to do so.

Rapa Nui, to give Easter Island its Polynesian name, is a roughly triangular island, a volcanic rock only 64 square miles in extent. Remote and geographically isolated—it is about 2250 miles from the island of Pitcairn to the north-west and 3300 miles from Chile to the east—it is linked culturally to Polynesia. Unlike most of Polynesia, however, it is subtropical, with a comparatively marginal local ecosystem. Polynesian explorers, like those who reached Easter Island, took a collection of animals and plants with them on their voyages. Some flourished on Easter Island, like bananas and sweet potatoes, though no trace has yet been found of dogs or pigs, which might have been expected. Chickens and Polynesian rats both survived and became useful, even vital, sources of food. The island did have indigenous birds but they disappeared, possibly wiped out by over-exploitation by the colonists (and their accompanying rats). The community which developed on the island had small villages of oval houses; crops were grown in walled fields, thus being protected from both the fierce winds and the salt-laden sea spray.

Above: Moai in the crater of Rano Raraku, where the statues were quarried and carved, and where many of them remain in various stages of completion. The soft volcanic tufa was ideal for making the statues, and over 95 percent of them came from here.

DID THE PEOPLE CAUSE THEIR OWN DESTRUCTION?

Estimates for the date at which Easter Island was colonized from Polynesia have traditionally settled on around AD 800, but this has recently been called into question. A new excavation has radiocarbon-dated the earliest actual evidence so far found for human occupation, and come up with AD 1200, which has thrown a lot of accepted ideas up into the air. This new date has not helped clarify what happened at all.

It has long been assumed that one of the reasons for the undoubted decline of the Easter Island community was over-population and the subsequent exhaustion of the fragile environment. There was certainly extensive deforestation; pollen analysis has confirmed that the island was once covered in palm forests. By 1722, when the European explorer Jacob Roggeveen "discovered" the island, it was bleak and there were relatively few islanders, probably only about 2000. It has always been thought that a large population was necessary to carve, move, and set up the moai or giant statues, and some estimates of past population levels have been as high as 20,000. However, estimates of population numbers for the past are very difficult to reach and are often based upon assumptions—like the numbers of people that might have lived in a house at any one time—rather than concrete evidence. The role of

Above: A "birdman" rock carving from the village of Orongo. In the final phases, the birdman competition became a way of selecting the island's chief. Each candidate would choose a young man to represent him, and these then had to descend the cliffs, make their way through shark-infested water to an offshore islet and await the return of the sooty terns. The one who swam back with the first egg secured the chiefdom for his master. This ritual was still developing when Europeans first arrived, and was ended by missionaries in the 1860s.

Opposite: Statues on the ahu or platform at Anakena Bay. This platform, Ahu Nannau, has a special place in legend and is associated with Hotu Matu'a, the ancestor who established society on the island.

other creatures that arrived with the settlers has also been highlighted recently; Polynesian rats love to eat palm nuts and could have had a serious impact. So the depletion of the island's resources may not have been entirely caused by people, and there may not have been as many of them as previously assumed anyway, and they may not have been there for so long... Research is ongoing and what had seemed to be clear is no longer so certain.

THE MOAI

The most striking feature of Easter Island for most visitors today—and also for Roggeveen in 1722—is the number of large statues or moai erected around the perimeter of the island. All of these are truncated human figures, stopping at the level of the lower abdomen. They have elongated heads with equally elongated ears, some of which are shown as pierced. Their arms are held tightly at their sides and their hands—with elongated fingers—almost meet at the level of the stylized loincloth. There are 833 known statues; they range in height from 6 to 32 feet and can weigh up to 82 tons. These were quarried and carved at the crater of Rano Raraku, where the soft volcanic tufa was ideal. Many thousands of basalt picks have been found and many statues still remain there, either prone or partly buried, and at different stages of completion. Some of the ones that were erected had pukao or topknots of red scoria added to their heads which came from another quarry, and some were also given eyes of white coral and obsidian.

Many of the statues—some 230—were transported to platforms around the coast. These ceremonial stone platforms, known as ahu, were put up by the islanders in the earliest stages of their occupation, and they gradually became bigger and much more numerous. The statues were set up on top of these, but not on all; in fact, less than half of the platforms have statues on them. Some of the major ahu sites became elaborate, multi-period structures. They have rubble cores and walls made from dressed stone which can support the enormous combined weight of several statues; one—Ahu Tongariki—has 15 figures and is the biggest on the island. Most of the moai face inwards, away from the sea and toward the villages. It has been suggested that they represent the ancestors.

MOVING THE MOAI

It has long been assumed that making and moving the statues would have involved huge numbers of people and there have been several theories, and even experiments, to try and establish how it was done. In the crater of Rano Raraku the statues were carved from the rock, eventually resting on a "spine" which was gradually undercut. Some of the figures which still remain in the quarry are immense but most of those which ended up

Opposite: A close-up of statues from Ahu Nannau. The red "topknots" came from a different quarry from the stones for the figures, and are not universal. They may have been added later, after the statues had been standing for some time.

Left: Archaeologists at work on Easter Island.

Above: Ahu Tongariki, the largest of the island's platforms, has 15 statues.

on the platforms are actually less than 20 feet tall. Transporting them may seem to outside eyes to have been the truly difficult part, but this may not have been as hard as it appears. Moving heavy canoes overland, ones capable of long voyages—and the materials needed to make them—was something the Polynesians were quite able to do, and this expertise may well have played a part when it came to transporting the statues.

It has been suggested that the figures were dragged horizontally on rollers, but they could also have been moved upright on a sledge. Two ways of doing this were tried, both on flat ground, and were found to be possible. However, they were rather risky and would possibly have been dangerous over rougher terrain. Recent experiments have exploited the similarity with moving canoes and one of these worked rather well. A concrete replica of a moai was placed on an A-frame sledge, lashed together in the shape of an outrigger canoe's hull, and the statue was firmly attached to it. This sledge was then tested using levers, rollers and a "canoe ladder" made from lateral rungs just over 3 feet apart on which a canoe could be slid along. The simple rollers did not work satisfactorily but the canoe ladder did, enabling the replica statue to be easily pulled along for about 300 feet. Admittedly this took place on relatively level ground, but the statue was also able to be moved up a ramp and onto a replica ahu, and was even erected using the sledge as a gantry.

How did the Polynesians Find Easter Island?

When Thor Heyerdahl sailed his Kon-Tiki raft from South America to Polynesia in 1952 he was attempting to prove that the Pacific Islands had been settled by people from South America, specifically from Bolivia. A little later he led expeditions to Easter Island trying to show that it, too, had originally been occupied by South Americans. Research since the 1950s has, however, shown no such phase in Polynesian prehistory, either at Easter Island or elsewhere, but there was clearly some contact, which is demonstrated by the presence of the sweet potato in Polynesia. This contact is now seen as having been sporadic and ephemeral, and as having involved Polynesian sailors rather than South American ones.

The Polynesians had an unrivaled knowledge of the seas around their island homes in the Pacific, and this was acknowledged by some of the earliest Europeans to encounter them, such as Captain Cook. He made a rough sketch map of the islands in the 1760s based only

on information given him by Tupaia, a Polynesian pilot. It covered a vast area of ocean, one at least as large as Australia, and Tupaia had all this information in his head. Pilots like him would have used their knowledge of winds and currents, built up and passed down through many generations, and their understanding of the sun and stars which they used like a compass. They also considered swell direction, the way waves were reflected off land in the distance, the movements of birds, and the presence of clouds when making landfall on isolated islands.

The double-hulled Polynesian canoes and sailing rafts were quite capable of enduring a long and dangerous voyage. These were constructed with flexible lashed joinery, but were at the same time very robust and seaworthy. To construct vessels like that, heavy timbers were required; these, often much larger than the largest of the moai, had to be moved and frequently transported over rough terrain. Abilities and knowledge gained in constructing canoes and rafts could easily have been transferred to other purposes.

The Americas

The Arrival of People

The ice sheets which had covered large areas of the world began retreating after about 18,000 years ago, and this withdrawal brought environmental changes in its wake. In the northern hemisphere, southern areas were no longer suitable habitats for the great migratory herds of reindeer and musk ox, or for the mammoths, all of them popular quarries for hunting bands of humans. Both the animals and their hunters moved northward and eastward, following the retreating tundra; as conditions continued to alter they moved farther and farther north. They finally reached Beringia, the land bridge that existed between Siberia and Alaska and which is now covered by water following the rise in sea levels caused by the continuing melting of the ice sheets.

The date of this first crossing of people into the Americas has been much debated. There are some very early dates from the North American end of this substantial land bridge—it was nearly 1000 miles wide—but they are disputed. The best evidence so far gives a date of 13,000 years ago; it comes from Bluefish Caves in the Yukon. Though parts of Alaska and the Yukon were free from ice at this time there were major ice sheets covering most of what is now Canada. A gap opened up, splitting these into two huge parts, and people were able to move southward. It used to be thought that this happened about 13,000 years ago but some sites that could have been reached only by means of this corridor, like Meadowcroft Rock Shelter in Pennsylvania, are producing dates which are earlier than that. Meadowcroft, for example, may first have been in seasonal use sometime between 19,000 and 17,000 BP. Other sites are apparently stunningly early like Pedra Furada in Brazil and Monte Verde I in Chile, where highly controversial dates of 33,000 BP have been obtained.

Whatever the truth of the very early dates, it is quite clear that by about 11,500 BP people had spread to almost all the habitable areas of the Americas. The consequent role of humans in the disappearance of large Ice Age animals has long been supposed to have been critical, but this is now being questioned. It seems as though the changing climatic conditions which enabled people to spread more easily through the landscape also made life more difficult for creatures like mammoths and mastodons, and that hunting by humans just accelerated their end.

MONTE VERDE

Monte Verde, close to the coast in Chile, is one of the potentially early sites and emphasises another possible method of colonisation—southward by boat, hugging the Pacific coast. In the late 1970s excavations revealed the existence of an early settlement which had been on the banks of a small creek. The preservation was excellent—the site had been covered by a layer of peat shortly after the inhabitants had left—and Monte Verde II, as it became known, produced dates of 15,500—15,000 years ago.

Opposite: Pedra Furada one of the oldest known human sites in the Americas.

Right: The site of Monte Verde is close to the Pacific coast of Chile.

Monte Verde I, which lies beneath it, is much more controversial: radiocarbon dates in the region of 33,000 BP have been disputed and the site is still being assessed. The traces of occupation have been described as "dubious."

Monte Verde II's preservation guaranteed some surprising survivals; wooden artifacts, for example, remained, as did much organic material. Tools made of worked bone and chipped stone were found, but the most remarkable evidence demonstrated other aspects of people's lives. A structure some 60 feet in length, made of hide and wood, had been in use. There was also another wood and hide structure, inside which traces of eighteen different medicinal plants were found. Tom Dillehay, the excavator, suggested that this might have been a place specifically set apart for healing. Pollen had generally survived remarkably well, and though some of the plants which had been used were local, others had been brought to the site from some distance, even from up to 430 miles away. It was also possible for the archaeological team to tell that water plants and wild vegetables, including tubers like the wild form of the potato, had been the most important part of the inhabitants' diet, though some meat had also been eaten. Salt came from the coast, as did some of the plants used—and bitumen also came from there; this secured flaked stone tools in wooden hafts. The inhabitants of Monte Verde II were clearly skilled at making maximum use of the environment in which they lived.

269

The Treasures of Sipan

The Peruvian tombs of the rulers of Sipan, found as recently as 1987, are the richest burials yet uncovered in the Americas. The first one, the tomb of the Lord of Sipan, as it has come to be known, was actually discovered by a group of looters, but they quarreled over their good fortune and one of them went to the police. The find was so significant that the police woke the archaeologist Walter Alva in the middle of the night, and research into the site still continues.

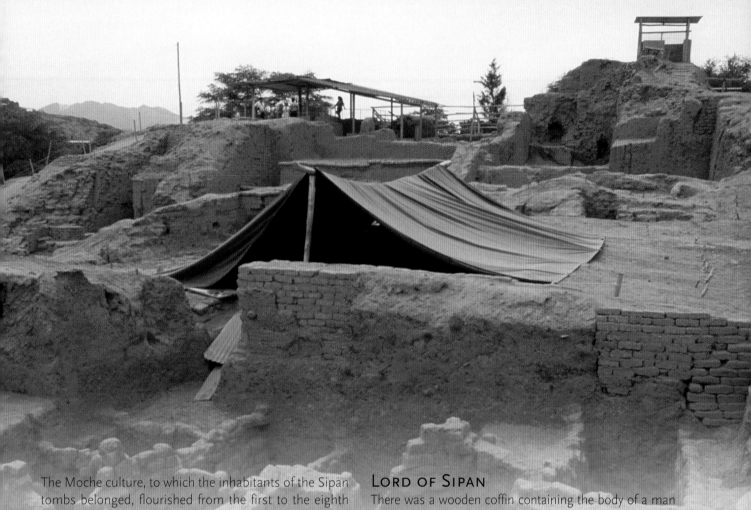

The Moche culture, to which the inhabitants of the Sipan tombs belonged, flourished from the first to the eighth centuries AD along the north coast of Peru. Moche pottery was well known and so were examples of metalwork and shellcraft; the enormous mud-brick pyramids were also a significant feature. These are now badly eroded and barely look man-made, and it was beneath a small pyramid that the looters had stumbled on their find. These robbers were just part of a long tradition. Theft from Moche sites stretches back to the Spanish conquest in 1532 and has been happening to such an extent that most of what was known about the culture came from objects illicitly removed from cemeteries and tombs. As such, nothing was certain about the context in which they had been found, something vital to a true understanding of the Moche world. The discovery at Sipan changed that.

The tomb which the looters had reached was investigated but most of its contents had gone. However, the archaeologists noticed something unusual, a place where mud bricks had been removed to dig a large hole, and they excavated further. The first thing they encountered was a body, the ancient remains of a man whose feet had been cut off. The supposition was that he might have been intended to be a guardian for another burial, and so it proved. He had actually been protecting a royal tomb, the first of several that were eventually found.

LORD OF SIPAN

There was a wooden coffin containing the body of a man aged about 40, filled with objects: jewelry in gold, silver, and precious stones; a gold headdress as well as feather ones; royal banners; clothing decorated in metal and other items. This evidently important man was dubbed the "Lord of Sipan." There were other coffins, too, lying around the main one; they contained the bodies of three women and two men, one of whom was accompanied by a dog. This was just the first; other tombs have now been found at Sipan, following the same pattern. They were all deep pits filled with offerings and attendants. The burial chambers were roofed after being filled with their occupants, and were then sealed up with adobe bricks. For once, they had been safe in their hidden locations within the pyramid.

The discoveries at Sipan have confirmed that some Moche pottery was decorated in scenes that had a basis in reality, something which had been debated by scholars. Many of the objects found there were already known from their representation on ceramics, but some of them threw new light on the culture, emphasizing, for example, the extent and variety of metalworking techniques. Much may yet be revealed as archaeological work continues.

Opposite: The contents of the tomb of the Lord of Sipan and (above) an excavation site at Sipan.

The Maya
Palenque and the tomb of Pakal

In the 1840s, two explorers called John Lloyd Stephens and Frederick Catherwood reported discovering "lost cities" smothered in the jungles of Yucatan. Their romantic accounts prompted interest in the vanished civilization of the Maya and many of the sites became famous. Palenque, toward the western edge of the territory covered by the Maya states, was one of these.

The prominence Palenque gained is not surprising as it is one of the most spectacular Maya sites. The existing buildings include a palace which has a tower four stories in height, a group of three temples representing Maya creation myths and the Temple of the Inscriptions. Mayan temples are often called "pyramids" because of their step-pyramid-like shape, but they differ from Egyptian pyramids in one major way—they were not intended for use as tombs. There is one exception, however, which is a relatively recent discovery.

THE TEMPLE OF THE INSCRIPTIONS

The tallest building in Palenque is the Temple of the Inscriptions. It rises in nine levels to a height of nearly 80 feet, and is topped with a sanctuary building. This was originally decorated with painted stucco sculpture, but most has not survived. The sanctuary is composed of a portico in front of an inner room with two side cells, and there are tablets covered in Maya hieroglyphs in both which give the temple its name. When considered together, these form the second longest Mayan inscription ever found.

The Mexican archaeologist Alberto Ruz Lhuillier was appointed director of research at Palenque in 1949. He became curious about the floor of the sanctuary in the Temple of the Inscriptions; one of the slabs in the central room attracted his attention. It had two rows of holes around its edges, depressions which had been fitted with stone plugs, and he thought that these might have been created so that the slab could be moved. He started to clean the floor next to the intriguing slab, where one of the others had also been damaged— possibly by treasure hunters who had been of the same opinion. Whoever they had been, they seemed to have been discouraged from continuing by a heavy infill of stones. Ruz Lhuillier began removing rubble and realized that the walls of the chamber didn't actually stop at the floor level; they went farther down. There had to be something underneath.

LHUILLIER'S EXCAVATIONS

Excavations began and the following day Ruz Lhuillier and his team uncovered a large stone forming part of a roof vault. It soon became obvious that they had found an interior staircase descending into the depths of the pyramid which had been filled up with rubble. Clearing this out proved to be a major task, extending over several field

Opposite: The palaces and temples at Palenque are situated on a wooded hillside which overlooks the flood plain of the Usumacinta River, in the western part of the Mayan lands. The palace complex, with its four-story tower, lies close to the Temple of the Inscriptions, the tallest building in Palenque. All the large buildings in the city were constructed in less than a century.

Right: A stucco relief from one of the temples at Palenque, Temple XIX, showing traces of color. Most of the carvings would originally have been brightly colored.

seasons, but as the team moved the infill from the four flights of steps they found a few offerings. Most of these—shells filled with red pigment, jade beads and earplugs, a pearl—were found at the bottom, against a wall blocking the passage which they reached in 1952. Again clearing the obstruction took time as it was feet thick, but eventually Ruz Lhuillier and his workmen reached a huge triangular slab, 6 feet high, covering an entrance. At its foot was a stone cist containing human bones. Though they had deteriorated badly, they were found to be the remains of six people; one was definitely female.

OPENING THE CHAMBER

Removing the triangular slab revealed an open doorway into an enormous chamber, 33 feet by 13, constructed on the pyramid's central axis and lying over 80 feet below the floor of the sanctuary. Over the years rainwater had leached through and the walls were encrusted with calcite, but Ruz Lhuillier was able to see that there had been decorations of carved figures. Most of the chamber was filled with a huge decorated monument, and at first the excavators thought they had found an altar. This was investigated the following season, in 1952, and Ruz

Lhuillier drilled into the monument from below, revealing the existence of a hollow space inside. The drilling showed that the space inside was colored red, a color often associated with the dead in Mayan culture, and frequently found in tombs. The monument was actually a huge sarcophagus resting on six stone supports.

The sarcophagus was covered by an immense carved stone, approximately 12 feet by 7, which had to be lifted—it weighed about 5.5 tons—and lifted carefully; it was already obvious that it was a significant piece of

Opposite: A deep relief from the Temple of the Foliated Cross at Palenque, which describes the birth of the god K'awiil.

Left: The Temple of the Inscriptions in Palenque which contains the burial of Pakal, the great seventh-century ruler. It seems to have been specifically constructed to act as his tomb and mortuary temple, but Mayan pyramids were not normally used for burials.

Above: Hieroglyphs from Palenque.

Maya Hieroglyphs

Maya society was, for a long time, viewed in a rather rosy, idealized light. Despite the fact that no one could decipher the details of inscriptions, it was known that the Maya had an interest in astronomical events, and some commentators saw them as peaceful "scholar princes." The decipherment of their hieroglyphic writing was to change all this.

There were plenty of inscriptions. Some, like those at Palenque, were long and presumably detailed, but nobody could read them. By the 1960s, however, this was becoming possible, and by the 1970s the Maya had joined other 'historical' societies whose records could be understood. Understanding Mayan history—which was evidently important to them, too, as they left so many records of their past—became possible, as did understanding more about Mayan religion. And as more was understood, the idealized vision of Mayan society was destroyed. It had been much more violent than anyone had assumed. The inscriptions on stones, temple staircases, even altars, describe wars and conquests between cities, and the capture—and sacrifice—of rival rulers and lords. The Maya had indeed been fascinated by astronomy, but celestial events were used for things like the propitious scheduling of battles, which particularly accorded with the cycle of the planet Venus. Because of detailed Mayan records it is now even possible to understand the shifting balance of power between the cities as they rose and fell.

Mayan art. Once it had been delicately raised a cutting could be seen beneath it, shaped rather like a womb. This had been sealed by a perfectly fitting slab, and that also had to be raised. Beneath it lay a cavity. The walls and base were red and there were human remains inside, of one person, covered with jade ornaments. There was a jade mask covering the face, a jade diadem, jade ear ornaments, necklaces, pectoral plaques, wrist guards; there was a jade ring on every finger and a piece of jade had been held in each hand. Two statuettes, also in jade, lay near the feet, and there had been more jade on the sarcophagus lid. Beneath the sarcophagus were two stucco heads, possibly portraits of the deceased, and pottery food dishes.

When the tomb was found, Mayan writing—hieroglyphs—was still undeciphered, so the identity of the occupant was unknown. He was later revealed to be Palenque's most powerful ruler, Pakal, who had reigned between AD 615 and 683 according to the Maya calendar, and the piers of the doorways in the sanctuary above depicted his son, Chan Bahlum, as a Mayan deity. The hieroglyphic texts from the sanctuary recorded Pakal's lineage and stressed his divine origin, and it appears that the whole temple was designed as a funerary monument for, and to, Pakal. Analysis of his skeleton showed that Pakal had been about 40 when he died, but the inscriptions state that he was twice that age. As yet there is no solution to this discrepancy.

THE SARCOPHAGUS LID

The huge carved lid of the sarcophagus was raised without sustaining any damage, and is indeed unique. It shows Pakal falling down into the Mayan underworld, curled in a foetal position, but from his body a tree grows, topped by a supernatural bird; a two-headed serpent winds about the tree. Around the side were carvings depicting ten rulers of Palenque, all springing from the ground, and the whole thing has been interpreted as an image of death and renewal. The sides of the lid were inscribed with the dates of death for Pakal's ancestors or predecessors, stressing his position and lineage. There was also a strange tube of mortar, modeled to look like a serpent, which led from the sarcophagus into a stone tube running up the 67 steps into the sanctuary, linking Pakal to the world of the living. To the Maya, this could have been a conduit for his spirit, connecting it to whatever religious ceremonies were being conducted in the sanctuary above.

Opposite: A carved skull which gave Palenque's Temple of the Skull its name.

Right: A Mayan ceremonial jade mask. The sophistication of its construction is evident in such areas as the lips, where the jade has been shaped into curves. Jade is thought to have signified eternal life.

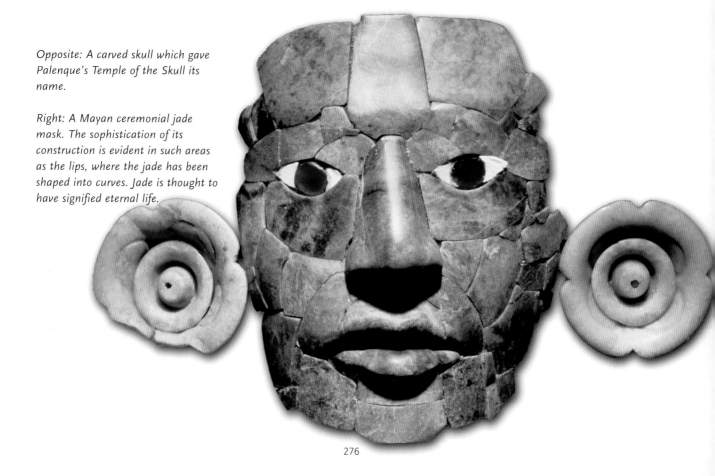

What Happened to the Maya?

In the ninth century, classic Maya civilization ended: official histories were no longer recorded, ceremonial sites were abandoned. This used to be viewed as an abrupt event, a calamitous sudden collapse, but the current picture is not so clear cut. It does not appear to have been a sudden catastrophe, nor did it affect all the Mayan peoples. The northern half of Yucatan remained civilized for some time; indeed, when the Spanish arrived hundreds of years later they found a comparatively civilized society. In the more southern and western areas there does seem to have been a general collapse, with kingdoms failing and most of the population disappearing, possibly moving elsewhere. Gradually, fewer and fewer construction projects were started and some were left unfinished; the monumental recording of scenes of court life stops and there are no more of the associated inscriptions. The kings, or a system based on them, seem to have vanished.

There have been many theories about why this happened. It used to be thought that as the kings disappeared, so did the lords and the people, but this is now known not to be the case everywhere. Noble residences were occupied at Copán for another 200 years or so, for example, and it took 400 years for the rest of the population to fade away. Among the wealth of theories are many that have now been eliminated, at least as sole reasons: peasant uprisings, epidemics, earthquakes, religious changes and ecological ones such as drought and soil erosion. Some, like earthquakes, are now seen as unconvincing, and most archaeologists agree that a combination of factors was probably responsible. Overpopulation combined with deteriorating agricultural conditions now seems to have been the key, with this triggering more warfare. One site, Dos Pilas, shows this change particularly clearly. Before AD 761 it had been a flourishing regal center; afterward it was in ruins, with defensive stockades running around it and small houses built apparently randomly over the central plaza. Overpopulation, environmental exhaustion and warfare would have triggered population movements and brought an end to the belief in rulers as protectors of their people, and may also have brought famine and disease in their wake. Something did undoubtedly happen, and by the time the Spanish penetrated the old Maya heartland in 1524 it was almost deserted.

Teotihuacán

The city of Teotihuacán in Mexico was never a lost city, unlike those of the Maya farther to the south; as with many monumental sites, its existence has been known by others since it was abandoned by its original inhabitants. The Aztecs, who knew the city much later, believed that the world had been created there: its name is an Aztec one which means "city of the gods." It has attracted archaeologists since the middle of the 19th century, and more recent work has revealed much about the city and its temples.

Teotihuacán flourished between AD 100 and 750, and reached its maximum extent—and probably power and influence, too—between the fourth and sixth centuries when it covered an enormous area and may have had as many as 125,000 inhabitants. There was a ceremonial core to the city, formed by a long straight avenue known as the Street of the Dead. This led, once all construction was complete, from the Temple of the Moon, past the enormous Temple of the Sun, to an immense enclosure which the Spanish thought had been the citadel and named accordingly. In the Citadel compound is the Temple of the Feathered Serpent, uncovered during major excavations between 1917 and 1922. All of the Temple's magnificent facades had collapsed, except for one, and this is now one of the most famous monuments in Mexico. Huge feathered serpent heads stick out of the facade, and are supposed to weigh about 4.4 tons each.

A further series of excavations here in the 1980s found burial pits containing a total of 120 people who seemed to have been some sort of offering, possibly connected to the Temple's dedication. Their bodies were grouped together in multiple burials of about 20 individuals, and were found in a flexed position with their hands tied behind their backs. Most of them appeared to have been warriors, judging by their dress, some elements of which appear to prefigure that worn by Aztec warriors much later. They had, for example, "mirrors": disks of slate encrusted with iron pyrites, fool's gold, which were worn in the small of the back. They wore necklaces, often rather gory ones: carved shell-shaped to resemble human upper jaws (one of them had a necklace made of the real thing), or shell necklaces looking like human teeth. These sacrificial victims had been accompanied by other offerings, thousands of ornaments in shell and hundreds of obsidian projectile points.

EVERYDAY LIFE

In the face of such extraordinary discoveries it is easy to overlook all the evidence of everyday life in Teotihuacán that has also recently started to emerge. The city has been the focus for an immense surveying and mapping project which has recorded its gridlike organization, with rectangular house compounds lined up along straight and narrow streets. Over 2000 of these have been mapped, but only a few have been excavated. It looks as though these compounds could have housed about 100 people, but they vary a lot: some are spacious and some

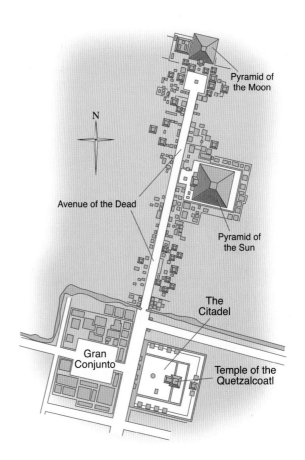

Opposite: The Temple of the Sun, with the Plaza of the Moon in the foreground. The Temple of the Sun is as large at the base as Egypt's Great Pyramid, and still stands 200 feet high. These grand buildings appear austere today; however, their plaster surfaces were actually painted with multicolored murals, some traces of which remain. The shape of both the Temple of the Sun and the Temple of the Moon was designed to echo the hills in front of which they stood.

Above: A plan of Teotihuacán.

are cramped. Some have elaborate courtyard shrines which were constructed over a burial, perhaps of an especially important individual or ancestor. Most seem to have been well built, with good drainage systems, and some are so beautifully decorated and apparently special that they could almost be described as palaces, while others are distinctly downmarket and shabby. There may have been some sort of hierarchical society, but that may not have been the whole picture; we just do not fully understand the nature of these compounds. Some may have been differentiated from others by their specialist functions, for example, but quite what these may have been is not yet known.

The Aztecs

Originally from the northern deserts of Mexico, the Aztecs migrated southward, one of many tribes. They, however, were to create the largest empire in Mesoamerica, stretching from one coast to the other, and they did so in a very short period of time.

Their capital city, Tenochtitlán, was founded in AD 1325 and grew swiftly to become the largest and most complex city in the Americas by the time the Spanish arrived in 1519. In 1521 much of it was destroyed by the Spanish. What remained was either demolished by them as they established control over their colony and constructed their own buildings, or is now inaccessible, buried deep below Mexico City. Some things come to light during modern building projects, such as the digging of the metro system, and have been excavated and studied, but much of what is known about the Aztecs comes either from their own accounts or those of the Spaniards.

One problem encountered by archaeologists working on what remains of Tenochtitlán is the very high water table. The Aztec capital was built on what was essentially an artificial island on a lake, Lake Texcoco, and

Opposite: An Aztec calendar depicting Tez-Calipoca and Quetzalcoatl. The whole of the calendar was sacred to various gods, who had to be propitiated at the appropriate time.

Right: An Aztec skull mask covered in turquoise. One particularly fine skull mask had the back of the cranium cut away and the edge lined with leather; straps were also attached so that it could be worn as part of a ritual costume.

Below: This ornament, which was probably designed to be worn on the chest, is made of wood covered with turquoise. The double-headed serpent was one of the symbols of the god Tlaloc, and it would most likely have been worn by his high priest. It may have been part of the treasure which Moctezuma sent to Cortès.

it was crossed by a network of canals. It was joined to the shore by an aqueduct and by various causeways, totalling 38 miless in length. This main island included the ceremonial center and the palace, but it also had a lot of ordinary residents living in one-story houses made of adobe. Estimates for population numbers vary, but there were probably at least 125,000 inhabitants of this main area which was largely constructed on a grid pattern. It was organized into neighborhoods which may have been defined by specific roles within Aztec society. Around Tenochtitlán itself were other settlements, including

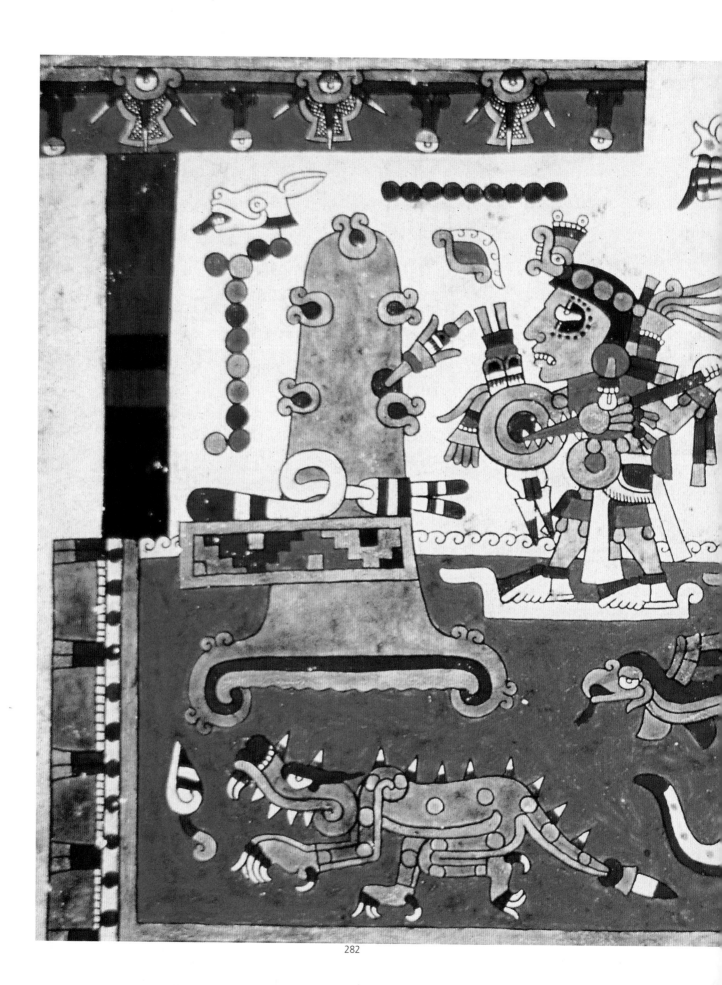

some set on smaller artificial islands or chinampas. These, which had been created by dredging the shallow lake bed and creating dry platforms between deeper canals, made intensive vegetable and fruit production possible. It has been estimated that the population of Tenochtitlán and its "suburbs" may have been as high as a million.

THE GREAT TEMPLE

Religion was central to Aztec life and central to Tenochtitlán was the Great Temple. It was the focal point of the city and stood in a large square enclosure which incorporated many other buildings and features, including other temples, a ball court, priests' dormitories, a school which trained the sons of the elite, and houses for warrior guilds.

Part of the Great Temple had been uncovered in 1948. By the late 1970s a more organized approach was being taken to working in Mexico City and the Museum of Tenochtitlán Project decided to investigate. In early 1978, before they were able to formally start work, electricity workers uncovered an immense carved stone in the relevant area. The archaeologists immediately became involved and a huge relief carving was revealed, depicting a dismembered goddess. This had evidently been central to the Great Temple and the Museum of Tenochtitlán Project became the Great Temple Project instead. Over the next four years its director, Eduardo Matos Moctezuma, revealed a surprisingly complicated picture.

It was surprising because nobody realized how much had survived of the Temple; it had been one of the buildings the Spanish had razed to the ground in 1521. However, the temple pyramid they destroyed had simply been the most recent in a series of rebuilding phases, with each new temple built on top of and around its predecessor,

Left: Aztec warriors standing on canoes which sail toward an island over a lake filled with monstrous fish. This is a page from a codex, an accordion-folded book.

HUMAN SACRIFICE AND RELIGION

The archaeologists found a lot of evidence of human sacrifice at the Great Temple, some of it architectural. There was a "skull rack" with a facade of grinning skulls; this was used to display war trophies—human bones. It was found north of the Temple at the Stage IV level which has been given a probable date of 1454—69. From Stage II, which has a date of 1390, comes a special wedge-shaped stone that was used to arch the bodies of sacrificial victims. Human sacrifice was a vital part of Aztec religion and the ritual for which they are best remembered was heart excision, where human hearts were cut from the chests of living victims and offered to the sun as nourishment. It has been suggested that the need for more and more victims was one of the main reasons for Aztec militarism.

According to the Aztec calendar, the year was divided into 13 periods lasting 20 days, each of which was associated with a specific deity, and during which elaborate ceremonies would be performed for that god or goddess. The natural world was controlled by a complicated pantheon of male and female deities, two of the most important being those to whom the Great Temple was dedicated, Huitzilopochtli and Tlaloc. There were also Quetzalcoatl, who governed the wind; Chihuacoatl, the earth; and Xoachiquetzal, who was connected to both the arts and sexuality. The sacrifices generally seem to have been made in order to maintain the existing balance and insure favorable conditions, whether that was bringing about military success or

enclosing it, going right back to the beginnings of Tenochtitlán. Nothing was left of the final version, the one the Spaniards destroyed, except its foundations. Like the others it had been a pyramid composed of successively smaller platforms, giving the whole a stepped appearance, and the top level had two large shrines built on it. These were dedicated to the war and sun god Huitzilopochtli, the Aztecs' patron deity, and to Tlaloc, the god of rain and water. Immense double staircases rose up to the shrines on one side.

As well as exposing the stages of construction, the excavators also found very many offerings, among which were sculptures in stone and terracotta, jade, and obsidian objects, and the skeleton of a jaguar which was found in a chamber belonging to the fourth stage; it had a ball of turquoise in its mouth. Many of the offerings were not of local origin and appear to have come from areas of the Aztec empire that would have paid tribute to the rulers. These were not, however, the only things that had been offered to the gods of the Great Temple.

insuring that it rained at the right time. They were essential for guaranteeing that the sun would continue to shine, and were also used to try and suppress disruption and disorder by placating the gods with the ultimate offering. The arrival of the Spanish, which came at a very ominous and inauspicious point in time, was marked by an apparent increase in sacrifices. It is worth emphasizing that human sacrifice was not a uniquely Aztec phenomenon, though it does seem to have been carried out on a particularly large scale; the Spanish left many shocked reports.

THE TREASURE OF CORTÈS

Quetzalcoatl was originally a Toltec god, and when the Aztecs arrived he fled eastward toward the Caribbean. He would, however, return and the time of his reappearance was predicted to coincide with a particularly dangerous point in the cycle of the Aztec calendar—one possibility was the equivalent of 1519. He was also a pale-skinned god, and when reports arrived at Tenochtitlán that year of the appearance of pale-skinned people from the east, obvious conclusions were drawn. The Aztec ruler Moctezuma therefore sent rich offerings to these mysterious people, and gave them permission to enter Tenochtitlán. Or so goes the tale.

Opposite below: A calendar stone from La Paz. Important events were dated in historical or genealogical records and certain cycles were thought to be significant. A full calendar "round" only occurred every 52 years, which was thought to be a particularly perilous point in time and, as such, was marked by more ceremonies and sacrifices than usual. One coincided with 1519, when the Spanish arrived.

Opposite above: A contemporary plan of the city of Tenochtitlán, the Aztec capital, most of which was destroyed or subsequently demolished by the Spanish to permit the construction of their own capital, now Mexico City. Little remains today, though sites are sometimes uncovered in construction work. The focus of Tenochtitlán was the Great Temple, and that has been rediscovered.

Right: Chacmool statues were a distinctive feature of some temples, and two were found at Tenochtitlán's Great Temple. It has been suggested that they served as a sort of opposite partner to the sacrificial stones, in that they symbolized religion and the life of the spirit rather than war and the fate of prisoners. They may have represented a divine intermediary.

The Spanish, spurred on by stories of their own and the desire for wealth, took full advantage of this and went on to conquer not only the Aztec empire but many others, aided by disease—smallpox ravaged Tenochtitlán, for instance—and disaffected vassal states. As a consequence many glorious pieces of Aztec art are the result not of archaeology but of misguided tribute, treasure-hunting, and looting and are without context. Some items remained intact; some were melted down.

A lot found its way to Europe. The first collection was sent to King Charles V of Spain by the Spanish leader Cortès and arrived in 1520; it was inventoried and, amazingly, the inventories have survived. Many of the items did not, though some can be found in European museums where they eventually ended up after a somewhat checkered history (including, in the case of a feathered headdress, being allegedly used as a dressing-up costume for ducal children).

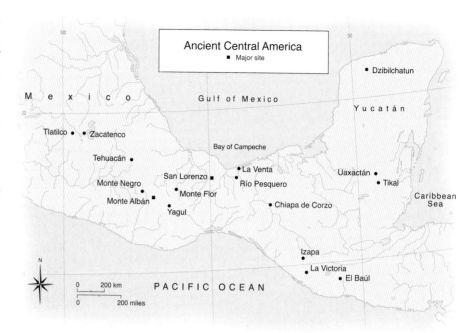

Moctezuma's tribute lists had alerted the Spaniards to the original sources of the gold, which had often come to the Aztecs as tribute in the first place. As a result they knew exactly where to look, and very little gold survives that had not been placed out of reach—below ground, in burials. A lot had come from the Mixtec, who were particularly skilled as goldsmiths. A cemetery near the Mixtec city of Monte Alban has produced many beautiful objects, and many more must have been lost.

The Ball Game

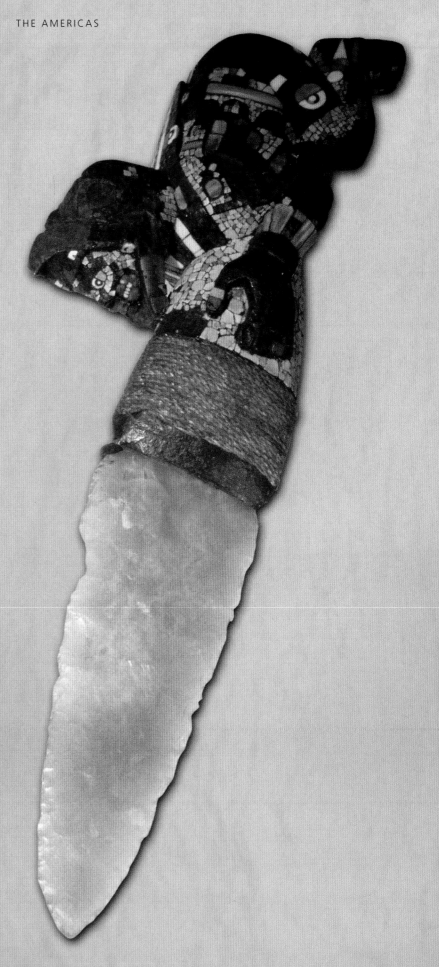

Among the structures in the Great Temple compound was a ball court. The ball game—often called the Mesoamerican ball game as it was a common feature of many societies over a long period of time and a huge geographical area—was usually played in a formal court though it could be played on any flat surface. Ball courts were generally long and rectangular with sloping or vertical sides and players scored by hitting a rubber ball through to the end, though they do not appear to have been allowed to use their hands or feet. Sometimes the game seems to have been purely recreational but, especially in earlier times, it also had a ritual significance; it may even have been associated with human sacrifice. It could act as a way for a ruler to entertain important guests from elsewhere, and there is also evidence of large wagers being made on the result of games.

Opposite above: A map of Central America.

Opposite right: A gold pendant of a ruler in full regalia. A lot of tribute came to the Aztecs in the form of gold, and this Mixtec piece demonstrates the skill for which they were noted. Much of the gold was removed by the Spanish, but some survived in tombs.

Opposite left: A pottery figurine of a mother and child. With the ceremonial sites and rituals like extensive human sacrifice, it is easy to forget that Tenochtitlán was a huge city with many "ordinary" inhabitants, probably as many as 125,000 in the central zone alone.

Right: A sacrificial knife with a chalcedony blade. The hilt is made of wood covered with a turquoise, malachite, and shell mosaic, and represents a warrior wearing an eagle headdress.

Machu Picchu and the Incas

On a July afternoon in 1911, Hiram Bingham, an American academic and explorer, climbed up to the top of a ridge high in the Peruvian Andes. The ridge connected two peaks, Machu Picchu and Huayna Picchu, and Bingham was chasing up reports of an Inca village that lay astride it which he hoped might be the remains of the Incas' last refuge from the Spanish invaders, their "lost capital." He saw plenty of ruins, beautifully constructed long terraces that stepped up the mountainside, maybe even a hundred of them. They had been partly cleared and were being used to provide crops for a group of local farmers who welcomed the independence that the remoteness of the place brought them.

Further investigation revealed many more buildings, some in excellent condition, but Bingham continued his journey in search of another Inca site. A few weeks later, however, he sent a team back to the remote mountain ridge to map the remains he had seen there. The following year he launched a major expedition, which received immense public attention.

Once the site had been cleared of the vegetation that had come close to smothering parts of it—some of this had already been removed by the farmers—it was obvious that the place had some fine Inca architecture. There were temples and religious shrines, including one temple with three windows which seemed particularly important. This led Bingham to formulate another idea about the site and suggest that Machu Picchu was the birthplace of the Incas: Inca legend stated that their ancestors had come from a cave with three windows. There were also residential buildings which would have been appropriate for members of the royal family and for their officials and staff; there were baths and watercourses, open plazas and all the terracing which

Opposite: Artificial terracing was constructed in many places in the valley which contains Machu Picchu, and these terraces were irrigated so that they could be used for agriculture. Those running down from Machu Picchu were the ruins that first attracted the attention of Hiram Bingham in 1911.

Above: The Temple of the Condor in Machu Picchu, one of many buildings only fully revealed once serious clearance began. Though the site had been used by local farmers, some of whom were even living in it, much remained overgrown when Bingham began work.

had first attracted Bingham's attention. The quality of the stonework was excellent, as it is at many other important Inca sites. The form of the site, the shape the settlement had taken, was determined by the ridge on which it was situated, but this had even been partly leveled to allow for the construction of more buildings. Whatever the truth of Bingham's hypotheses, it was obvious that the site had been important, one on which a lot of effort had been invested.

Inca Construction

The Incas frequently reshaped the landscape itself, something seen very clearly at Machu Picchu—where the top of the ridge was leveled off—but also common elsewhere. Canals were constructed to improve irrigation, and an existing system of agriculture on terraces was reinvented and expanded around major settlements like Machu Picchu. All this was possible because the Incas imposed taxes on the many people of their vast multi-lingual, multi-ethnic empire, and these taxes could be paid in physical labor as well as goods.

The main feature of Inca architecture is the use of enormous stone blocks that were cut to size so that they fitted closely; mortar was not used. The huge blocks were moved into place using human strength with a combination of levers, pulleys, and rollers, resulting in buildings so strong and solidly constructed that they stand firm even today, having survived earthquakes which have destroyed buildings put up since then.

Close to Cuzco, the capital from which the Incas ruled and which they considered to be the center of the world, lies the site of Sacsahuaman. Here the elaborate stone walls provide remarkable evidence for the skill of Inca masons; apparently there was a labor force of up to 20,000 who worked on the site for decades. Cuzco itself also has many surviving Inca walls. It was a truly imperial

city; only the royal family, state and religious officials were permitted to live in the city itself and it had a profound significance. Cuzco was carefully planned, as were other Inca sites like Machu Picchu. All of this organization came to an end with the arrival of the conquistadors.

Machu Picchu in its Setting

The Inca lords transformed the valley of the Urabamba river into what was, in essence, an imperial park. The river was canalized, its vertical banks faced in stone which still survives in places, the hillsides were terraced and irrigation canals were constructed. Though the landscape is very different today, it was once highly productive agricultural land, terraced and irrigated. A series of settlements were constructed in the valley and Machu Picchu is one of these. Vast resources must have gone into its construction, turning an unpromising mountaintop into a sophisticated royal retreat. With no emperor or court to provide a reason for its continued existence, it is likely that Machu Picchu would have been abandoned very soon after the Spanish conquest.

Higher up this valley is Ollantaytambo and like Machu Picchu, it had served as a rural palace, building up into a complex of temples and large residences which is still very well preserved. Following Atahualpa's capture and murder, remnants of the royal court retreated there, but they were driven down the Urabamba and into the jungle.

Pizarro's band of conquistadors set about plundering the cities and dismembering the empire, something they did very effectively. So effectively that it is still difficult to understand many aspects of the Inca state.

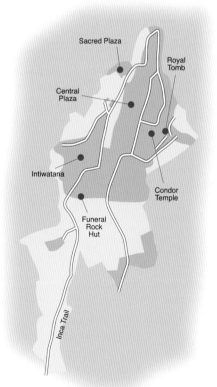

Opposite: Hiram Bingham, the "discoverer" of Machu Picchu.

Above: Many Inca walls built without the use of mortar have lasted longer than much subsequent work, which has proved more vulnerable to earthquakes.

Left: A plan of the settlement of Machu Picchu.

Hiram Bingham
"Discoverer" of Machu Picchu

Hiram Bingham had an extraordinary life, and bringing the famous Peruvian site of Machu Picchu to the attention of the world was just part of it. He was born in 1875 on a mission run by his grandfather outside Honolulu, and attended Yale University. He briefly became a pastor in Hawaii himself, but soon met his wife Alfreda, who was heiress to the Tiffany fortune. He abandoned his career and worked to save some money with which to travel to California and begin graduate studies. The couple married and he began doctoral work at Harvard, where they were subsidized by her family.

Despite being an academic for many years, Bingham always preferred to be recognized as an explorer, part of his career which began while he was teaching at Princeton when he undertook his first research journey south. Soon after his return he was appointed to Yale as a lecturer, and became a full professor there. In the meanwhile Bingham had become obsessed with the secret capital of the Incas, the city from which they were supposed to have led resistance to the Spanish invaders after the fall of their capital, Cuzco. In 1911 he set off on an expedition to Peru, and eventually found the place he claimed to be the ruins of this secret city, Machu Picchu. He began serious archaeological excavations at the site in 1912 and worked there for several seasons until he was forced to leave because he had allegedly contravened Peruvian laws relating to archaeological exploration. He never went back.

His life after Machu Picchu was, however, similarly colorful: he became a flyer in the First World War, giving up teaching to do so, and then went into politics. He died in 1956, and will always be remembered as the man who excavated Machu Picchu.

Pueblo Farmers of the Desert

The Pueblo dwellings in the deserts of the southwestern parts of the United States have long fascinated travelers and archaeologists, attracting their attention since the beginnings of American archaeology. The extraordinary sites often looked as though they had only just been abandoned, and the dry climate preserved many artifacts such as pottery, baskets, and textiles. Early finds even included things like sandals made from yucca plants and pots still containing corn. But the remains of the buildings are probably the most spectacular surviving aspect of the culture.

Archaeologists separate the farmers of the American southwest into three basic groups, though their cultures share some common characteristics and there seems to have been some physical overlap. The Four Corners area of the Colorado plateau—where four states, New Mexico, Colorado, Utah and Arizona, meet—was occupied by a people who used to be known as the Anasazi, but who are now generally called the Ancestral Pueblo. It is thought that the Hopi, Zuni, Zia, and Acoma people, who inhabit parts of the region today, are their descendants. They were known as Pueblo peoples because they lived in settlements: "pueblo" means village or town in Spanish.

The deserts of the southwest are a harsh environment, one which was occupied by hunter-gatherers for thousands of years. However, about 2000—2500 years ago things started to change. The inhabitants began growing crops which had been domesticated earlier in Central America, such as squashes, maize and beans, and adopted a more settled way of life. Initially there was some reliance on hunting and gathering as well, but the overall contribution of farming increased and the people started living in settled houses which were sunk partly into the ground. They also began making pots; containers prior to this had been woven: baskets made from yucca fibers, twigs, bark, and grasses. Tobacco and corn were gradually added to the crops planted but the people were not reliant on domesticated animals, except

Opposite: Mesa Verde, meaning "green table" in Spanish, is so called because of the forest of trees that grows along the top of the cliff. Situated in the state of Colorado, the buildings were offered some protection when the area became a national park in 1906 but it was not until 1978 that the site was designated a World Heritage Site.

Above: A kiva from Chetro Ketl in Chaco Canyon, northern New Mexico, under snow. Though Pueblo Bonito was the largest of the sites in the canyon area, comprising over 600 rooms, there were twelve others. They have some features in common, and kivas, even multiple kivas, are one of these. At Chetro Ketl there are 12 kivas and several hundred rooms.

Left: Grinding stones from Mesa Verde. Maize was one of the major crops grown by the Ancestral Pueblo people; beans and squash were also important.

turkeys and dogs. By this point they were skilled farmers, adept at achieving the maximum they could in such a demanding environment. Initially they used only rainfall, known as "dry farming," but irrigation systems were developed—and in some places became very elaborate—to channel water on to the fields. Most of the crops were grown on the mesas, the flat-topped mountains of the region.

About AD 900 there seem to have been significant population changes in the area—this is much debated—and a corresponding change in the way people lived. The nature of the settlements altered, with small individual farmsteads giving way to bigger communities. These were centered on what are known as "great houses," communal buildings constructed of masonry rather than adobe. The exact function of these is also much debated, but they are a common feature in sites across a wide area.

CHACO CANYON

New Mexico's Chaco Canyon is one of the best known of the Ancestral Pueblo sites. There are 13 in the area and one, Pueblo Bonito, has the largest great house—with 600 rooms covering about 2 acres. Great houses like this were constructed in Chaco Canyon between 900 and 1140, which must have been a period of considerable prosperity or, at the very least, of considerable communal effort. Some materials had to be brought to the canyon, probably from some distance: for example, the building of the 12 great houses would have required 200,000 wooden beams with an average length of 16 feet and a diameter of about 8 inches.

Great houses contain a number of kivas, some very large. These are round structures, and probably had a communal role. Kivas exist in modern Pueblo villages, and serve a variety of functions—social, political, and religious. As there seems to have been considerable

Opposite: The cliff dwellings at Mesa Verde are some of the most spectacular archaeological remains in the world. Wedged into the cliffs or under giant overhangs, they have provoked fascination and debate since the Europeans first encountered them.

Above: The Cliff Palace at Mesa Verde is the largest of the sites below the mesa's overhang. It had a total of 150 rooms and 23 kivas.

Right: Pueblo Bonito included several kivas, which probably fulfilled the same purpose as their modern equivalents do in today's Pueblo villages—communal meeting places for social, political, and religious functions.

continuity in the form of kivas over the past 1500 years, it is assumed that their function has also remained fairly constant. Some archaeologists have suggested that the great houses were temples rather than places where people lived, however.

There were extensive trading systems. Chaco Canyon sites were linked to each other and these links extended farther afield, but trading networks went much farther than the immediate region. Imported materials such as shell from California, from both the Gulf and the coast, and turquoise from New Mexico were used in craft workshops. Chaco Canyon was a thriving community, but for some reason building ceased in the middle of the 12th century.

MESA VERDE

There were early semi-subterranean pit houses at Mesa Verde, north of Chaco in Colorado. But the most spectacular Ancestral Pueblo sites here were constructed later, in the 12th and particularly the 13th centuries. The cliff

settlements at Mesa Verde itself are amongst the most extraordinary archaeological survivals in the world. They were tucked under steep overhangs, and form almost hive-like complexes of interlinked dwellings. Cliff Palace, at Mesa Verde, had 150 rooms and 23 kivas and, like all these sites, the buildings were of stone, wood, and plaster. Fields were scattered along the mesa tops and were reached by specially cut stairs running from the cliff settlements.

Some of these settlements seem to have been situated in clearly defensible positions, and there is some evidence of violence in the Mesa Verde area during the 13th century. Indeed, after 1000 there is evidence from skeletons that some people had been deliberately killed: they had injuries which would match being battered or sustaining arrow wounds, suggestive of individuals perhaps being ambushed. However, by the 12th century there were mass killings, demonstrated by disarticulated and fragmented—intentionally fragmented—human bones. Some archaeologists have seen these as an indication that cannibalism was being practised. At one site, Castle Rock Pueblo, in Colorado, 41 people had been killed at one time, an incident which happened about 1280. It is possible that there was increasing competition for agricultural land, but whatever the reason, it highlights one of the central mysteries of American archaeology. Why were the sites abandoned? What actually happened?

WHY DID THE PEOPLE LEAVE?

Hundreds of years later the first European researchers encountered sites like Mesa Verde's Cliff Palace, the largest of the dwellings beneath the overhang of the mesa. It looked as though the town had just been deserted, they noted. There have been many theories about what happened, some applying just to the Mesa Verde area, some just to Chaco—where the situation has its own name, the "Chaco phenomenon"—and some being more general.

Environmental change is a recurring theme. It used to be assumed that Chaco had been a fertile oasis, well wooded and watered, and that this had altered to the landscape of desert and scrub present in the area today. However, evidence to the contrary began appearing in the 1980s, and it seems that Chaco may never have been wooded to that extent. This new geological evidence has also shown that a large, relatively temporary, natural lake may have existed at the northern end during the 11th century, when construction in Chaco was at its height. This is also the area of the canyon where most of the great houses are. The water from this lake may well have given people a reason to settle in the area but its role is, as yet, unclear.

There may also have been significant droughts and periods of cold weather, and unfavorable climatic conditions would have made it difficult to sustain agriculture, and ultimately life, in these comparatively marginal areas. The question of the impact the people themselves had on the environment has also been raised, but population levels are notoriously difficult to establish with any degree of certainty and they are key to assessing this factor.

Then there are social issues. Environmental pressure could have created social unrest and competition between different local groups, or change might even have been independent of environmental issues. It has been suggested, for example, that the people could have been attracted somewhere else, rather than been forced to flee against their will, and that a new religion could have provided the impetus for such a move.

Opposite and right: The dwellings under the cliffs at Mesa Verde must have hummed with activity when they were at their height. Fields were situated on top, on the flat surface of the mesa, and steps were especially cut to allow the inhabitants to reach their crops.

Most archaeologists now think that it was a combination of factors that made areas like Chaco Canyon and Mesa Verde much less attractive, so much so that the people left. The Pueblo people of today, however, simply see it as one migration of many, part of a continuing pattern which has run throughout their history.

Index

Left: Hatshepsut's mortuary temple of Deir el-Bahri on the west side of the Nile.

Bibliography

Allchin, B. and Allchin, F.R., The Rise of Civilization in India and Pakistan, Cambridge, 1982

Andronikos, M., Vergina, the Royal Tombs and the Ancient City, Athens, 1984

Bahn, P., (editor), The Cambridge Illustrated History of Archaeology, Cambridge, 1996

Bedoyere, G de la, Hadrian's Wall, Stroud, 1998

Butterworh, A. and Laurence, R, Pompeii: the Living City, London, 2005

Cadogan, G., The Palaces of Minoan Crete, London, 1991

Carter, H. and Mace, A.C., The Tomb of Tut.ank.amun, London 1923–33 (3 vols)

Chadwick, J., The Decipherment of Linear B, Cambridge, 1958

Coe, M.D., The Maya, London, 2005 (7th edition)

Coles, J. M., and Harding, A. F., The Bronze Age in Europe, London, 1979

Collis, J., The European Iron Age, London, 1984

Collis, J., The Celts, Stroud, 2003

Coulston, J. and Dodge, H. (editors), Ancient Rome: the Archaeology of the Eternal City, Oxford, 2000

Cunliffe, B. (editor), Prehistoric Europe, Oxford, 1997

Curtis, J., Ancient Persia, London, 1989

David, R. and Achbold, R., Conversations with Mummies: New Light on the Ancient Egyptians, London, 2000

Davidson, J., Courtesans and Fishcakes: The Consuming Passions of Classical Athens, New York, 1997

Dickinson, O., The Aegean Bronze Age, Cambridge, 1994

Dillehay, T., The Settlement of the Americas, New York, 2000

Evans, A., The Palace of Minos at Knossos, London, 1921–35

Evans, S.T., Ancient Mexico and Central America: Archaeology and Culture History, London, 2004

Fagan, B., Eyewitness to Discovery, Oxford, 1996

French, E., Mycenae, Stroud, 2002

Gamble, C., The Paleolithic Societies of Europe, Cambridge , 1999

Harding, A. F., European Societies in the Bronze Age, Cambridge, 2000

Higham, C.F.W., The Civilization of Angkor, London, 2001

Jones., M.K., The Molecule Hunt, London, 2001

Kemp, B.J., Ancient Egypt: Anatomy of a Civilization, London, 1989

Khurt, A., The Ancient Near East, c 3000–330 BC, London, 1995

Ling, R., Pompeii: History, Life and Afterlife, Stroud, 2005

Macdonald, W.L. and Pinto, J.A., Hadrian's Villa and its Legacy, New Haven, 1995

Macnamara, E., The Etruscans, London, 1990

Mattingley, D.J. and Aldrete, G.S., 'The Feeding of Imperial Rome' in Coulston and Dodge, Ancient Rome, 2000

Mee, C. and Spawforth, A., Greece: An Oxford Archaeological Guide, Oxford, 2001

Mithen, S., After the Ice, London, 2003

Moseley, M.E., The Incas and their Ancestors: the Archaeology of Peru, London, 2001

Morwood, M.J., Visions from the Past: the Archaeology of Australian Aboriginal Art, Sydney, 2002

Mulvaney, J. and Kamminga, J., The Prehistory of Australia, Sydney, 1999

Phillipson, D.W., African Archaeology, Cambridge, 1993

Plog, S., Ancient Peoples of the American Southwest, London, 1998

Prag, J. and Neave, R., Making Faces, London, 1997

Rawson, J., The Mysteries of Ancient China, London, 1996

Reeves, N., The Complete Tutankhamun, London, 1990

Renfrew, C. and Bahn, P., Archaeology: Theories, Methods and Practice, London, 2000

Scarre, C. (editor), The Human Past, London, 2005

Schnapp, A., The Discovery of the Past, London, 1996

Stringer, C. and Andrews, P., The Complete World of Human Evolution, London, 2005

Van der Mieroop, M., A History of the Ancient Near East, Oxford, 2004

Yadin, Y., Masada, New York, 1966

Picture Acknowledgments

The publisher would like to thank the following picture libraries for their kind permission to reproduce their photographs in this book:

Ancient Art & Architecture Collection Ltd: 3, 4, 14,16, 17, 18, 19, 20, 21, 22(t+b), 24, 25, 26(r+l), 27, 28, 29, 30(t+b), 31, 32, 33, 38, 40(r+l), 41, 42(b), 43, 44, 45, 46, 47, 48, 49(r+l), 50, 51(t,m,b), 52, 53(t+b), 54, 58, 62, 63, 64, 65(t+b), 66, 67, 68, 69(r+l), 70(t+b), 71(r+l), 72, 73, 76, 77(t+b), 78, 79, 80, 81(t+b), 82, 83, 85, 86, 87, 88, 89, 91, 94, 95, 97, 98(t+b), 99, 100, 101(t+b), 103, 104(t+b), 105, 106, 107, 108, 110(t+b), 111, 112, 113(t), 114, 115(t+b), 116, 117(t+b), 118, 119, 120(t+b), 121, 122, 123, 124, 125, 126(t+b), 127, 130, 131, 132, 133, 134(t+b), 135, 136, 140(t+b), 141, 144(t+b), 145(b), 146, 147, 148, 149, 152, 153, 154, 155(t+b), 156(t+b), 157, 158(t+b), 160, 161, 162, 163, 164, 165, 166, 167, 1168, 170, 171, 172, 176, 177(t+b), 178(t+b), 179, 180(t+b), 181, 182, 183, 184(t+b), 185, 186, 187, 188, 189(t+b), 190(t+b), 191, 192, 193(t+b), 194, 196, 197, 198, 200, 202, 203, 204, 205(t+b), 208(t+b), 209, 210, 211, 212(t+b), 212, 214, 215(t+b), 216, 218, 219, 220, 222, 223(r+l), 224, 225(t+b), 226, 227, 228, 229, 230, 232, 233, 234, 235, 236(t+b), 237, 238, 239(t+b),240, 242(t+b), 243, 244, 246(t+b), 247, 248, 249, 250, 251(t+b), 252, 253, 254(b), 255, 256, 257, 258, 260(t+b), 261, 262, 263(t+b), 264(t), 265, 266, 273, 274(t+b), 275, 276, 277, 280, 281(t+b), 282, 284(t+b), 285, 286(t+b), 287, 288, 289, 290, 292, 293(t+b), 294(t+b), 295, 296, 297

Corbis: 6, 8, 9, 11(t+b), 12, 13, 34, 35, 36, 37, 39, 42(t), 55, 60, 90, 92, 93, 96, 102, 113, 128, 159, 155, 173, 174, 206, 254(t), 264(b), 268, 270, 271, 278, 291

Getty Images: 10, 74, 217, 272

GNP: 56, 57, 59(t+b), 61(t+b), 138(t+b), 139, 143, 144(t), 145(t), 146(t), 150(t+b), 151(t+b)

Front cover images: Stonehenge © Getty Images, Roman amphitheatre © Getty images, statue of Ramses II, Luxor, Egypt © Corbis, diver holding a ceramic vessel © Corbis
Back cover: Baalbek, Lebanon © Getty Images

Maps on pages 37, 84, 78, 109, 137, 143, 175, 240 courtesy of Cartigraphica.

The publisher would also like to thank Michelle Williams, Haruko Sheridan and Etty Morris at the Ancient Art and Architecture Collection for all their help in producing this book. Thank you also to Simon Taylor.